William Aldis Wright

Generydes

A Romance in Seven-Line Stanzas

William Aldis Wright

Generydes
A Romance in Seven-Line Stanzas

ISBN/EAN: 9783744674461

Printed in Europe, USA, Canada, Australia, Japan

Cover: Foto ©Thomas Meinert / pixelio.de

More available books at **www.hansebooks.com**

Generydes,

A ROMANCE IN SEVEN-LINE STANZAS.

———

EDITED FROM

THE UNIQUE PAPER MS. IN TRINITY COLLEGE, CAMBRIDGE

(ABOUT 1440 A.D.),

BY

W. ALDIS WRIGHT, ESQ., M.A.,

HONORARY FELLOW AND BURSAR OF TRINITY COLL., CAMBRIDGE,

EDITOR OF 'BACON'S ESSAYS,' 'THE BIBLE WORDBOOK,' ETC.; JOINT EDITOR OF THE 'CAMBRIDGE SHAKSPERE,' ETC.

LONDON:

PUBLISHED FOR THE EARLY ENGLISH TEXT SOCIETY,

BY N. TRÜBNER & CO., 57 & 59, LUDGATE HILL.

——

MDCCCLXXVIII.

PREFACE.

THE present version of the story of Generydes is printed from a MS. in the Library of Trinity College, Cambridge, where it forms part of the Gale collection, and is marked O. 5. 2. From the fact that in the same volume are Lidgate's *Siege of Troy* and his *Siege of Thebes*, the whole volume was catalogued as *Lidgate's Poems*, and consequently the existence of an entirely unknown poem was not suspected. When Mr. Furnivall was engaged upon his edition of the Helmingham MS. of *Syr Generides* for the Roxburghe Club in 1866, my attention was directed to some printed fragments of another version of the story in seven-line stanzas which had been discovered by Mr. Bradshaw in the binding of an old volume in our Library, Michaelis Menoti *Sermones Quadragesimales*, Paris, 1525; a volume which had formerly belonged to Edmund Castell, the well-known Oriental scholar. After copying these for Mr. Furnivall, I found some other fragments of the same version among the papers of Sir John Fenn, the editor of the *Paston Letters*, which were in the possession of Mr. Philip Frere of Dungate, who had inherited them from his father, Sergeant Frere, the nephew and adopted son of Lady Fenn. These also I transcribed and forwarded to Mr. Furnivall, and a week later, accidentally opening the volume of *Lidgate's Poems* among the Gale MSS., my eye was attracted by the name 'Generydes,' and to my great satisfaction upon further examination I discovered that the MS. contained all but one leaf of the seven-line stanza version. It is a large folio, measuring $17\frac{1}{4}$ inches by 12, vellum, and was written about the middle of the 15th century. No inference can be drawn from the fact that it is bound up with Lidgate's *Sieges of Troy and Thebes*, for it appears, upon closely examining it, to have been originally in a volume by itself, or to have formed a part of another volume. The evidence of this is that the edges of the book are adorned with coats of arms, but these ornaments do not extend over the portion occupied by the story of Generydes, which was therefore, in all probability, originally distinct. At the end of the *Siege of Troy* occurs the signature 'Antonius Thwaites me possidet,' and at the end of the volume 'Henry Thwayts' and 'Henry Thwaites.' Anthony Thwaites may have been the son or descendant of John Thwaites of Hardingham, Norfolk, who married Anne, daughter of Sir William Knevet, and died 22 Henry VII., leaving a son Anthony (Blomefield's *Norfolk*, v. 1198, folio ed.). The book has evidently been in the Thwaites and Knevet families, for their arms are found in various combinations on the margins; and as the Thwaites arms do not appear in the first part, which contains the story of Generydes, whereas the Knevet arms are of frequent occurrence, it is possible that this may have belonged originally to the Knevet family, and may have been bound up with the Lidgate portion after the above-mentioned marriage of John Thwaites with Anne Knevet. The other coats of arms I have been unable to trace with any certainty. To do so would involve a minute and curious, but certainly lengthy investigation, and is altogether foreign to the purpose of this preface. As a further proof that the Generydes portion of the volume was originally distinct from the rest, I may add that the signatures of the quires, which, except the last, consist of eight leaves, are quite separate from those of the quires that follow, which evidently began a volume. Of the Generydes part there were originally 38 leaves, but one of these has been cut out, leaving a gap of 187 lines in the MS. after l. 4619. There are two columns in a page and an average of 45 lines in a column. The handwriting is very like that of the *Siege of Troy* and the *Siege of Thebes*, which follow, and all may have been the work of the same scribe.

The questions of the authorship of the English version and the source of the story are as obscure now as they were when Mr. Furnivall's edition of the other text appeared. I have applied to both M. Gaston Paris, and M. Paul Meyer, but neither of them has met with any French version of the story. It must have been sufficiently popular to have been twice translated into English, and possibly may still be lying hid in some unexpected quarter. The disappearance of the original is scarcely more remarkable than the almost as complete disappearance of the printed edition, of which only a few mutilated fragments are known to exist. These, in all probability, belong to that which was licensed to Thomas Purfoote, as appears by the Registers of the Stationers' Company for the year 22 July, 1568—22 July, 1569, where the following entry occurs (*Arber's Reprint*, i. 389) :—

purfoote Receyvd of **thomas purfoote** for his lycense for pryntinge of a boke intituled *GENERYDES* iiij^d

From the poem itself we get no clue as to the original. The translator, to eke out his verse, occasionally introduces such phrases as 'the story tellith it me' (651), 'Mynne Auctour seith' (686), 'myn Auctour tellith me' (967), 'as the writeng seyth' (1081), 'myn Auctour doth witnesse' (1166), 'the story doth witnesse' (1348), 'the Story tellith me' (1648), 'the story makith mynde' (2131), 'I me reporte onto the letterys blake' (4526), 'as my Auctor doth write' (6002), 'in the story leke as I do fynde' (6732) ; but he tells us no more. In the Roxburghe Club version there is a French original spoken of, and a Latin translation from it by a clerk at Hertford, but here the information ends.

'Now of a geste that was sum tyme,
That was radde in frensh ryme :
A clerk itt in to latyñ tooke
Att hertford out of a booke,
There in latin was it wretin,
As clerkes wele knowen and weteñ.'

In order that those who read the story may not be interrupted by the gap which occurs in consequence of the loss of a leaf from the MS., I give in brief the missing portion from the other version.

After the slaughter of Sir Yuell, Generydes makes his way to the ship in company with Clarionas and the lavender, and reaches Persia in safety, where they are welcomed by the Sultan, who makes a great feast in honour of their return. After the first course had been served, appear three messengers from Auferius to the Sultan, begging him to send his son Generydes to assist him in recovering his lost kingdom

of India from Sir Amclok. The Sultan, who now hears for the first
time that Generydes is a king's son, offers him half Persia and
his daughter Clarionas in marriage. Generydes in return asks for a
hundred knights, that he may win his father's heritage, and desires
that his marriage with Clarionas may be put off till he comes back as
a conqueror and can make her Queen of India. The Sultan grants his
request, and allows Darel and those who were knighted with Generydes
to accompany him. But when the plan was communicated to Clarionas
she was filled with dismay.

The story then goes on as in the text.

I have in almost all cases printed the MS. as it is written, except
where there was an obvious error destructive to the sense of a
passage. In such instances I have sometimes corrected the text,
putting the MS. reading at the foot of the page, and sometimes have
introduced the correction in the Glossary. But I have not always
attempted to fill up the defective or correct the irregular lines,
and have sometimes left the reader to amend the text for himself.
Professor Zupitza, in the first volume of *Anglia*, pp. 481—483, has
printed some conjectural emendations, some of which I had already
made in the margin of my own copy. They are included in the
following list of correction :—

In 34 after *pite* insert *was*. In 39 for *lesse* read *lest*, as Professor
Zupitza suggests. In 146 for *sothe* read *soche*. In 307 for *also* read
al so. In 308 Professor Zupitza conjectures that we should read
preyse for *plese*. In 335 omit *be*. In 414 omit *to*. In 454 for *hem*
read *me*, as Zupitza suggests, where the MS. has *he*. In 601 for
fourth read *fourth with*. In 707 for *renew* read *remew* = *remeve*. In
864 the MS. has *tell vs att it is*, for which I originally conjectured
telle what it is, or *telle all as it is*. I now think the true reading is
telle it as it is. Zupitza conjectures *as att* (= that) *it is ;* but when
at or *att* in this poem is used as a relative it is always preceded by
'that.' See 347, 591, 4388. In 1042 for *send* read *sendeth*. In
1163 the reference to the foot-note is omitted before *Ayre*. Omit
full-stop at end of 1190. In 1330 for *obeyed* read *obeye*. In 1383
after *all* insert *that*, and omit *that* in 1386. In 1446 omit the
second *he*. In 1455 Zupitza conjectures *wrought* for *sought*. In

1460 Zupitza suggests that *Anasere* should be printed instead of *Anasore*, because it is made to rhyme with *prisonere* and *ther*. Perhaps he is right, though in another passage, 2061, I had changed *ther* to *thore* for the sake of the rhyme, as the form *thore* occurs in 3394, 4316. The same correction would apply to 1725 (MS. *Anasare*), 2059, 2592, 2858, to which may be added 5575. In the present text, however, the forms of the name vary between *Anasore* and *Anasare*, while in the Roxburghe Club version we find *Anazaree* and *Anazare*, and I do not feel certain that after all the instances noticed by Zupitza may not be cases of imperfect rhymes. In the various readings given from the printed fragments at p. 224 it will be seen that in 2059 the printed text has *Anazere*, but then in the next line the reading is altered to *that there were*. To proceed with the correction of the text : in 1556 omit *hoole*. In 1633 Zupitza conjectures *ye rebuke* for *he rebukith ;* perhaps the single change of *he* to *ye* would be sufficient. In 1765 put a comma at the end of the line. In 2130 read *traytourly*. In 2481, 2482 something is wrong. Zupitza proposes to omit *That* in the first line. I would suggest the insertion of *it ranne* after *bak* in the second. See 2678. In side-note against 2524 for *Mountenor* read *Mountoner*. In 2576 the MS. has *hyn*, which I have corrected to *hym*, a form of *hem* which occurs more than once in the poem. Zupitza suggests *hem*. In 2682 *withoute moo* should not be between inverted commas. See Zupitza's note on Guy of Warwick, 719. In 2831 for *man of age* we should probably read *maner age*. In the side-note opposite 3018 for p. 60 read p. 69. In 3087 Zupitza suggests *left* for *lost*. In 3125 there is a corruption. We should probably read *Thus* for *This*, and the next word may be read *towardly* in the MS. In 3246 for *on* read *on to*. In 3297 for *to fight* read *for to fight*. In 3347 for *his* read *he his ;* but there is still a corruption in the passage, as is seen from the faulty rhyme. Perhaps we should read *whanne he him understode*. In 3392 for *knew* read *knew how*. In 3412 for *take* read *to take*. In 3414 after *councell* insert *the ;* and in 3416 after *sone* insert *be made*, as Zupitza suggests. In 3570 for *specially* read *speciall*. In 3635 for *swiff* read *swift*. In 3695, 3696 transfer the comma from *voyse* to *courte*. The number of leaf 20 should be opposite 3712. In 3761 for *said* read *saide*, as MS. In 3780 omit *Iuell* and the full-stop at the end of the line, and in 3781 insert *ride* after *cowde*. At the end of 3859 omit note of exclamation. In 3921 the MS. has *on on ;* perhaps we should read *and on*. In 4069 for *after now* read *now after*. In the marginal note opposite 4201 for *Four* read *A few*. For 2467 read 4267 (p. 136). In 4489 the line should be amended by reading *at all aventure*. In 4702 for *be* read *he*, as MS. In 5333 for *noo* read *non*. In 5628 for *lorde* read *lady ;* and in 5651 omit *on* after *lay*. In 5664 omit *mayde ;* and in 5705 for *hir* read *his*. In 5718 after *please* insert *it*. In 5821 insert *on* before *apace*. In 5858 for *ganne yei fall* read *yei fill*. In 5894 omit *ought*. In 6029 for *thorough* read *thorough out*. In 6087 for *euerychone* read *euerych ;* and insert *so* before *stronge* in 6091. In 6195 for *them* read *hym*. In 6271 the metre may be amended by reading *Ther to Abide to tyme,* &c. In 6296, 6297 there is some corruption, probably due to the omission of some lines. At the end of 6443 omit comma. In 6569 for *swounyng* read *swoune*. On p. 211, l. 9614 should be 6614 ; and in the following line *non* should be inserted after *of*. In 6619 insert *the* before *tideng*. In 6640 for *place* read *pales* = palace. In 6693 for *in* read *in to*. In 6718 insert *was glad* or *was fayn* before *of*. There is a corruption in 6821, but I do not see my way to a restoration of the text. In 6966 read, for the sake of the metre, *All as myn Auctour doth reherse*. In the marginal note, 3435, for *untrew* read *untrue ;* and add ERBYS, *sb.* herbs, 6821, to the Glossary.

Besides these there may be many others, but they are not such as to cause a reader any difficulty, and the remedy is generally very obvious.

The Glossary will, I trust, be found fairly complete.

W. A. W.

Trinity College, Cambridge.
   December 7, 1878.

GENERYDES.

In olde Romans and storys as I rede,   1   [leaf 1]
Of Inde Somtyme ther was a nobyll kyng,   Auferius, king
Ientill, curteys, full trew in worde and dede,   of India,
Wyse and manly preuyd in euery thyng,   4
To his people full good and eke lovyng,
Mighty and ryche, a man of nobyll fame,   a man of noble
And Auferius this was the kynges name.   7   fame,

This worthy prince hadde weddyd in serteyne 8 married a
A fayre lady, and comne of nobyll kynne ;   fair lady,
And what pleasure he cowde for her ordeyne,   Serenydes,
                          daughter to the
That shuld be do, ther was noo lette therin ; 11 king of Africa,
In euery thyng he dede hyr loue to wynne,
He hadde nomore to lese and that he knewe,
ffor afterward she was to hym vntrewe.   14 who was
                            unfaithful to him.

Hire fader was a man of grete powre,   15
And kyng of aufrike as I vnderstonde,
his doughter quene of Inde as ye shall here,
kepyng right grete estate withynne the lande, 18
And all the reme obeyed to hyre hande ;
And of hyr name to telle withoutyn lese,
The story seyth she hight Serenydes.   21

This kyng of ynd, of whom I spake before, 22
hadde a Styward a man of grete renown,   His Steward,
he gouernyd the contre bothe lesse and more, Sir Amelok,
                            who governed
Also he hadde the Rule of euery towne,   25 the country,
And namely tho that longyd to the crowne :
him for to plese the pepill were full fayne,
And ser amelok his name was for sertayne. 28

was very intimate
with her.
Not long after ther felle suche aqueyntaunce   29
Betwix the Quene and hym, that allway stiH
hire mynde, hyr thought, was sette to his plesaunce,
All his desire hooly for to fulfiH,   32
And whenne he lyste she was aH atte his wille ;
Gret pite that she in suche a wyse
Shuld sette hyr wurchippe atte so litiH prise.   35

One day the king,
Vppoñ a day the kyng' for his disporte   36
An huntyng' went onto a fayre forest,

witn four or five
attendants,
Whanne he was sadde to putte hym in coumfort,
he lefte his meñ at home bothe most and lesse,   39
Save iiij or v suche as hym semyd best,

rode a hunting
into a fair forest,
And forth he gothe ther as the hartys hye,
his houndys were oncopelyd by and by.   42

An hert was fownde among the holtys hye,   43
And vppe vppoñ his fete he was a noñ ;
The houndys went after witH a mery crye,
The kyng rode after aH hym self alone,   46

and was
separated from
his companions.
TyH he hadde lost his knyghtes euerychone,
The houndes and the hert that was be fore,
Withynne a while they harde of them nomore.   49

So rode he fourtH as noo thyngge he rougHt,   50

He lost his way,
hys game was lost, his knygHtes forþe be hynde,
And specially on them was aH his thougHt,
For hougHe they were he wyste not them to fynde, 53
Thus rydilH he sore trobelyd in his mynde ;
The day was gonne, wherefore rigHt hertely
To god he prayd to send hym) some remedy.   56

but rode on
till he came to
a road which
led to a house,
And, As god wold, hym) happyd in a waye,   57
Whiche brougHt hym) streyte to a goodly place ;
And as his goodis is redy to purvaye

ffor good people in euery nedefuH case,　　　　　　60
With that counfort he rode a better pase,
And whenne that he was come nygh hande *therate*,　　*when a fair maiden opened*
A fayre mayde ther openyd hym) the gate.　　　　63　*the gate*

She seid he was welcome to that ostage,　　　　64　*and welcomed him.*
Ther were nomore but she and other twayn),
One of them was a man) right ferre in age,　　　　*She and her maid and an old man*
The toder was hyr mayden) in *sertayne*,　　　　67　*were the only inhabitants,*
To make hym chere they dede ther besy payn),
To hyr chaunbyr she brought hym) verily,　　　　*and she brought him*
Whiche was arayed right wele and richely.　　　70　*to her chamber,*

In that chaunber ther was an hanged bedde,　　　71　*where was a bed with curious*
Of sylk and gold fuH curyously wrought,　　　　*hangings.*
And ther vppon) a shete of launde was spredde,
As clenly dressed as it cowde be thought:　　　74
'And nowe,' quod she, 'that ye be hedyr brought,
Yow to counfort is holy myñ entente,
This howse is aH atte your comaundement.'　　　77

Anone vppon) as she these wordis saide,　　　　78
Ther come an hert in att the chaunber dore　　　*A hart came in at the chamber door,*
AH embosed; the kyng' was sore dismayede,
Semyng' to hym), as it passid in the flore,　　　81
It was the same he chased in the more;　　　　*which the king thought was the*
This is, thought he, for me some maner trayne,　　*same he had*
And ther with [aH] she seyde to hym) ageyn):　　84　*chased.*

'Be not a ferde of this sodeyñ aventur;　　　　85　*'Be not afraid,' said she, 'it is all*
It is for no harme, it is aH for your beste,　　　　*for the best,*
This old fader he knowit very sure,
Of vij Saugys callid the wysest　　　　　　88　*as the old man knows, who is the wisest of the*
That was in Rome, but *ther* he myght not rest,　　*7 Sages of Rome.*
ffuH wekydly he and his vj felawes
In to the see were cast among the wawis.　　　91

When he was cast adrift with his fellows, he was thrown on the coasts of Syria, where my father is king,

And as the grace of god it wold ordeyne,   92
In Surre was this goodmaɳ cast a lande,
Where my fader is kyngᵗ and souerayne,
Seke and wery ye may wele vnderstonde;   95
And whanne that he was founde oɳ the sand,

and became the chief of his council.

he sent for hyɱ to come and not to fayle,
And whenne he came was made chefe of his councell.

He sayde the land of Surry shuld be lost   99
By a Gyaunte, and all for love of me;

By his advice I was sent here,

Wherefore be his avyse in to this cost
I am come here, in lyke wyse as ye see;   102

and I pray you now pardon me for what I shall say,
[leaf 1, back]

And forthermore I praye yow take iu gre,
That I shall in your presence declare,
As fortune will for youre ease and welefare.   105

And in this case to telle the mater playne,   106
Of very trougth and make no more delayes,

for to-night a child shall be begotten between us that shall do wonders.

This nyght *ther* shall be goteñ betwix vs twayne
A child that shall do mervelys in his dayes,   109
And moche a do he shall haue many wayes
With grete travell, and all eskape right wele,
This old fader canne tell this euery dele.   112

For this cause the hart led you hither.

Only for this, and for noñ other thyng,   113
The hert that ye haue chased all this daye,
he was trewly the cause of yourᵗ comyngᵗ,
And to this place he gidyd yow the weyc;¹   116
This is the very trougth as I yow saye,

Yet you must know that the queen is untrue to you,

Yet most ye knowe a thynge that is bc hynd,
Touchyng the quene, whiche is to yow vnkynd   119

And vtterly ontrew in euery thyngᵗ;   120
She and the Stiward bothe of oɳ assent,
With thor sotilte and false Imageninge,

¹ MS. *wepe.*

Yow to distroye that is ther hoole entente, 123 and with the Steward has plotted your death.'
ffor she is hoole at his commaund[e]ment;
And aH to do yow hurte and hynderaunce,
Whiche afterward shalbe to your plesaunce.' 126

For these tidynges the kyng abasshid sore, 127 The king was sore abashed,
But ayenward whanne he thought ow that mayde
Anone his cher amendid more and more,
Remembryng' the wordis that she sayde 130
Of his abideng' ther; thenne he hyr prayed and asked to know the real cause of his being there,
To late hym) wete the very certente,
And she answerd ayen) that myght not be. 133

'This old fader that is my felaw here, 134 but she said the old man could tell him,
he canne telle that as wele as eny wight.'
The kyng' hast[ed] to here of this mater',
And prayed that man) that he wold telle hym) right.
he answered hym) and saide, 'as for that nyght and this he promised to do next day.
Go to your rest, for that is my councell,
To morow shaH ye knowe withoute fayle.' 140

Anon vpon) ther soper' was redy, 141
She seruyd hym, in[1] like wyse as hym) ought, At supper the lady waited upon him, and
And euery thing Accordeng' by and by,
For his plesur' trowly ther lakkyd noght, 144
With aH deyntes trevly as cowde be thought;
Hyre chere, hyr porte, it was in sothe awyse,
That more goodly that cowde noman devise. 147

After soper, withynne a litiH space 148
She brought hym) to his bedde with torche light, after supper brought him to his bed.
And eyther stode so wele in otheris grace,
That she with hym) layde in armys right; 151
And what plesure they hadde as for y[t] nyght,
Peraventure fuH good, who so it wist,
I canne not saye, deme ye as ye list. 154

[1] MS. and in.

But how that euer it was be twix them thwaync, 155

It so happened
that a child
was begotten,

It happith, so the writeng' doth expresse,

That nyght ther was a child goten certeyn ;

After his hunteng' and his besynesse,   158 ·

ffor his travell and his grete werynes

after which the
king fell asleep,
but the lady
lay awake
sighing,

he felle a slepe, and for to saye yow more

She sleppyd not, but lay and syghid sore.   161

With hyr syghenyng' a non with Alł she wept,   162

letting her tears
fall on his shirt;
so that he
awoke,

And oñ his armys dede the terys falle,

That thorough his shirte he felt it as he slept ;

Right sodenly he brayded and wooke with Alł,   165

And curtesly oñ hyr he beganne to calle,   ·

saying be feared
she repented of
his coming.

'I drede me sore,' quod he, 'in myn entente

That of my comyng heder ye repente.'   168

'Nay,' said she,
'but my sorrow
is for your
departing.'

'Repente,' quod she, 'nay, nay, I yow ensure,   169

Your' departeng' is cause of all my smerte,

Only for that I do this payne endure,

ffor I shall lose the plesur' of myn hert,   172

And all my Ioye, I may it not asterte,

Withoute socour' or helpe O warentice,

My disteyney hath shape it in this wyse.'   ·   175

'Fair lady,' he
said, 'I hope
we shall not
part so soon,

'My fayre lady,' quod he to here Ageyne,[1]   176

'I haue good hoope we shall not parte so sone,

And if we do, I seye yow certeyn

My chefe counfort is all to geder doon ;   179

To morow shall we wete or it be none,

but to-morrow
the old man will
tell us.'

This old fader that ye kepe with you here,

he shall telle vs the trougth of this mater.'   182

When it was day and it was tyme to rise,   183

This old fader on to the kyng' he goth,   ·

And whanne he cam he spak in this wise ;

[1] MS. *Areyne.*

'That I shall sey, leve me withoute othe,   186   At daybreak the
This nyght is geten a sone betwix yow both,   old man
                                                                told him that he
Whiche shalbe suche, myn auctour doth expresse,   must leave,
That all contres shall speke of his prowesse.   189

Here may ye a byde no lenger in this place,   190
ffor very trough for causes more thanne on;
But of your shirt I must telle yow the cause,   and that the
                                                                tear-stained shirt
Vppon the whiche hir terys fell vppon: 193   could only be
                                                                washed by the
Ther shall non wassh them owt but she alone,   lady herself.
Not be no maner of craft, take this of me,
But she sette handes therto it will not be.   196

And now to yow, madame, thus I saye;   197   The lady he
                                                                warned to return
Yow must departe, and I shall telle yow whye,   to her father,
The kyng youre fader is right seke this day,
And lythe ner' vppon the poynte to dye;   200   who was dying.
And but ye ryde this day right hastely,
And leve aparte all other thyng therfore,   [leaf 2]
Ye are not lyke to speke with hym nomore.'   203

When he seid all that he thought to seye,   204
Ther nedid noo displeasur' to be sought;
The kyng knewe wele ther was non other way,
They must departe, and that was all his thought;   207
Thenne were they bothe so ferre in sorow brought,
Be cause of ther' so sodenly departeng,
They cowde not speke a word for erthely thyng.   210

He toke his leve in sorowfull maner,   211   The king took his
                                                                leave in sorrow,
hym for to be holde it was a grete pite;
And furthe he ridethh with full heuy chere,
With his knyghtes to mete and it wold be: 214
And at the last it happyd hym to see,   and in a fair
                                                                valley fell in with
Where as they rode in a full fayro vaile,   his knights,
he sporyd his hors and theder toke the way.   217

They hym perseyued sone, and forthe they went,   218
A none they mette the kynge vppon the waye,

who saw that he
was sad.

he was no thyng mery to ther entente,
That wist they wele yet durst they noo thyng seye,   221
Withynne his brest he kept it day be day;
And whanne that he came home, I yow ensure,
Of his councell ther wist non erthely creature.   224

Now to this lady lete vs turne ageyn,   225

The lady went
her way to Syria
with the old man
and her maid,

Whiche to Surry hath take hir viage,
And in hir companye no man but twayn,
hir mayde and the old man ferre in age;   228
So atte last they come to the village,
Ther for to rest as for a nyghtis space,
A dayes Iurney owt of the kynges place.   231

She Rode to court in grete hevynesse,   232

and came to her
father,

And furth with all she came to the kyng,
Which was febyll and sokyd with sekenesse;
Yet not for thy he hadde trew knowleginge   235

who gave her his
blessing,

Of his doughter, and gave hyr his blyssyng,
his land, is good, withoute eny stryffe,

and died,

And so to god he passed owt of his lyffe.   238

. There was wepyng and many a hevy chere,   239
Among them all grete sorow ganne they take,
And as it is the custom and maner,
Anone they were arrayed in clothis blake;   242
And sone[1] vppon ordenaunce ganne they make,

and was royally
buried.

In all the hast posible as for his beryeng,
In Ryall wise accordyng to A kyng.   245

This yong lady so goodly and so faire,   246
The lordes all and the Comyns of the lande,
Be cause she was his doughter and his ayre,

---

[1] MS. sone A.

They toke hir for ther queno I vnderstonde, 249 *His daughter was crowned queen,*
And crowned hir with septer in hyr hande ;
And afterward, as is tho right vsage,
The lordys all to hir dede homage. 252

She was full wele belouyd in certeyne 253 *and was well beloved,*
Of hir lordes and of hir comenaute,
And of hir name sho was callid Sereyne,
ffro tho first day of hir natiuite, 256 *but refused to marry.*
ffull humbly they hir be sought that sho
Wold be maryed, for that was ther a vise, *Her name was Sereyne.*
But that she wold not in no maner a wyse. 259

The tyme came that hir wombe be ganne to grow 260 *At length, when her womb began to grow, she took*
Som dele gretter thanne it was wont to be,
But yet sho wold not it hadde ben knowe ;
here mayde sho callid furth in priuite, 263 *counsel with her maid Medeyn,*
Meden she hight, tho story tellith it me,
To whom the queno hadde a right fey[th]full trost,
ffor to that mayde sho myght sey what here lyst. 266

And whan she came, she told here all the case, 267
lyke as it was of all here aventur :
'Madame,' quod sho, 'I shall with goddes grace *who promised to be true to her,*
ffull trewly kepe your councell be you sure :' 270
So went she fourth hyr scosynne to endure, *and so it went on till the time of her delivery arrived.*
Till atto last, be goddes purvyaunce,
The tyme was come of hir delyueraunce. 273

Thenne was ther non of councell saue Medeyn ; 274
Ther was no noyse, nor ther was noo cryeng,
I canne wele thynk tho gretter was hir payne ;
her meny hadde non other knowleginge, 277
But hir sekenes was of some other thinge :
So this lady, full debonerly and myld, *She brought forth a son;*
Brought furth a sonno whiche was a threfte child. 280

but none knew
save Medeyn,
who took it to a
lavender to be
brought up.

Medcyne it toke and in hir lappe it leyde,   281
She brougħt it streyght on to a lavender ;
'This is sothely my Suster sonne,' she sayde,
'I wold it were kept in good maner.'   284
'Maistres,' seyde she, 'care not for this mater,
I shaħ it bere oñ to A good noryse,
Whiche shaħ it kepe right wele o warantyce.'   287

A nurse was
found for the
child,

First to a norise, as fast as euer they canne,   288
They brougħt the child withoute eny lese ;
And thanne to chircħ to make a cristenmañ,

who was christ-
ened Generydes.

And callid it be name Generydes ;   291
Thenne his moder, after aħ hir dissese,
Askyd medeyñ if she hadde done wele
And she seid yae, and told hir euery dele.   294

As soon as he
could speak

Whenne the tyme was come that he cowde speke and goo,
And vnderstonde what folkys did hym) calle,

the queen sent for
Medeyn to bring
him to court.

The quene anoñ, withoute wordes moo,
Callid Medeyñ, and she came furtħ with aħ :   298
'Medeyñ,' quod she, 'my wiħ in[1] especiaħ
Is for to haue my sone Generydes
In courte[2] with me his honour to encrese.'   301

[leaf 2, back]

To curte he came a pratye yong seruaunt,   302
But what he was ther wyst noo creature,
Saue only this that Medeyn) was his Aunte,[3]

He came,
and grew up at
court,

And so fourtħ in courte he dede endure,   305
Tiħ he was wexen) of a goodly stature,
And ther witħ also Ientiħ and curteys,
That[4] aħ the countre[5] right gretely did hym) plese. 308

till one day he
asked Medeyn of
his father.

Vppoñ A day he axkid of Medeyn)   309
Of his ffader, and hougħ is moder was,
She answeryd hym), and this she sayde ayen),

---

[1] MS. *is in.*   [2] MS. *contre.*   [3] MS. *Aunte.*
          [4] MS. *Thall.*   [5] *? courte.*

'I yow besecho of respite in this case   312
Till on) the morow, and thenne with goddes grace
All that ye haue desired now of me,
Sone shall ye knowe tho very serteynte.'   315

Of his desire tho quene hadde knowleginge,   316
She sent for hym) and seid, 'Generydes, .
Of ynde suerly your' fader is the kyng',
And I your moder am withoute lese ;   319
But ye must kepe this mater husht and pece,
ffor ther is now that knoweth it sauc we twayne
In all the court, but if it be Medeyn).'   322

And whenne he knowe this mater very right,   323
Streyght to the quene he seid for eny thing' ;
Besechyng' hir of licence that he myght
So the courte where his fader is kyng' :   326
ffor as hym) thought it were right wele semyng',
ffor to do hym) seruice as in that case,
And rather ther thanne in a stranger place.   329

And he wold so demene hym) furth with all,   330
That in tho countre ther shuld no maner weight,
But if it were the kyng' in especiall,
Wete what he¹ were be countenaunce or sight.   333
The quene Answeryd and seyd, 'all is but right
That ye desire, and therfore be myn) Assent
Is and shalbe to forder your ente[nt].'   336

And furth with all sho callid Natanell,²   337
A Ientill man right connyng and courteyse ;
To hym) sho told this mater euery dole,
Of hyr and of hir sonne Generydes,   340
And who is fader was withouten) lese,
And how that his desire in eny wise
Is for to do his fader some seruice.   343

¹ MS. *I*.   ² MS. *Natarell*.

'Therfore,' quod she, 'I prae yow feithfully,   344
That ye witt do the pleasure that ye may
Onto my sone, and teche hym throughely
That att longith to hym to do or saye ;   347
ffor his expencez and for his aray,
ffor hors or men that maye be for your spede,
he shatt not lakke no thyng' that hym nede.   350

whom she warned to beware of the Steward, But be wett ware that the Stiward knowe not this, 351
Whiche is ontrewe and hath be many a daye ;
ffor if he may knowe who is sonne he is,
he witt suerly distroye hym and he maye :   354
Wherefore whanne ye come ther this shatt ye seye,
A Dukes sone he is and born in Greke,
To se the kyng' and wurchippe for to seke.   357

And whanne ye maye fynd good leyser and spase,   358
That sekerly ye may speke with the kyng',
Ye shatt me recomaunde on to his good grace
and to convey a ring from her to the king. ffutt humbly, and take ye hym this ryng',   361
he gave it me atte our' last departeng';
When he it seth it shatt his thought renewe,
And suerly knowe that your massage is trew.'   364

This Ientitt man gave answere[1] in this wise :   365
Natanell promises to obey her wishes. 'Madame,' quod he, 'my witt is and shatt
To do your' sone pleasure and seruice,
As ye shalbe right wele content withatt,   368
With goddes grace and what that euer befatt,
Better or werse or what aventure be tyde,
Ye shatt witt wete I witt with hym a byde.'   371

Furthe on his way Rideth Generydes,   372
lakkyng' no thing that cawde be hadde in mynde ;~
And of his labour' wuld he neuer sese,

---

[1] MS. an answere.

TiH he come streyght atte Reme of ynd, 375   They come to India, to the chief city

Thenne for*ther*more as reasone wold hym) bynd,

Of dyuerse folke he asked where laye the kyng' :

Att parentynne, they seid withoute feyning', 378   Parentine,

Off aH the land named the chefe Citee : 379

Then) NatanеH as sone as euer he myght,

The best loggyng' of aH that he cowde see,   where Natanell took a lodging,

ffor his maister he dede it redy dight, 382

And ther he toke his rest as for that nyght,

And on) the morow in good and riche araye,   and on the morrow they

he went to see the kyng' ther as he laye ; 385   went to court.

And NataneH with hym) in companye. 386

The kyng' was sette and *ser*ued in the haH,   The king was in the hall among his lords.

With knyghtes and Esquyers throughely,

In grete astate among the lordes aH ; 389

Thanne NataneH the porter' ganne to calle,

he came anon withoute taryeng',

And curtesly gaue them) ther welcomyng'. 392

Furthe anon in to the halle they ganne goo, 393

And to the kyng' they made Reuerence,   They made their reverence to him,

lyke as it was accordyng' for to do.

Thenne NataneH in opyn) audience, 396

Before his lordes in his hye presence,

ffuH connyngly in aH his demeanyng',

Right in this wise he seide onto the kyng' : 399   and Natanell said

' Ryght noble pr*ince*, this Ientilman) present 400

To yow is come ferre out of his contre,

A dukes sone of Greke born) by disente,   that Generydes was the son of

here in your' court desireng' for to be, 403   a duke of Greece,

To lerne connyng' and wurchippe for to see :   [leaf 3]

The Duke his ffader wold he shuld do so,   who desired to be in the king's

And be right gladde ye leste excepte hym) so.' 406   court.

When he hadde seid and made his Reuerence,　　407
The kyng⸳ anon⸳ thanne answeryd to Nataneħ,

The king gave them welcome,
And seid he was welcome to his presence,
Be holding⸳ wele his face and euerydele;　　410

and was reminded of the lady who had harboured him so well,
Thenne that lady that harboryd hym⸳ so wele
ffeħ in his mend, and thought be his visage
he was fuħ lyke to be of hire lenage.　　413

He loked fast oñ to hym⸳ in stede fast wise,　　414
thinking Generydes might be his son.
And thought alway his sonne that he shuld be:
Whenne mete was do the kyng⸳ be ganne to ryse,
To nataneħ his maister thanne saide he:[1]　　417
'This yong⸳ Esquyer is right welcome to me;
he shaħ lak noght, I say yow for certeyn⸳;'
And he right lowly thanked hym⸳ ageyn⸳.　　420

They hadde mantellys and aħ of on⸳ makyng⸳,　　421
Whiche were right sone departed bothe in fere;
Generydes gives his mantle to the butler,
Generydes withoute taryeng⸳
Gaue his mantiħ on to the Boteler⸳,　　424
Thenne Natanell, in right curtes maner⸳,
Natanell his to the porter.
To the porter he gaue that was his owne,
In thankefuħ wise the better to be knowen⸳.　　427

And so they live in court.
Thus in the courte dwellid Generydes,　　428
Right wele belouyd of euery creature,
So weħ wexen that he was doutelys
A very goodly man⸳, I you ensure:　　431
With good vesage, fuħ metely of stature,
his porte, his chere, and all his behavinge
ffuħ like a Ientilman⸳ in euery thyng⸳.　　434

After a time, as the king was alone in a gallery,
It happyd so withynne a litiħ space,　　435
The kyng⸳ a lone went in [a] Galery;
Thanne Nataneħ aspied where he was,

[1] MS. *he saide.*

And to the kyng' he went trewly,   438
To late hym) wete his erand by and by,
lyke as he was comaunded for to sey,
And thus he seid withoute more delay :   441

'Syr, if I durst be bold as in this case,   442
My message wold I say, if it yow please,
The quene Sereyne commanditħ hir to *your* grace,   Natanell gave
And sent yow here your' sonne Generydes :   445   him the ring
Be cause ye shaħ think it is noo lese,   and message
                                                                from Sereyne.
She chargyd me to take yow this ring',
Ye gaue it hir atte your bothe departyng'.'   448

The kyng' toke gode avise vppon) the reng',   449
It was his owyn), and that anon) he knowe ;
To Nataneħ he seid withoute feyni[n]g',   The king recog-
'Gramercy, frend, for your massage is trew,   452   nized the ring
Ye haue brougħt hym) that dotħ my ioye renew ;   and thanked
                                                                Natanell.
Whanne he come first hem[1] thougħt it shuld be he,
Wherefore I prae yow bryng' hym) on) to me.'   ·455

Thanne furtħ with aħ departed Nataneħ,   456
Generydes he brougħt on to the kyng' ;   Generydes was
Whanne he was come the kyng be held hym) weħ,   then brought
                                                                to the king,
And liked hym) rigħt wele in eu*er*y thyng',   459
God wote he was so gladde of his comyng',
That ther cowde noman) deme betwix hem) twayne,
Whiche of them) bothe were gladder in certayne.   462   and both were
                                                                glad.

Whanne this was do he went to his *seruice*,   463
The kyng dede caħ on to hym) Nataneħ,
And chargod hym) in eny man*er* wise,
Aboue aħ thyng' that he shuld kepe hym) welle ;   466
Thanne *seruyd* he the quene att eu*er*y mele,   After this Ge-
Bothe att hir mete and soper decently,   nerydes attended
                                                                upon the queen,
The whiche he dede fuħ wele and manerly.   469

[1] MS. *he.*

Withynne a[1] while it happyd in y[is] wise,   470
The quene beheld Generydes so well,

who liked him
so well that all
her love was
set upon him,

And liked hym so wele in his service,
That all hir loue on hym was euery dele,   473
And in hyr self she cowde non other fele ;
Withoute that she myght have his loue ageyn,
She were on don for euere in certayne.   476

and one day,
when the king
was gone a-
hunting, she
told him all,

Not long after the kyng on hunteng went,   477
Generydes that day abode behynd,
The quene knew that, and sone for hym she sent,
And told hym all that lay sore in hir mynd ;   480
'Generydes,' quod she, 'if I myght fynd
That ye wold loue me best and so endure,
I shall do yow the same I you ensure.   483

Full long agoo I was in this purpose,   484
Butt thenne I myght not telle yow what I ment,
Desireng yow to kepe this mater close,
And lete me haue knowlage of your entent ;   487

promising him
great worship
if he would
assent.

I promys you if ye will assent,
In grete wurchippe I shall yow wele avaunce,
And alway do that may be your plesaunce.'   490

Generydes stode still in grete musyng,   491
And to the quene gaue answere in this case :

Generides said,
'I am the king's
man, and can-
not be untrue
to him,'

'Madame,' quod he, 'I am bounde to the kyng,
To be his man her and in euery place ;   494
And I so moche am hold to his grace,
That for to haue his Reme myself alone,
I wold not be ontrew to his person.'   497

and took his
leave.

With that he toke his leve and furth he went ;   498
And whanne she sawe it wold non other be,
She threte hym sore, and seid he shuld repent,

¹ MS. *ai.*

She rente hir here, a wonder thyng' to see,   501 The queen en-
And broughܕ hir self clene owt of charite;   raged, tore her
The Stiward came and sawe alܭ was amys,   hair and threaten-
'Madame,' quod he, 'what grete affraye is this?' 504

'Afraye,' quod she, 'so may ye wele it calle.'   505 telling the
'But who did this?' quod he, 'I prae yow saye;   Steward
Telle me the sothe, and late me dele withalܭ,
ffor I shalܭ sone a wreke alܭ this arraye,   508
What euer he be he shalܭ repente the daye
That he was bold, in ernest or in game,   [leaf 3, back.]
To do to yow this villany and Shame.'   511

'It is,' quod she, 'that fals Generydes,   512
Be cause he myght not haue his wilܭ of me;
ffor by noo prayour' he wold neuer sese,
But thus he hath arayed me as ye se.'   515 that Generydes
And whanne the Stiward hard that it was he,   had offered her
'Madame,' quod he, 'be ye no mor' displesid,   violence.
ffor in this case your' hart shalܭ sone be eased.' 518

He toke a naked sward and forth he goth,   519 The Steward
Generydes to slee if that he myght;   took a sword
But he wist wele beforn) the quene was wroth,   and went forth
Wherefore be tyme he went owt of hir sight: 522 to kill Generydes;
To his chaunber' the Stiward goth fulܭ right,
In euery place he sought hym) vppe and don),
And he was atte his logging' in the town),   525 but he had gone
                                     to his lodging
                                     in the town,

Owt of daunger, and with hym) Natanelܭ   526
To whom) he told this mater alܭ in feere;   and told Na-
Quod he ageyn), 'here in we shalܭ do welܭ   tanell, who
Tilܭ that the kyng' come home we wilbe here, 529 advised him to
Thanne wilܭ it be good tyme to draw yow neer', await the king's
And do seruice like as ye did be foore,   return.
What euer falܭ they shalܭ preyse yow the more.' 532

The kyng came home, with hym his knyghtez aH, 533
Generydes, as he was wont to do,
ffuH wele and goodly seruyd in the haH :
The Stiward hadde fuH grete enuy therto, 536
And in his hand he bare a staff also ;
So goth he furthe in myddes of the prese,
In grete auger threting' Generydes 539

Withoute reason), and seid, ' what dost yᵘ here ? 540
here is noman) content of thii seruice.'
Generydes he gaue hym) non answere ;
' Why spekist thu not ?' quod he, ' thu art not wise.'
And with that word, in fuH creweH wise,
he toke hym) be the heere ther as he stode,
And smote hym so that his nose braste on blode. 546

And whanne the kyng' perseyuid aH the case, 547
Thow he were wrothe ther ought noman hym) blame,
To see his sonne so wrongyd as he was ;
he callid on to the Stiward bi his name, 550
' Traytour,' quod he, ' god geve yᵉ uery shame,
This yong' Squyer suerly dede non offence,
And thou hast smetyn) hym) here in my presence. 553

Not only now thu dost me villany, 554
Butt here afore thu hast do many moo : '
And with his knyff he smote hym)[1] hastely
Thorough the arme, and when) he hadde so do, 557
' Out of my sight I warne the that yᵘ goo.'
With that the quene was wroth in hir maner,
Thought she anon this towchith me right ner. 560

Owt of the court the Stiward went his weye, 561
To his casteH he toke the wey fuH right,
And made hym strong' of men) and of array,

[1] MS. hym hym.

And euermore his thought was day and nyght   564   and plotted
To avenge hym) of the kyng if that he myght ;   vengeance.
To that purpose he sette aH his entente,
And moche people he hadde of his assent.   567

Now late vs leue aH this as for A space,   568
And to Generydes I wiH returne,   Generydes was so
So rebukyd and skomfite as he was,   discomfited
he cowde not make no chere but alwey mourn),   571   that he could not
And lenger ther he thought not to sogeourne,[1]   remain,
But hastely to make his departeng,
And furth withaH he came to the kyng.   574

He knelid down) and seid right in this wise ;   575   and begged the
'Ser, if it please your goodnesse for to hire,   king
WitH yow I haue contynued my seruice
In pese and rest, and now ye[2] Stiward her'   578
hath smete me in fuH crueH maner,
And hath putte me to Shame in your' presence,
And wile I wote I dede hym) non) offence.   581

I may not ease my hert as in this case,   582
That doth me harme whanne I remembre me,
here afterward I shaH, be goddis grace,
Think ther vppon) whanne I a seasone see,   585
I wiH no lenger dwelle in this contre,
Wherefore, I you beseche, sithe it is so,'
That ye wiH graunte me licence for to go ;   588   to let him go.

And whiH I leue your' trew man shaH I be,   589
Where euer I traveH to and fro,
To do yow pleasur' that at lithe in me,
ffor right gretly am I holden) therto.'   592
And whanne the kyng knew weH that he wold go,   The king
And that ther was non) other meane to fynde,
God wote he was right heuy in his mynd.   595

       [1] MS. *sogeourur.*   [2] MS. *now is* y'.

and all his knights were sorry

The knyghtes aH, and the squyers truely,   596
Were fuH sory of his sone departeng,
Notwithstondyng ther was noo remedy,
But furth he goth withoute more taryeng,   599
Right vmbly he toke leue of the kyng,
And so fourth he went thorough owt yᵉ haH,

when he took leave.

ffuH curtesly he toke leue of them) aH.   602

Generydes and Natanell

Generydes and also NataneH   603
To ther logging they toke the redy waye,

trussed up their harness

And trushed ther' harnes euery dele,
Whanne that was do Generydes ganne saye,   606
'Now late vs here appoynt for our' Iurnay

and resolved to go

In to what land or contre we shaH goo.'
Quod nataneH, 'that hold I wele to do: 609

[leaf 6]

To Surry ward, hough seye ye now be that?   610
The quene Sereyne wold right fayne se you *ther*.'
'AH that is sothe,' quod he, 'but wote ye what?
In stranger' place fayne wold I that we were,   613
ifor I am now of age harmes to bere;
And to be knyght as I see other be,
The more wurchippe the better think[eth] me.'   616

'AH this is very sothe,' quod NataneH,   617
'To your entent I canne right wele agree;
Ther is a land I am remembryd wele,

to Persia.

Men) call it Perse, a plenteuous contre,   620
Ther and [yow] wiH the Sowdon) may yow see,
The whiche is knowyn) bothe ferre And nere,
A myghti prince, a man) of gret powre.'   623

Generydes thanne answerd in this wise: 624
'To that contre I rede we take the waye,
ffor ther we may not fayle of good seruice,

As ye suppose, tell me what ye seye.'   627
'Kepe still,' quod he, 'your purpose I yow praye,
To myn entent ther is best abydeng,
I wote he will be gladde of your comyng.'   630

Ther hors, ther men, were redy euerychon,   631
To that contre they toke the wey full right,
And on hir wey so ferre fourth were thei goon,
That of the Citee sone they hadde a sight,   634
Theder they came be thanne it was nyght,
And fourth withall to ther loggyng they went,
The best that they cowde fynde to ther entent.   637

It was the best Citee of all the lande,   638   They came to the chief city, Mountener,
And mountener it hight withoute fayle,
Therin the Sowdon was I vnderstonde,   where the Sultan Goffore dwelt,
In a castell full riche of apparell.   641
Generydes thanne after his grete apparell,
And Natanell they bothe in good aray,
To the Sowdon they toke y⁰ redy way.   644

And whanne they came ther as the Sowdon was,   645
Ther wer knyghtes and Squyers many on,
hym self walkeng in his disporteng place,   and found him walking in his pleasure ground.
They all awaiteng vppon his persone,   648
Generydes and Natanell anoon·
Avaunsed them the sowdon for to see,
Goffore he hight, the story tellith it me.   651

Whanne[1] he hym saw he did to hym obeseaunce,   652
ffull manerly and seyd right in this wise;
'Ser, if it be your will and your pleasaunce,
her am I come to offer my seruice   655   Generydes offered him his service,
To your lordshippe, right as ye list to devise,
Now please it yow to take me for your man,
And I shall do suche seruice as I canne.'   658

¹ MS. *Thanne.*

The Sowdon) stode and hard hym) euery dele,   659
he toke good hede att hym) in euery thing';
And dougħt ye not he lekid hym) rigħt wele,
Bothe his person) and aħ his demeaneng',   662
And furthwith gaue hym) his welcomyng'
ffuħ curtesly, and seid in Ientiħ wise;
'I am) content of you to haue seruice :   665

What¹ is your' name? I prae yow teħ it me.'   666
'My name,' quod he, 'ser, is Generydes.'
'Generydes,' he said, 'wele mote ye thee ;
A Ientilman) ye seme withouten) lese,   669
And in wurchippe rigħt lekely to encrese ;

and was accepted. Wherefore of suche as do to me seruice
I wiħ that ye be nexst in eny wise.'   672

The Su'tan's daughter, The Sowdoñ hadde his dougħter and his ayre   673
In his palys vnder his gouernaunce,
And for certeyne she was rigħt inderly fayre,
And, as the writeng' makith remembraunce,   676
ffuħ womanly of speche and countenaunce ;
In suche wise hir' name beganne to sprede,
That euery man) spake of hir' goodlyheed.   679

And as the Sowdon) was sett att his mete,   680
Generydes softely he beganne to calle,
The best deynte that before hym) was sett
he toke it hym), and badde hym) goo with aħ   683
To his dougħter : 'my lord,' quod he, 'I shaħ.'
So fourth he gotħ ther as this lady was,
Clarionas, Myune Auctour seitħ she higħt clarionas.   686

loved Generydes, This fayre lady beholde Generydes,   687
In stedefast wise on) hym) she cast hir eye,
Aħ his maners so wele it did hyr plece,

¹ MS. That.

That she constreyned was in certeynte 690
To loue hym best, it wold non other be;
She thought it dede hir good on hym to thynk,
And of hir cuppe she offeryd hym to drynk. 693

He toke it of hir hand full curtesly, 694
And ferthermore, as I this mater fele,
In his conseyte, I say[1] yow certeynly,
hym liked neuer creatur so wele: 697
his mynde, his thought, was sett oon hir yche deell;   *and his mind was set on her.*
And, as I cowde perseyue in myn entent,
There hartes bothe were sone of on Assent. 700

Generydes he toke his leue anon, 701
To sone she thought as after hir avise,
Yet or[2] that he departed was and goon,
To kysse hym she forgate not in no wise, 704
he thanked hir and offerid hir seruice,
To be hire man and alway to be trew,
So to endur and neuer to renew. 707

Vppe from hir mete arose clarionas, 708
And on hir bedde she leyde hir fourth with AH;
hir mayden had grete mervell what it was,
And full softely on hir she be ganne to calle, 711
'Madame,' quod she, 'what thing is now be fall?
Of your dissese I prae yow telle it me,
To wete yow seke it is a gre[te] pite.' 714   *[leaf 4, back]*

Ther with the lady gaue answere ageyn 715   *She told her maid, Mirabell,*
Vnto hir mayden, Mirabell was her name;
'Of my dissese,' quod she, 'yf I shuld layne   *of her disease,*
Only to yow, I wis I were to blame; 718
I haue founde yow, in ernest and in game,
Att all tymes full secrete and full trew,
And soth to saye I neuer other knewe: 721

MS. *sam.*   [1] MS. *of.*

And for to telle you plenly of my dissese,   722
This is the cause ; ther is on) specialy
hath don) me harme, god wote causeles,
I neuer offendid hym) truly ;   725
And me think ther is noo remedy',
ffor I was neuer seke on) this maner',
A fore this tyme now knowe ye all in fer'.   728

' Not all,' quod she, ' madame, that may not be ;   729
ffor yet I haue no knowlage whiche he is.'
' It is,' quod she, ' a yong Squyer', parde ;
he is but late come to my lord, I wis,   732
A very goodly man), so haue I blisse.'
' All this may be, and I beleue the same ;
But good madame,' quod she, ' what is his name?'   735

and that unless
she could see
Generydes,

' To seye yow sothe,[1] Generydes he hight.'   736
Quod she ageyñ, ' now wote ye euery dele ;
Butt I of hym) right sone may haue a sight,

it would not
long be well
with her.

With me I wote it will not long be wele,   739
ffor hym) only is all that euer I fele,
And alway more and more it doth encrese ;
God wote I am no thing' in hertys ease.'   742

' Madame,' quod she, ' dismay yow neuer a dele,   743
Be of good chere, hurt not yow to soore ;
Doughte ye noo thing' All this shalbo right wele,
ffor I shall trewly do my part ther fore   746
With right good will, and for to say yow mor',
ffor [2] this mater I shall do wele ordeyne
That ye suerly shall speke with hym ayen).'   749

With that anon) clarionas be ganne   750
To take hir' chere mor' comfortably,
Notwithstondyng' she was bothe pale and wanne,

---

[1] MS. *the sothe.*   [2] MS. *And for.*

And to hir ma[y]de she seid full soberly,   753
'love Myrabell, I thank yow hertely,
ffor of myn payne now I haue some respite,
And if I leue I shall it yow wele aquyte.'   756

Now late vs leue apart clarionas,   757
And to Generydes turne we ageyn,   Generydes, on his part,
Whiche for hir sake stondith in hevy case,
As full of thought as he myght be certayn ;   760
Out of the cowrt he went for very peyn,
Streight to his logging hastely he hym spedd,
Whanne he came ther he leyde hym on his bedd.   763

His maister had mervell what it ded mene   764   told his master of his case.
So sodenly to see hym in that case,
All distemperyd and out of colour clene,
he mused sore what maner a thing it was ;   767
And whanne that he myght geto a metely space,
Right thus he seid to Generydes,[1]
'I prao yow, ser, Telle me your dissese.'   770

'Mayster,' quod he, 'all that lythe in my hert, 771
What euer it be, to yow I wolle not layn
Why and wherefore I suffer all this smert,[2]
Clarionas she causith it certayn,   774
ffor hir only I suffer all this payne,
And for to sey the very certaynte,
I wote not why she shuld do this to me.'   777

'Ye wote what, ser, after myn avise,   778   Natanell promises to speak with Clarionas.
Bo mery and that is my councell,
In this mater I shall do yow seruice,
And peraventur sumwhat it shall prevaile ;   781
To morow I shall be ther withoute faile,
And spcke with hir as touching this mater,
And what she seith ye shall haue pleyno answer.' 784

---

[1] MS. *Gerocrydes.*   [2] MS. *this certeyn smert.*

'Maister,' quod he, 'I thank you hartely,   785
To yow only is all my very trost,
And what ye think that I shall do trewly,
In this mater' demeane me as ye list ;   788
hough I shall spede fayne wold I that I wist.'
'Wele, ser,' quod he, 'I canne noo ferther saye,
To my power I shall do what I may.'   791

With that he partid fro Generydes,   792

And on the morow, whanne he hadde tyme and space,
Onto the court he went withouten lese,
Therfor to speke with fayre clarionas.   795
Whanne he¹ was come ther as she was,

Myrabell came and this to hym ganne seye,
'Where is,' quod she, 'your' maister, I yow prae?' 798

'Att his loggyng', foll ill att ease,' quod he,   799
'And so a be a sithe afore yester day ;
What hym aylith I woote noo thing' parde,
His comfort and his chere is all awaye,   802
Butt after myn entent this dare I saye,
All this is grow, to tell the mater clere,

Sithe he now last was with my lady here.'   805

Whan Mirabell perseivid what he ment,   806
And what desire he hadde thanne was she fayn,

All this goth wele, thought she, to myn entent.
'Wele, ser,' she saide, 'to yow I will be playn ;   809
Sithe your' maister was here, I will nott layne,
My lady hath be seke bothe day and nyght,

ffor she hadd neuer rest I yow be hight.   812

Yet not for thy, if ye haue ought to saye   813
ffor your maister be his comaund[e]ment,
Goo forth anon with owt more delaye,

¹ MS. she.

And telle hir all tho trougth of your entent,   816
To speke with yow she wilbe wele content.'

So furth withall, after his purpose was,
Streight fourth he goth on to Clarionas.   819

'Madame,' quod he, 'my lord Generydes   820

To you hym recomaundith for certayne,
A wofull man, clene owt of hartes case,
And for to telle yow all tho mater playn,   823
If it please yow ye may respite his payn,
Of your goodnesse to graunt hym that licence,

That he may come on to your nobill presence.'   826

Whenne she had herd these wordes euerydele,   827
'Come nere,' she said, 'Mirabell, I you p[r]aye.'

'Madame,' quod she, 'I vnderstonde hym wele ;
As me semyth with your wurchippe ye may   830
Send me for hym and here what he will saye,
his maister here right sone for hym will goo.'
'I am content,' quod she, 'that it be so.'   833

Myrabell came and toke hym owt Aside ;   834
'Do after me,' quod she, 'as in this case :
Att this wyndow my lady shall abide,
ffor thorough owt the gardeyn he shall pace,   837 into the garden.
And ther he shall haue good leyser and space,
To saye what that hym list in secrete wise ;
Now goo furth for this is myn aviso.'   840

Furth on his way departith Natanell   841
To his maister, and founde hym passeng' sadde :
'What tidynges now,' quod he, 'will it be wele?'
'Right wele,' quod he, 'be ye noo thyng adred :   844
Whanne ye knowe all I wote ye will be glad,
As for tho first, now take this of me aloon,[1]
She will that ye come speke with her anon.'   847

[1] *aloon* added in another hand.

Who was glad
now but Ge-
nerydes?

Now who was gladde, and who was well apayde,   848
And endly mery but Generydes,
Remembryng⁴ what Natanell had seid?
So furth he goth, and neuer wold he sese,   851
Into the courte in myddes of the prese,

He went to the
garden to
Clarionas,

And so furth on vn to Clarionas,
In the gardeyn) where apoynted was.   854

Whañ he hyr saw, he fayled countenaunce,   855
Where with suerly he was not wele apayed ;
And in like wise, to sey yow in substance,
On here behalf she was somwhat dismayde ;   858

and told her

Yet atte last right thus to hir' he saide,
'Madame,' quod he, 'be cause I hadde licence,
I am more bold to come to your' presence :   861

And for to sey yow myñ entent I wis,   862
As for my self this is the mater playn),
ffor I must suerly tell vs att¹ it is ;

of his pain of
heart for her
sake.

My hert is ouercome with very payn)   865
All for your' sake, and so hath beñ certeyñ
Sithe I was here oñ massage sekerly.'
'hoo so?' quod she,² 'I haue grete wounder why. 868

What³ cause haue ye to putte me in this witte?   869

The truth was
soon known on
both sides

As for my part I do no thyng⁴ nee sey,
I rede putte suche thougthes in respite ;
Where I haue not offendid be this day,   872
Wherby ye shuld be hurt by eny way :
Wherefore,' quod she, 'in ernest and in game,
To putte in me the defaute ye are to blame.'   875

'Trewly, Madame,' thenne seid Generydes,   876
'Of me ye ought no magry to purchase,
And for to con) yow thanke for my dissese,

---

¹ So MS. ; perhaps for *telle what*, or *telle all as.*
² MS. *he.*   ³ MS. *That.*

Now trewly that were a strange case.   879
Yet be the meane of fauour and of grace
Ye may me helpe all only and no mo,
O trewth it were your wurchippe so to do.'   882

Quod she ageyñ, 'if it were for to blame,   883   though after
My wurchippe were amendes for to make ;   some bashfulness
                                                              on Clarionas's
And in like wise ye aughht to do the same,   part,
If ther were eny suche that for your sake   886
had so sufferyd payn or heuynesse had tak ;
Peraventour I myghht be oñ of thoo,
What will ye sey,' quod she, 'and it be so ?'   889

'Madame,' quod he, 'I here yow speke right wele,   890
ffull fayne, god woote, I wold that it wer soo.'
'Trewly,' quod she, 'it is thus euerydele,
I yow ensure, I may not goo ther fro ;   893
But my wurchippe may not avowe it soo.
This is the very trouth withoute feyning,
ffor loue will haue his course for eny thing.'   896

Wheñ Myrabell had hard all this array,   897
'After this werr,' quod she, 'god send vs pece :
I canne will think it will not lest alway.'
'Now god defende it,' quod Generydes ;   900
'I must depart,' quod she, 'withoutyñ lese,
As for A tyme your pleasur for to spare;
Of evill speche it is good to be ware.'   903

And shortly for to say you as it was,   904
A full [a]corde was made betwix theñ twayñ :
he gaue a ryng oñ to Clarionas,
And she toke hyñ Another for certeyñ ;   907   and they ex-
                                                              changed rings.
With trew promys eyther for ioye or payñ,
In stedefast wise ther hertys to ensure,
Neuer[1] to chaunge but alway [to] endure.   910

¹ MS. Nouer.

And by that tyme fer passid was the day,   911
Mirabell seyd, 'it is hye tyme for to goo.'
Thanne wist he wele ther was non other waye,

[leaf 5, back] he must departe wheder he will or noo :   914
he toke his leue, wherewith he was full woo ;
And as for hir she was nott wele contente,
Yet not for thy she kist hym or she went.   917

Full of[te] tymes ther[1] were betwix hem[2] twayne, 918
They often meet Dayes apoynted to mete in secrete wise :
in secret. Notwithstondyng I say yow for certeyn,
To hir wurchippe was thought noo preiudice,   921
Butt only to owe hir his seruice,
As feythfully as cowde be thought or ment,
Ther was non other thyng in ther entent.   924

So furth he goth full streyte in to the halle,   925
To do seruice hym thought it for the best ;
And for to sey yow soth among them All,
In court there Thorough owt the court he was the goodliest,   928
was none like
Generydes, In his demeaning the most Ientilest,
And with a spere to renne in warre or pece,
Ther was non like on to Generides.   931

Havkyng, hunteng, he cowd good skill ther on ; 932
And what that eny Ientilman shuld do,
ffor very trougth in all the courte[3] was non,
Knyght or squyer, so wele willyng ther to :   935
and all loved him Thorough owt the courte[3] he hadde the love also
save Malichias. Of euery creatur, bothe more and lesse,
Saue of A knyght callid ser Malichias.   938

As [for] a tyme leue we Generydes,   939
His father's (the And late vs now speke of the kyng of ynd,
king of India's)
Steward And of his Stiward whiche wold neuer sese,

---

[1] MS. they.   [2] MS. hym.   [3] MS. contre.

But of malice compasing' in his mynd   942
AH maner weyes som treson¹ for to fynd ;
With aH the helpe that he cowde geto certeyn),
ffor to distroye his lord and souereyn).   945   plotted against
                                                                                 his lord,

And to performe aH that he haddo take in hand, 946
This fals Stiward he had gaderid people grete,   and gathered an
                                                                                 army
To the nowmber' of iiij or v thousand,
Of men of warre the best that he cowd gete ;   949
And in A busshment fuH sone he had them) sett
Nyhand the town), his treson) to be gynne,
And be that meane the cite for to wynne.   952   to win the city.

Off his tresone the quene knowe wele also,   953   The queen knew
                                                                                 the treason.
It to performe she did aH hir entent,
And of hir councell ther were lordes² moo,
And certeyn) of them) were of hir' dissente :   956
Of aH this werk the kyng' was innocent,
And of ther falsed no thing' perseyuyd,
The more pite he shuld be so dissoyued.   959

And shortly to procede whan this was do,   960
There were iij lordes came on to the kyng',
Desireng' hym) on huntyng' for to goo,
ffuH ontrewly ther with ymagenyng' ;   963
To ther desire the kyng' was welewillyng',   While the king
                                                                                 was hunting with
So fourth on) huntyng' he rode certeynly,   three lords
The iij lordes with hym) in companye,   966

And ij Squyers, myn) Auctour tellith me ;   967
And while he was most besy in his game,
This fals Stiward had goten) the Citee,   the Steward took
The whiche was callid parcyntyn) be name,   970   the city
And made hyn) self proclamed in the same   and proclaimed
                                                                                 himself king.
AH openly bothe kyng' and souereyn),
Ther was no man) that durst saye ther ageyn).   973

          ¹ MS. *tresom*.   ² MS. *lordes*.

The king heard thereof from a forester,

þe kyng' hym self knowe noo thyng' of this case,   974
Till atte last a forster came rideng';
And, wete ye wele, so sorowfull he was,
That he onnethe myght speke to the kyng',   977
And ther he told hym euery maner thyng',
Of his Stiward and of his fals treasone,
And what people he hadde withynne the town).   980

'I must,' quod he, 'telle yow myn) avise and entent ;
The quene is cause of this on) happy case,

and that the three lords were traitors also.

ffor these iij lordes ar' of hir Assent,
That are Abideng' with you in the chase ;   984
And whanne the kyng' perseyuyd hough it was,
All his huntyng' was don and his besynesse,
An hevy mañ [he was] and coumfortles.   987

In this musyng' he rideth furth a pase,   988
The iij lordes they mette hym) on the waye :
'Traytours,' quod he, 'god geve yow euyll grace
ffor your' seruice that ye haue don) to me,   991
So vntrewly your' prince for to be traye,
Whiche neuer hurt nor harme on) to yow ment,
I trost to god ye shall it sore repent.'   994

All his wordes they sett Att litill price,   995
ffor whye they drede hym) not the soth to saye :
And to the kyng' [they seyd] right in this wise,
'Take it in gre the fortune of this day.'   998
And whanne he saw ther was non) other way,

He drew his sword and slew one.

he drow his swerd And smote on) of them so,
And[1] from the grownde he myght noo ferther goo, 1001

Butt felle down dede then) in continent.   1002

The others fled,

his felawes fledde as fast as euer they myght ;
The kyng' sawe that, and after them) he went,

[1] ? *That.*

And ouer toke them) long or it was nyght.   1005
So ferthermore to saye yow the very right,
he slew them) bothe And sayde, 'traytours erante,
Of your falshed ye shall yow neuer avaunte.'   1008

And vppon) this he turned bak ageyn)   1009
To his squyers, whiche were right ferre behynd,
And in this wise he dede to them) complayn) :
'I have,' quod he, 'founde yow bothe trew and kynde,
Now lak I good where with I shuld yow fynd,
And for to counfort me now in my nede,
I canne noo more but Ihesu be your' spede.'   1015

Whenne his squyers had hard hym) thus complayn),
They answerd hym ayen) in goodly wise ;
'Ser, think you not but we shall do our' payn)
To coumfort yow, and do yow suche seruice,   1019
As our' connyng' And Powre may suffice,
And though your' hart be now noo thing' in rest,
With goddes grace All shalbe for your' best.'   1022

The kyng was plesid wele with ther coumfort,   1023
And as hym) thought he prayed them) for to saye
To what contre it were best to resorte,
That for hym) self he myght some what purvaye.   1026
One of them) seyde, 'lo yender lyght the waye ;
Streyght to the Reme of Trace it will yow bryng',
Wherein dwellyth a prince, A[1] nobyll kyng'.'   1029

Toward that land he toke the waye full right,   1030
Whiche was callid a plentevous contre ;
Whanne he came ther, as fast as euer he[2] myght
To se the kyng' he went in certayn[t]e,   1033
In humble[3] wise, besechyng' hym) that he
Might do hym) seruice with his squyers twayne,
In like wise as his pleasur' wold ordeyne.   1036

The kyng⸵ was wele contente of his comyng⸵,   1037
and entered the
king's service,
And of seruice he seid he shuld not fayle ;
What he shuld do he told hym⸱ euery thing⸵,
That myght only to his wurchippe prevaile ;   1040
And so alway, after thought and travaile,
God send rest and coumfort, be ye sure,
To euery wele disposid creature.   1043

Thus in that contre abideth still alway   1044
The kyng⸵ of ynd, vnknowen⸱ in euery wise,
With his ij squyers, a wayteng⸵ day be day
hym⸱ for to serue as they made ther promys ;   1047
And so this prince contynued in seruice,
Right well be trost and cherishid with the kyng⸵,
ffor he cowde please hym⸱ in euery thing⸵.   1050

All that he dede was done so wittely,   1051
his demeanyng⸵ was suche thorough owt the place,
That euery man⸱ hym⸱ preysid by and by,
And he so wele stode in the kyngges grace,   1054
That he hym⸱ gaue, withynne a litill space,
and was made
Steward.
Of all his lande the Stiwar[d]shepe to holde,
And full power to rewle it as he wold.   1057

When he dede as wele as cowde be thought,   1058
Onto the kynggez honour⸵ in certayne,
Iustice was kept like wise as it owt,
Ther was noman⸱ be resan⸱ myght complayne ;   1061
And for he shuld his charge wele susteyn⸱,
The king gave
him an Earl's
land.
The kyng hym⸱ gaue clerly an⸱ Erlys lande,
The whiche but late was com in to his hand.   1064

Now of this mater⸵ a while let vs sese   1065
As for a tyme, And speke of quene sereyne,
That was moder on to Generydes,

And hougȟ that she hadde herd the tidenggez playn,
hougȟ ontrewly his fader be a trayn
Of his lordes made after ther entente,
he was putte owt of his land by ther Assent.   1071

Sereyne
heard how the
king of India had
been put out of
his land.

Off hym and of there sonne Generydes   1072
Was vtterly her mend and aȟ here thought;
And trewly to leue in hartes case,
That cowde she nougȟt tiȟ that she hadde hym sougȟt;
Of her estate no pleasure she no rougȟt,
Saue only for to knowe the certeynte
Of auferius the kyng where he shuld be.   1078

And fourtȟ with aȟ she ganne an erle to calle,   1079
The whiche in sothe hadde widded hir Cosyn,
Rigȟt as the writeng' seytȟ in especiaȟ,
A fayre lady and nexst of Aȟ hir kynne;   1082
The Erle to truste was noo daunger in,
ffor he was ware and wise I yow ensure,
And therwith trew as eny creature.   1085

and sent for an
Earl

She told hym Aȟ the grounde of the mater   1086
In euery thing', and how it was be faȟ,
Of auferius and of hir sonne in fere,
And hougȟ the kyng betrayed was withaȟ,   1089
'Wherefore·my purpose is in especiaȟ
To take on me the labour' and the payn,
Where euer he were to fynd hym in certeyn.'   1092

Then[1] to the Erle she seid in this maner: 1093
'Ye shaȟ here haue the rewle and gouernaunce
Of this contre, with aȟ my full powre;
My men shaȟ be vnder your' obeiseaunce,   1096
And hougȟ it be be disteyne or chaunce,
What euer falle, if I come not Ayon,
Ye[2] shaȟ be here botȟ lord And souerayn.'   1099

to take the
rule of the
country while
she went in
search of
Auferius and
Generydes.

---

[1] MS. *When*.   [2] MS. *ke*.

'Madame,' he seid, 'to gouerne this contre   1100
It is noo liteH thing to take in hand ;
ffor yow it is moche bettyr thanne for me ;
Yet neuer the lese, sithe I vnderstonde   1103
Your purpose is to depart owt of the land,
I wolle fulfille your pleasur in this case,
And trewly as I canne be goddes grace.'   1106

Queen Sereyne
set off,

Now Gothe quene Sereyn fourth on hir Iurnaye,   1107
And in hir company she hadde a knyght,
A trosty man, and othe[r] squyers twaynne,
With but few moo ther hors for to dight ;   1110

came to India

So to the Reme of ynd they went fuH right,
And sone vppon ther labour and traveH

to Parentine,

To parentyne she came with owt fayle,   1113

A towne whiche is rehersid here by fore.   1114
Anon withaH was purveyd a logging

[leaf 6, back]

ffor this lady ; and, for to say yow more,

and lodged with
the faithful
forester,

hire oste was sumtyme dwellyng with the kyng,   1117
The same forster that brought to hym tidengge,
Of his Stiward and of his fals treson,
As he rode in the forest vppe and down. ·   1120

As for a nyght ther toke she hir loggyng,   1121
And made on calle the good man of the place,
'Good ser,' quod she, 'telle me where is the kyng ;
I haue grete nede,' quod she, 'on to his grace.   1124
Sumtyme a lady weH att ease I was,
And now be force,' quod she, 'siche is my chaunce,
I am putte ow[t] of myn enheritaunce.'   1127

'Madame,' quod he, 'here is noo remedy :   1128
The kyng suerly is putte owt of his right
By grete tresone, I saye yow certenly,

By his Stiward and by the quenys myght,   1131
Whiche I may soore repent bothe day and nyght;
ffor now A dayis I lese all that I wanne,
Where here before I was[1] a threfty man.   1134

Wherfor to hym I will, this is noo naye,   1135 *whom she prevailed upon*
Where euer he be, I say yow certaynly.'
Thanne sayd the quene, 'good ser, I yow pray,
That ye will come with me in companye;   1138 *to come in search of the king.*
hym for to fynd I purpose vtterly,
And I shall paye your costez euery dele.'
Quod he, 'madame, I gre me wele   1141

In your presence to travell day by day.'   1142
So on the morow departed quene Sereyne,   *On the morrow they departed*
As erly as she cowde on hir Iurnay,
With hir to goo the forster was right fayn.   1145
So many dayes she laboryd certayn,
That of the Reame of Trace she had a sight,   *for Thrace,*
And thederward they toke the wey full right.   1148

When they came ther the[y] sawe a faire cite,   1149 *and came to a fair city*
As full a pepill as it cowde suffice,
The fayre Reuer grete pleasur for to see,
With shippez grete of dyuerce merchaundise,   1152
All goodly thing that eny cowde wele devise;
And as the Story makith remembraunce,   *of which Auferius was governor.*
kyng Auferius had ther the gouernaunce.   1155

And ther he was purposing to Abyde,   1156
As for A tyme for materys for the kyng:
The quene Sereyn was be the Ryuers side   *The queen lodged by the river side.*
Right Wele loggid, and whan she hadde tideng   1159
A[nd] trew knowlage of Auferius the kyng,
hough he but late was come to the Citee,
God wote full wele therof apayed was she.   1162

[1] MS. *wis.*

For hir' disporte she goth to take the Ayre,   1163
And to the Reueres side she ganne hir dresse ;

Ther was a brygge full strongly made and fayre,
And ther she sawe, myn Auctour doth witnesse, 1166
iij lavenders ded all ther besynesse
A sherte to wassh ; thanne seid she to them iij,
' What do ye here, fayre susters myn ?' quod she.

Quod on of them, 'that were good to be knowe, 1170
It is a wonder wark withouten dought ;
We wassh a shirte, and euer shall I trow,

ffor this ij yere we haue ben it abought,   1173
And yet we cannot gete the spotte[s] owt,
Wherefore they calle vs noo good lauenders,
And we haue vsid it thus many yerez.'   1176

' Shewe me yᵉ shirte,' thanne seid the quene Sereyn,
' And I shall se what I shall do ther to :
Whanne I haue do, ye shall haue it ageyn,
And do ther with what ye list to do.'   . 1180
She toke the Shirte withoute wordes moo,

And wesht it onys and ryneshed it so clene,
That afterward was noo spotte on it seen.   1183

When she had don, she toke it them ageyn,   1184
Or tyme that she departed fro the place ;

To hir logging went the quene Sereyn,
The lavenders hadde wonder of that case,   1187
They mused sore and mervelid how it was :
And home they went the women euerychon,
Whanne it was drye they bare it fourth anon. 1190

To auferius the kyng where as he laye,   1191
In a castell full goodly to behold ;
And whanne he sawe his shirt in that aray,

¹ MS. Araye.

Withoute spotte, he beganne to be cold,   1194   who called to
                                                                    mind what the
To thynk hough that a good old man hym told,   old man had
                                                                    told him.
Bothe of [the] shirte and other thingez aH,

Whiche sith that tyme fuH trewly hath be faH.   1197

The same forster that came with quene Sereyn,   1198   The forester
                                                                    who came with
To the castiH he toke the way fuH right,   the queen went
                                                                    to the castle
To se his lord, god wote, he was fuH fayn.

Whanne he came ther of hym he hadde a sight,   1201

And spake to hym as sone as euer he myght ;

The kyng hym knew, wherof he was fuH glad,

Not withstondeng he fond hym passyng sadde.   1204   and found the
                                                        king sad.

'Ser, if it please your lordshippe,' thanne quod he,   'Sir,' said he,
                                                        'why is this
'I yow beseche teH me your heuynesse :   heaviness?'

To wete yow in this plight it grevith me,

ffor if I myght I wold it fayne redresse ;   1208

And oftentymes it hath be sene expresse,

In grete materys, withouten eny fayle,

A sympiH mannys counceH may prevayle.'   1211

To hym Ayen seid Auferius the kyng ;   1212   The king

'I knowe your trowth, and soo hath doon Alway,

And for to sey yow [sothe] withoute feyneng,

AH this is come to me sithe yester day,   1215

And hough and in what wise I shaH yow saye :'

And so fourth he tolde of quene Sereyn,   told him of queen
                                                         Sereyn,
And hough a child was gote betwix them twayne,   1218   [leaf 7]

And of his shert where on hir[1] terys felle,   1219   and of her tears
                                                         on his shirt which
That now shuld wassh them owt saue only she :   none but herself
                                                         could wash out.
'Now is it clene, whiche lekith me fuH ille,

ffor thus I thynk It canne non other be ;   1222

But she is dede in very certente.'   'But she is dead.'
                                                         'Nay, Sir,
'Nay,' quod he, 'ser, I trow it be not soo,

ye shaH here better tydengez or ye goo.   1225

[1] MS. *his*. But see ll. 162, 193.

I saw a fair
lady wash a
shirt by the
river's side.

I saw but late vppon the Ryueres side   1226
One wassh a shert, I wote not whose it is.'
Whanne he[1] hard that he wold not long abide
But askid more, 'now telle me who did this,'   1229
Quod auferius, 'so haue ye Ioye and blysse.'
'A fayre lady,' quod he, 'I yow ensure,
And for to chese a goodly creature.   1232

I came with her
out of India to
seek you.'

I came with hir owt of the Reme of ynd,   1233
And atte myn howse ther toke she[2] hir loggyng;
She askid me where that she shuld yow fynde,
And I told hir I hadd no knowlachyng;   1236
So fourth she went and left all other thing,
At a venture your welefare for to see,
And so came I with hir to this citee.'   1239

'Now, help me
to see her,'
said Auferius.

'Now, for my loue, helpe that I may hir see   1240
In eny wise,' quod Auferius the kyng;
'ffor I canne think right wele that it is she,
Whom that I loue aboue all other thing.'   1243
The forster seid, 'ser, on to hir loggyng,
When euer it please yow, I shall be your gyde;
ffor she is here by vppon the Ryuerez side.'   1246

In this mater ther was no more to saye,   1247
No lenger avise nor lenger abyding,

Without delay
he went to her
lodging.

Butt furth he rideth vppon his hakeney,
Vppon the Reuerys side to hir logging: 1250
And whanne she had knowlache of his comyng,
Remembryng hough that she shuld hym see,
Wete ye right wele a glad woman was she.   1253

When he was come and knewe that it was she,   1254
ffor very glad he wist not what to saye;

When she saw
him

Whenne she hym sawe it wold non other be,

---

[1] MS. *she*.   [2] MS. *che*.

Butt furth with aH in swounyng ther she[1] lay.   1257
As sone as he hir sawe in that armye,
God wote he was aw hevy maw therfore,
And ther with [all] abisshid more and more.   1260

Yet Atte last full Ientilly he went,   1261
And toke hir in his armys for sertayw,
hir to commfort he did aH his intent ;
With that she came vnto hir self ageyw.   1264
Thanne was ther ioye betwix them twayw,
ffor to teHe yow aH it were a wounder,
And ofte they kist or they woldł part A sonder.   1267

Thanne was ther not ferre owt of the Citee   1268
A fayre casteH, and thederward he went
Owt of the Citee, not[2] ferre past ij myle or iij,
That was his owew att his comaundment.   1271
Whanne [he] came ther for moche people he sent,
The whiche held of his lordshippe and fraunchesse,
That *thei* shuld come to hym in eny wise.   1274

And so they dede moche people in certayw ;   1275
Whanne they were come he told them aH the case,
Desireng them to goo for quene Sereyne
To the Citee, and bryng hir to this place ;   1278
ffor he purposith sone, with goddes grace,
In as short tyme as he cowde wele devise,
hir for to wedde in honorabiH wise.   1281

To this casteH they came with quene Sereyw,   1282
Right wele a compayned in euery wise,
Of hir comyng the peopiH were fuH fayw,
And offeryd hir right lowly ther seruice ;   1285
Atte hir pleasur and atte hir owyn devise,
In that casteH she tared for to rest,
Onto the tyme they purvayed for the fest.   1288

[1] MS. *se.*   [2] MS. *nor.*

Meanwhile
the king fell
sick

In this meane while, the kynges massenger   1289
To Auferius he came withoute fey[n]ing.
Curlus he hight and seid in this maner:
'My lord,' quod he, 'ye must come to the kyng   1292
In aH the hast, and make noo taryng';
I drede me sore he may not long endure,
ffor he is passyng seke I yow ensure.'   1295

When Auferius the kyng herd that he saide,   1296
AH sodenly he waxhid bothe pale and wanne;
ffurth on his waye to ride he hym purvayde
Vnto the kyng As fast as euer he canne,   1299
And wete ye wiH he was an hevy man:
ffor by the tyme he came vnto that place,
and died   The kyng was dede, whiche was a hevy case.   1302

For hym was made grete ordenaunce I yow ensure;
The peopiH wept, ther hertys were fuH sore,
And for to purvaye for his sepulture
They besyed them echon, bothe lesse and more,   1306
Thanne was ther made an ordenaunce therfore,
ffuH rially witH aH maner seruice;
As feH to his estate in euery wise.   1309

W[i]thynne a while after aH this was do,   1310
A non ther was callid a parlement,
By Auferius and other lordis moo,
ffully concludid AH by on Assent,   1313
without heir.   Be cause the kyng left non of his disente,
Nor of his blode of that land to be kyng,
To chese them on And lefe aH other thing.   1316

The parliament   And whanne they were Assemelyd euerychone,   1317
And them Avised them wele in euery thing;
They were fully Accordid aH in one,

That Auferius suerly shuld be ther kyng: 1320
he was to them so trew And so loving,
And so rightwise in euery Iugement,
That so able was now to ther entent.   1323

chose Auferius
to succeed him.

[leaf 7, back]

And shortly to procede in this mater,   1324
They chase hym kyng by voice of the land,
The lordes and the Ientilles all in feere,
To hym dede homage as I vnderstonde,   1327
With full promes ther feithes in his hand,
Atte all seasones to hym to owe ther seruice,
And hym obeyed in eny maner wise.   1330

Whanne this was do he sent for quene Sereyne,   1331
And in as goodly hast as it myght be,
The mariage was made be twix them twayn,
With grete honour and grete solempnite,   1334
So grete a gaderyng was neuer in that contre ;
ffor to that fest he bedde his lordes euerychone,
Theder thei came and ladys many on.   1337

The marriage
was made
betwixt him and
Queen Sereyne,

And whanne the fest was all to geder don,   1338
Not long after withynne a litell space,
The quene Sereyne was with child full son
And whanne tyme came, as god will geve hir grace,
She bare a sonne, a threfte child he was ;
And whanne that he was growe to mannys age,
he was callid Ismaell the Savage :   1344

and in due
time she bare a
son,

Ismael the
Savage.

For he was wild in all his demening,   1345
Vnto the tyme he drew to more sadnesse,
Thanne afterward he was withoute feyning
A nobyll knyght, the story doth witnesse :   1348
Now late vs thenne speke of Generydes,
What payn he hadde for fayre clarionas,
By grete envy of cursid malichias.   1351

Now let us
speak of
Generydes.

One morning he
went to speak
with his lady.

In a mornyng' arose Generydes,   1352
To his lady he toke the way full right,
To speke with hir as for his hartys ease ;
This Malichias of hym he had a sight,   1355
And after hym, as fast as euer he myght,
ffull secretly he goth hym to aspye,
hym for to do sum shame and velanye.   1358

Malichias hid
in a tree to
hear what
they said,

And to perfourme all his purpose in dede,   1359
Vppe in a tree he stode full secretly,
That what they seid therof he toke good heede,

and told the
Sultan all that
he could say to

And to the Sowdon told it by and by :   1362
And where as he dede noo thyng' ellys trewly,
But spake with hir to telle hir' his entente,
he hym reportid wers thanne euer he ment,   1365

her dishonour.

To hir dishonour all that he cowde say.   1366

The Sultan
sware they
should die,

Whanne the Sowdon had knowlage of this case,
he sware his othe ther was non other waye,
Butt bothe they shuld be dede be goddes grace.   1369
To hym anon thanne sayde Malichias,
' Of your' doughter ye may not avenge yow soo,
But as for hym ye wote what is to do.'   1372

Yet in his wraugth this thought he euer among',   1373

but could not
kill Generydes
for fear of the
people.

If he shuld avenge hym sodenly,
All his pepill wold say he did hym wrong',
Withoute Iustice to cause hym so to dye ;   1376
And to eschew the Rumber and the crye,
his purpose thanne he chaungyd all in feere :
And Malichias was wroth in his maner,   1379

And thought he was myst1[est]ed vtterly,   1380
Be cause the Sowdon dede not as he ment ;
ffor he was fayn to think that he shuld dye,

Butt for aH he myst of his entent,   1383   Malichias
did not leave
his malice

Yet in his malice he was so fervent

he wold not leve, butt stille alway opece[1]

Dede aH that he cowde to hurt Generydes.   1386   against
Generydes.

So on a tyme fuH streyght he toke the waye   1387

To the Sowdon, and seid in this maner ;

'My lord,' quod he, 'ye love not that I saye,

And if it please yow my councell for to here,   1390

Ye shaH haue knowlache of this mater clere.'

'Wele thanne,' quod he, 'if I may fynd it soo,

Ye shaH sone wete what I shaH do therto.'   1393

'In a mornyng, if it please yow to rise,'   1394   He took the
Sultan one
morning

Quod Malichias, ' I canne say yow nomore,

But[2] ye shaH se your self in euery wise

The very trougth, as I haue seid before ;   1397

And wete ye wiH it grevith me fuH soore,

That ye shuld me mystrest by eny waye,

I wold not that for more thanne I wold saye.'   1400

The[3] Sowdon sayde, 'as towchyng this mater,   1401

I wolle gladly be after your avise.'

Soo on a day the wedder was fuH clere,

In a mornyng the Sowdon ganne to rise,   1404

As erly as he cowde in eny wise ;

flurth on he goth, and with hym Malichias,

Streight to the chaunbour of Clarionas.   1407   to the chamber of
Clarionas,

Save Malichias with hym ther was noo moo,   1408

Atte A wyndow they stode hym to Aspye.   where they
watched the
lovers from a
window.

Generydes, as he was wont to do,

fluH sone after he came fuH secretly,   1411

As oft tyme As he came, yet trewly

he mystrestid neuer erthely man be fore,   Generydes
was sad

Yet As he Stode he Seighed wonder soore.   1414

[1] MS. *opece*. Perhaps we should read *alway stille opece*.
[2] MS. *Be*.   [3] MS. *She*.

To hym anoñ thanne seid Clarionas,   1415
'Ye seigh gretly, I prae yow telle me why.'
'Madame,' quod he, 'for certayn it was,

for a dream he had dreamt of Malichias.

This nyght I hadde a wonder dreme trewly   1418
Of Malichias; noo mo but¹ he And I
Were in A place, this is the certeyn[te],
And of my clothez ther he robbid me.   1421

I drew my swerd to reskewe hym ageyn,   1422
Butt in that case I myght not haue my wiH,

[leaf 8]

The Sowdon came and cast me downe, I wene,
In a depe pitte, whiche grevid me fuH iH: 1425
With that my swerd owt of myn hand it feH
On Malichias and gave hym suche a wounde
Vppon the hede that downe he felle to the grownde.

Yet cowde I not eskape owt of the pitte,   1429
ffor aH the craft that I cowde wele devise ;
Butt atte last, as god wold fortune it,
Ye aH only, and by your interprise,   1432
Owt of daunger ye causid me to rise.'
To hym anone thanne seid clarionas,
'I am a ferde,' quod she, 'of Malichias ;   1435

Clarionas also had had a dream.

For I dremyd that he wold haue me slayn,   1436
Save it lay not in his powere to do,
ffor he purposith by some maner trayn,
Whanne he may see a tyme to shew vs woo.'   1439

When they had spoken

And whanne thei had to geder spokeñ soo,
Supposyng wele that aH had ben in pece, .

the Sultan took Generydes

The Sowdon came and toke Generydes,   1442

In grete anger rebukyng hym fuH soore,   1443
And chargid Malichias in aH the hast
To bynd hym fast, and also ferthermore

¹ MS. *be.*

That he in prison depe he shuld be cast,   1446 *and ordered*
Ther to abide while that his lyff may last;   *him to be put*
                                                                 in prison.
Or ellys he shuld by[1] Malichias avise
Be putte to deth in a right shamefuH wise.   1449

For his doughter he sent fuH hastely,   1450 *His daughter he*
And in his hete gave hir a grete repreff,   *called by a*
                                                                 shameful name.
And callid hir, god wote, right shamefully
AH other wise thanne he cowde make the preff: 1453
And in his hert it was an vtter greff,
ffor he demyd on hir that she ne sought,[2]
Whiche afterward fuH gretely hym for thought.   1456

Now Generydes goth with Malichias,   1457 *Generydes was*
his handes bounden as a prisonere,   *put in a tower,*
Streyght to a towre wherein the prison was;
And hym delyueryd onto Anasore,   1460 *under the*
A gentiH knyght keping the prison ther,   *charge of*
                                                                 Anasore,
To kepe hym hard and strayte in his office,
Withoute favour in eny maner wise.   1463

And for to shew his malys vtterly,   1464
With strong yrons this cursed Malichias   *and fettered*
he feteryd hym, and that soo grevously   *grievously by*
                                                                 Malichias.
The blode sprange owt in many dyuerse places;[3]   1467
And whith an hevy hammer that ther was,
On his leggys so sore he lette hym falle,
Att euery tyme he brake the skynne with aH.   1470

Thanne Anasar was wrothe in his maner,   1471
And in this wise seid to Malichias,
'Ye do me wrong, sithe I am keper here,
To do that is myn office in this case;   1474
ffor his offence[4] or how that [euer] it was,
It is agayn aH reson in certayne,
To do [to] hym this importabiH payn.'   1477

---

[1] MS. *be by.*   [2] So MS.; perhaps for *that he ne ought.*
[3] So MS.; perhaps for *place.*   [4] MS. *office.*

For noo prayer yet wold he neuer sece,   1478
But trewely did as he did before :
Longer suffer myght not Generydes,

*At length
Generydes smote
him that he died.*
Nor nought he wold thow he shuld die[1] *therfore,* 1481
And with his fist he smote hym) wonder soore,
That bothe his eyne owt of his hede ganne falle,
And sodenly he died furth withall.   1484

*The keeper
gave out*
And whanne the keper sawe that he was dede,   1485
Thanne was he sory for Generydes ;
If it were knowen) that he were don) to ded,
The Sowdon) wold be wroth withouten) lese,   1488
Owt of reason) that noman) cowde hym) sese :
Wherefore he founde a meane to his entente,
By there avise that were with hym) present.   1491

How[2] Malichias whanne he came fro the towre,   1492
And don) that the Sowdon) bad hym) do,
*that he fell down-
stairs and brake
his neck.*
his fete fayled in vnhappy oure,
And down) he felle and brake his nek in ij ;   1495
And for to make a preff that it was soo,
They toke hym) vppe and layde hym) soft and fayr',
Down) Atte lowest foote of all the stayre.   1498

Thus were they all accordyd euerychone,   1499
Generydes to quyte all vtterly ;
Among' them) all ther was on,
A knight Darell
A knyght that alway was in companye   1502
With anasor, and lovyd hym) trewly ;
And as he wold the toder wold the same
In euery thing', and darell was his name.   1505

*was chief of the
council in this
matter,*
In this mater' he was chef of councell   1506
With anasor to helpe Generydes :
he bad hym) goo and in no wise to fayle

[1] MS. did.   [2] MS. Now.

To the Sowdon, and telle hym the processe,   1509
And he wold be[1] on of his cheff witnesse.
Thanne anosor ther as the Sowdon was
ffull sone he went, and told hym all the case.   1512

and Anasore went to tell the Sultan,

Yet or [that] he departyd was and gone,   1513
ffull streyte he went vnto Generydes,
And of his bandis losed hym anon,
That he somewhat myght be att his hartes ease.   1516
ffor though[2] ther were a noyse among the prese,
Yet wist he wele as for fayre Clarionas,
That he was no thing gilty in that case.   1519

first having loosed Generydes.

Furth in his waye goth now the Chastelyn,   1520
And to the Sowdon saide in this maner :
'I shall yow telle of a ventur certeyn,
And that a strange, if it please yow to here,   1523
hough Malichias, withynne my office here,
Toke vppon hym as for Generydes
All that ye bad me do withoute lease.   1526

He tells his tale,

And ouer that he dede full trewely,   1527
With strong Irons and feteryd hym full sore,[3]
The blode ranne owt and that full petevously ;
Whanne he had don, to seye yow ferthermore,   1530
Downne of the greses he felle the hede before,
And brake his nek, it myght non other be,
ffor this he died in very certeynte.'   1533

[leaf 8, back]

Whanne the Sowdon hard this, I yow be hight   1534
Ther myght no man be wrother thanne was he,
'What, serys !' he seith, 'this goth not All a right :
Thow Chastelyn, in what wise may this be ?   1537
All this is done but for a sotilte,
To hide your falshede vnder a coverture,
But he shall dye to morow be ye sure.'   1540

and the Sultan was wroth and suspicious.

¹ MS. *he.*   ² MS. *thought.*   ³ MS. *fast.*
GENERYDES.   4

To hym anon answered the Chastelyn;   1541
'Ser, if it please your' lordshepe for to here,
ffor your' wurchippe yow most your' self reteyne,
And take a good avise in this mater,   1544
See that your' grounde be very good and clere,
To your' entente accordeng¹ to the same,
Or ellys it is but slaunder to your' name.'   1547

The more he spak the more he lost his payn;   1548
Whanne Anasar' saw that he went his wey:
The Sowden callid fourtĥ his chaumberleyn,
'Goo,' quod he, 'as fast as euer ye may,   1551

and ordered
Malichias to be
buried.
And see that Malichias in good arraye
Be caryed thens, ther as his body is,
To the temple in honorabiĦ wise.'   1554

Now gotĥ the chaumberlayn furth on his way,   1555
With aĦ the hoole howse att his comaundment,
His body was
found torn to
pieces by hounds. And whanne they came ther as the body lay,
It for to bery after ther entent,   1558
Ther they founde it witĥ hundes alto rent,
Some rede, some blak, and some of dyuerse hude,
Ther cowde no man nownber the multitude.   1561

Eche of them bare a pece away,   1562
Of flessĥ ne boon ther was no thyng behynd;
The chammberleyn whanne he sawe that arraye,
he went furtĥ sore musyng in his mynde,   1565
And told the Sowdon as he shuld it fynde ;
In euery thyng thanne was he grevid soore,
The Sultan was
more wroth, And more wrother thanne he was before.   1568

Thanne for his lordes ¹ furtĥ witĥ aĦ he sent,   1569
That they ² shuld come withoute eny fayle :
Whanne they were come anon incontynent,

¹ MS. lordes thanne.   ² MS. he.

Generydes was brought owt of the Iayle,   1572
ffull sore aferd as it was noo mervaill;
And ther he stode before them euerychone,
Right in this wise the Sowdon sayde anon: 1575

'This felaw her, this yong man that ye see,   1576
Generydes,' he saide, 'that is his name;
he was suerly the man that plesid me,
Wenyng' to me that he hadde be the same;   1579
Butte now he hath don me an vtter shame,
ffor he hath done my doughter villanye,
And layne be hir I sey yow certenly.   1582

I saw hym speke with hir in secrete wise,   1583
Wherefore I wote it may now other be;
And I shall wele aquyte hym his seruice,
ffor he shall dye therfore, now trostith me;   1586
That other may ensampyll take and see,
To be ware how they in suche case
here afterward offende in eny place.'   1589

With that anon answerd Generides: 1590
'My lord,' quod he, 'if ye cause me to dye,
Ye do me wrong, I take god to my witnesse;
And wele I wote ther is no reasone whye,   1593
ffor in this poynt I am no thyng gilty,
And that I shall make good, I yow ensure,
On knyght or Squyer whill my lyff endure.'   1596

Whanne the Sowdon had hard all that he seid;   1597
'Trowist thu to fyght,' quod he, 'as in this case?
Nay think it not, thy bost shall sone be layde,
ffor thu shalt [dye] to morow withoute grace,   1600
And what that euer be withynne this place,
That wolle for the entrete in eny wise,
he shall not spede I yow promysse.   1603

to condemn him
to death.

Wherefore I wold ye gave your' full assent   1604
Among yow all this processe to fulfille,
Accordeng' plenly to that Iugement.'

All were silent
but Anasore .

And ther withall the lordes were ful stille,   1607
And seid noo word neyther good nee ill,
Thanne Atte last the Chastelyn alone,
like as a knyght spake afore them euerychone :   1610

'My lordes All,' he seid, 'hough may this be ?   1611
This is a thyng whiche I neuer sawe,
The Sowdon doth vs wrong, As thinkith me,
To make vs deme a man withoute lawe ;   1614
And for my part, for favour or for awe,
I shall neuer assent to this mater,
Consideryng what he hath proferyd her.'   1617

Thanne was the Sowdon owt of pacience   1618
With Anasor', And spake full hastely ;
'Ye are,' quod he, ' to bold in my presence,
Ayenst my will to speke so vtterly,   1621
It is noo sygne of very loue trewly,
Not withstondeng I wote wele what ye mene,
But troste me wele it goo not as ye wene.'   1624

and Darell, who
took the part of
Generydes.

Thanne came Darell and putt hym self in prese,   1625
Where here be fore rehersid is by name,
Of nobyll kynne he was withouten lese,
The more bolder he was to take a blame   1628
In this mater accordyng' to the same ;
And in this wise he seid be fore them all,
And to the Sowdon in especiall :   1631

' As for my felawe her, the Chastelayn,   1632
I haue mervell that he rebukith hym soo ;

[leaf 9]

And wele I wote that he hath don his payn,

ffor your' pleasur' in aH that he cowde doo,   1635
And vtterly this wiH I saye also,
he that wiH do Generydes a shame,
I yow ensure he shaH do me the same.'   1638

Thanne to the Sowdon furtH witH aH they went, 1639
The lordes and the knygHtes euerychone,
And prayed hym) to respite the Iugement,
ffor certenly his wurchippe laye ther on) ;   1642
And wele they wist that reson) was ther [n]on),
A man) to deme, in eny maner case,
Withoute lawe and in so litiH space.   1645

The lords then prayed the Sultan to respite the judgment.

The Sowdon) was as wrothe as he mygHt be,   1646
That in noo wise he wist not what to saye ;
Thanne was ther on), the Story tellitH me,
A knygHt whiche hadde be witH hym) many a day,
And wele cheryshed witH hym) he was Alway,
like as he wold the Sowdon) wold the same
In euery thyng', and Lucas was his name.   1652

The Sultan was wroth,

but was pre-vailed upon by Lucas,

Vnto the Sowdon) he seid thus anon) :   1653
' Me think, ser, as ferre as I canne fele,
These lordes and these knygHtes euerychone
In this mater they haue not seyde but wele,   1656
hasty processe wiH shende it euery dele,
Avise yow wele and do be good counceH,
And that shaH gretly yow honour and provaile.' 1659

Whanne the Sowdon) had hard hym) euery dele, 1660
Withynne a while he was rigHt temperate,
Of aH his wordes he remembryd wele,
And witH hym) self he was half atte debate ;   1663
he thought he wold noo more be obstenate,
And gaue them) respite be fore them euerychon),
TiH one and xxti dayes were come and goon). 1666

and gave a respite of xxi days.

Therof was all the felashepe full fayn),　　　　1667
And wele content that he hadde suche [grace]

Generydes to prisone went ayeyn),
Atte hartes ease meche better thanne he was ;　　1670
ffor Anasore hadde graunt hym) all the place
ffor his Disporte, to take it as hym) list,
In hym) he hadde no maner of mystrest.　　　　1673

Whille he was stille in prisone a bideng',　　　1674
his thought was all on) Clarionas ;
And euer in his mynd remembryng',
how fayre [1] of hewe and womanly she was ;　　1677
And if he myght stonde in so good a case,
hir to reioyse and haue hir atte his wissh,
Of all his payne he wold not sett a rissh.　　　1680

She was vppe on) A chaunbyr still opece,　　　1681
And euery man) that passid to and fro
She askyd fast aftur Generydes,
In very trougth if he were dede or noo ;　　　1684
They seid he was ageyn) to prisone goo,
And was a lyue they knewe it for certayn),
The whiche some what conforte[d] hir Ayeyn).　1687

The Sowdon) charge[d] them to kepe the day,　　1688
In eny wise what thing that euer fall :
And so they dede his pleasure to obeye,
Theder they came ichon) in generall ;　　　　1691
Thanne was the place to litill for them) all,
Wherefore the Sowdon) anon) dede ordeyne
A larger place all owt vppon) the playn).　　　1694

And for to determytte this mater,　　　　　　1695
Generydes was brought owt of the gaile ;
The Sowdon) thanne rehersid thanne in fere

───────────

[1] MS. *good fayre.*

his displeasur' withoute eny fayle, 1698 and the Sultan related his displeasure,
hougħ he mygħt best to his entente prevaile ;
And sodenly, among them euerychone,
ffurth witħ ther came a massanger anon, 1701

In hast[y] wise as fast as he cowde ride, 1702
And to the Sowdon he seid, rigħt in this wise :
' I am not come my massage for to hide, when a messenger came from the King
But boldly for to telle you myn aviso. 1705
Ther is a kyng not ferre from thise partise,
In aħ contres ther as men riden and goon,
Vnder hovyn so grete ther leviħ non. 1708

Kyng' of Egipte he is, the sotħ to saye, 1709 of Egypt,
And haue mervell, sithe ye be hold soo wise,
That ye so long haue putte it in delaye,
And come not furtħ to offer your' seruice ; 1712
Wherefore he wiħ that ye in eny wise
Yeld vppe your' land att his comaund[e]ment, demanding the Sultan's land.
And vtterly obey to his entent : 1715

And for to take avise in this mater, 1716
he grauntitħ yow a moneħ day of space,
And by that day to geve a playn answere,
As ye wiħ be demeanyd in this case ; 1719
And your' dougħter also clarionas, and his daughter.
I counceħ yow to send hir to the kyng,
ffor your' ease and welefare in tyme comyng.' 1722

Whanne he hadde seid his massage aħ in feere, 1723
The Sowdon was displeasid for certayn ;
And furtħ witħ aħ he chargid Anasar',
To take witħ hym Generydes ayeyn, 1726
And ther to kepe hym suerly on A payn,
ffor he mygħt not procede furmabely,
Because the tidyngez came so hastely. 1729

'Now telle what maner a man is he,'   1730
Seid the Sowdon, 'that is of suche powre ;

[leaf 9, back] And sey me now the very certente.'
To hym anon thanne seid the Massenger,   1733
'If it please yow to wete, that ye shall here :

Belen the Bold is the King of Egypt's name. Belen the bold his name is ouer all,
And kyng of kyngges now men do hym calle ;   1736

His loggyng is vppon a fayre Ryuer,   1737
Callid teger, not ferre owt of this cost ;
And there he lith with right a grete powre,
his owne persone and also all his oste ;   1740
he will that it be knowen to litill ¹ And most,
That fro that grownde he will nott part Away,
Till he haue redy word what ye ² will saye.'   1743

The Sultan refused his daughter, The Sowdon thanne gave Answere furth with all, 1744
And in this wise seid to the massanger ;
'Of my doughter, as for the principall,
I lete yow wete, for pleasur' nee for fere   1747
Think not ther on, for she shall not come ther',
Nother in no nother place I yow ensure,
The whiche myght sownne onto here dishonour. 1750

and for the rest of the message, As for the Remenaunte of your' message,   1751
Be cause I will not lette yow of your' waye,
Whanne euer ye will ye may take your' viage,
ffor your' Answere I will that ye shall sey,   1754

he would answer it in a month. I will send word withynne a moneth day
Vnto your' prince, where euer he be present,
All vtterly the fyne of myn entent.'   1757

The messenger left, and the Sultan consulted his lords, The massanger anon he toke his leve,   1758
And furth he went whanne he hadde his answer'.
The Sowdon anon he ganne his councell to meve

---

¹ MS. *likill.*   ² MS. *he.*

Of that mater that towchid hym) soo nere,   1761
And Askid ther aviso in this mater,
Not on) nor twayne, but aH in generaH,
Thanne spake ser DareH, and Answerd furth with AH :

' These lordes here, that ben) of your counceH   1765
And my falow, and I be on Assent
In that mater to se what may prevaile,
As we seme [1] best we shaH shewe our' entent.'   1768
Thanne spake lucas anon) encontinent,
' Ser, dought ye not,' quod he, ' in this case
It shaH be purvayde fore with goddes grace ;   1771

Sithe tyme of mend this land ded neuer soo,   1772   who advised
And as for vs we wiH not [now] begynne.'   him to resist
his lordes aH Assentid wele therto,   Belen,
And thought that lucas seid right wele therin.   1775
' We trost,' quod they, ' the victory for to wynne,
Vppon) that prince so myghti in his strength,
Or ij monethys be fully drawe o length.   1778

But this we wiH require yow euerychone,   1779
To shew your' grace on to Generydes ;   and to release
ffor wele we wote offence he hath do non),   Generydes.
Vs thynk he shuld the soner haue his pece ;   1782
We yow beseche your rancour for to sese,[2]
ffor att this tyme he may do good seruice,
And suche as shaH please yow in euery wise.   1785

And in this wise, yf it please yow to here,   1786
Be myn) aviso ye shaH send [3] for your ost :
And these lordes that ben) with yow here,
lett them) send for ther men) in euery cost,   1789
In aH ther best army both lesse and most ;
And so shaH yow, with aH your' baronage,
Defende your' lande that it pay noo trewage.'   1792

---

[1] So MS. ? deme.   [2] MS. sesee.   [3] MS. sent.

The Sultan

The Sowdon markyd wele ther wordes all,   1793
And thought it was but reason that they scide.
'Now, seris,' quod he, 'sithe yow in generall
ffor this young man so specially hath prayed,   1796

agrees to free
Generydes,

That ye desire of me shall nott be nayed ;
Ye may telle hym he shall stonde in my grace,
like as he dede before in eny place.'   1799

They were right glad and thankyd hym icheon,   1800
That they for hym had sped so wele that day;

and Anasor
and Darell

Thanne Anasor and Darell went anon
Vnto the towre where he in prison laye.   1803
'What tydinges now,' quod he, 'I praye yow saye.'
'Be of good chere,' quod they, 'dought ye no dele,
Your pece is made, and all shall be right wele.'   1806

set him free.

They toke his feters of incontenent   1807
ffrom his leggis, and whan they had so do,
Thanne was he glad Inow, and furth he went
To the Sowdon as fast as he cowde goo,   1810
With Darell and ser Anasor Also ;
And whanne that he come to his presens,
ffull vmbely he did his Reuerence,   1813

Generydes begs
for the Sultan's
favour,

And to the Sowdon seid right in this wise ;   1814
'I wold beseche yow, ser, graunte me your grace,
I neuer offendid yow in my seruice,
Nother to yow nor to Clarionas.   1817
But hir to wurchippe as my dute was
In that that I cowde do, I yow ensure,
As long as I in seruice dede indure.   1820

And more ouer, as for the massanger,   1821
It grevid me full ill to here hym speke :
he sett his wordes in soo grete maner,

That I wold fayn on hym haue ben wreke ;   1824

With your licence his purpose shaH I breke,

And if I may your pleasure vnderstonde,

With that prowde kyng I wiH fight hand be hand. 1827

and offers to
fight the king
of Egypt hand
to hand.

He shaH not do your doughter dishonour,   1828

As long as god wiH send me lyff and space ;

Nor of his pride shaH neuer come that our

That ye shaH paye trebute, be goddis grace,   1831

This land shaH neuer stande in suche case ;

And if ye geve me leve, withoute fayle

ffor aH his strength I wiH hym onys assayle.'   1834

[leaf 10]

Whanne the Sowdon had hard hym sey so wiH,   1835

'Generydes,' quod he, 'I goue yow grace,

AH myn eviH wiH I for geve euery dele,

And ye to stonde in soo good a case   1838

As euer ye dede withynne eny place ;

ffor now I know that ye, in euery wise,

haue contynued fuH trew in your seruice.   1841

The Sultan
restored Gene-
rydes to favour,

And ferthermore, withoute more dalay,   1842

To morow suerly I wiH make yow a knyght ;

And for your sake an hundred more that day

Ther shaH be made, and then with goddes myght   1845

I shaH purvay as for the landes right,

It to defende, and that it may be clere

ffrom aH seruage and clene owt of daunger.'   1848

and promised
on the morrow:
to make him a
knight.

Thanne was his thought vppon Clarionas,   1849

Sithe he hir saughe hym thought passing long ;

That she myght stonde in his favour and grace [1]

like as she dede, for he had don hir wrong ;   1852

And that he cowde remembre euer among :

Wherefore he thought hir to recompence,

he sendith for hir to come to his presence.   1855

He then sent:
for Clarionas,

[1] MS. his grace.

Thanne Anasore was chargid for to goo   1856
Vnto the chaunbyr of fayre Clarionas,
To bryng her furth the Sowdon bad hym soo,
That euery man myght see withynne the place,   1859
hough wele she stode with hym in euery case :
And whanne she came befoore hym, for certayn,

and took her
in his arms.

The Sowdon toke hir in his armys twayn.   1862

'Doughter,' he seid, 'for yow I am to blame,   1863
ffull wrongfully to me ye were accusid,
And not gilty I will recorde the same,
To say the soth it may not be refusid ;   1866
So hold I yow all vtterly excusid
In euery thing¹; and here, or where ye be,
Att All tymes right wele come on to me.'   1869

Clarionas was fayn whanne this was doo,   1870
Of hym she toke hir leve full curtesly ;
Thanne was Generydes full glad also,
Be cause hir pece was made so trewly :   1873
And as she went he cast on hir his Iee,
So as he durst, to saue hym self fro blame,
And she ayenward Aquyte hym with the same.   1876

Thanne was ther sone Assigned knyghtez twayn   1877
To bryng hir to hir chaumber furth with All,

Next day
he assembled
his knights,

And on the morow the Sowdon for certayn
With his lordes he come in to the hall,   1880
And ther anone [among] his knyghtez all,
And, soth to say, the first of eny man

Generydes the
first of any.

Generides the order ther beganne.   1883

They took
their leave,
and went to
make ready.

The lordes toke ther leve on be on,   1884
To make them redy atte ther owyn devise ;
The ffelischepe departid euerychon

¹ MS. *think*.

To goo and come ageyn) to ther seruice,   1887
And euery man) in defensable wise,
hors and harnes withoute eny more delay,
To muster withynne a moneth day.   1890

Furst the Sowdon) sent his letters owt,   1891 The Sultan sent
With massengers as fast as they cowde ride,   letters to the
                                                             kings and
To kynges and to princes aH abought,   princes
The nexst that were marching on) euery side,   1894
Desireng them) armour to provide
And in aH goodly hast for them) he sende [1]
To come to hym) his contre to defende.   1897 to help him.

These lettres came on) to these princez aH,   1898
hym) for to helpe they grauntid euerychone,
Whanne they were come, furst in especiaH   There came
Croves the kyng of Arabye was on) ;   1901 Croves, king
                                                             of Arabia,
.ij. thousand knygHtes came with hym) alone,
Be side archers a nowmbyr fuH notabyH,
Whiche for werre Were right good men) and able.   1904

The kyng' was wele in age I yow ensur',   1905
And anasor' his sone was for certeyn)   father of Anasor,
A goodly prince and comly of stature ;
Of his comeng' the Sowdon was fayn) ;   1908
Notwithstondyng it was to hym) a payn)
So ferre owt of his contre to travaH,
But his promesse was suche he wold not faylo.   1911

Nexst after hym) ther came owt of turkey   1912 a prince of
                                                             Turkey, and
A myghti prince, and with hym people grete,   his two sons,
A thousand helmys with hym) in companye,
O[f] his contre the best that he cowde gete,   1915
his sonnes bothe with hym) were not [2] for yete,
And for to sey yow soth, and not to feyn),
Trewly they were fuH semely knygthez twayn) ;   1918

        [1] MS. sent.   [2] MS. not ferre.

Off grete wurchippe and of right nobiH fame,   1919
David and Abell,   The eldest hight *ser* Dauid, as I rede,
The yonger sone *ser* AbeH was his name,
Whiche of his enmys[1] had but litiH drede ;   1922
The kyng hym self was a lest man in dede,
Also he louyd wele fayre Clarionas,
Butt she hadde sette hir hert in other place.   1925

the king of   Thanne came the prince of Cesare sone vppon,   1926
Cæsarea,
With vij hundred knyghtes of his own lande ;
[leaf 10, back]   The Story seith his name was Cherydone,
Cherydone,
the father of   And *ser* DareH his sonne was, I vnderstonde :   1929
Darell,
This prince was hold fuH manly of his hande,
his archers and his foote men wele arrayed,
The Sowdon of hym was right wele apayd.   1932

Obeth, king   Thanne came the fortht, whiche was of SesiH kyng,
of Sicily,
A wurthy prince, And Obeth was his name ;
.v. honderyd knyghtes he dede with hym bring,
And men a foote accordeng to the same ;   1936
The prince hym self of good and noble fame,
Theder to come he was right wele content,
As sone as he his lettres to hym sent.   1939

the king of   Nexst after come the kyng of Nicomede,   1940
Nicomedia,
Esaunce,   iij. thousand men he brought on to the Citee ;
(with 3000 men as
black as coal,)   As blak as cole icheon thei[2] were in dede,
Save only ther tethe ther was noo white to see,   1943
Strong men they were the story tellith it me :
Esaunce he hight, the story doth witnesse,
A curtese knyght and fuH of gentilnes.   1946

the king of   From Ethiope ther came another kyng,   1947
Ethiopia,
ij thowsand knyghtes att his gouernaunce,
With[3] meche pepiH on foote Att his leding :

---

[1] MS. *elmys*.   [2] MS. *ther*.   [3] MS. *Whiche*.

Thanne after came A riaH ordenaunce,   1950
Too mygliity princes with a grete pusaunce,
ffro Masedeyn) and owt of Arkadye,   *and the princes*
                                                            of Macedon
Ther cowde no man) the nowmber specific.   1953   *and Arcadia,*

Thanne came Moab, of Capadoor the kyng,   1954   *Moab, the king*
                                                        of Cappadocia,
To the Sowdon) as fast as he cowde hye
With ij knyghtes in felashepe rideng,
Balam the tone And yeferus trewly,   1957
The kyng of Damask and of Ermonye,   *the kings of*
                                                        Damascus and
Of knyghtes wel Arrayed with spere and Shelde,   *of Ermonye,*
xv. thowsand they brought in to the feld.   1960

Sone after come the kyng of orkenay,   1961   *the king of*
                                                        Orkney, and
In his companye ther came also   *after him two*
                                                        kings more,
Another kyng in good riche Arraye;
And after hym) ther came ij kynggez moo,   1964
O thirde CesaH the kyng was on) of thoo;
And what peopyH they brought among them) three,   *and a third Cesall,*
Mynne Auctour seith it is a wonder to see.   1967

Now haue I here rehersid in substaunce   1968
xv kynges, As shortly as I myght,   *15 kings in all,*
With ther powre and AH ther hoole puysaunce,
Whiche was so grete, to sey yow very right, 1971
The Cite myght resscyue them) day ne nyght ;   *and met in a*
                                                        wood without
Butt vnder nethe a woode withoute the town),   *the town.*
Ther was sette vppe the Sowdones pavilyon)   1974   *The Sultan's*
                                                        pavilion

Vppon) A playn), and made of silk and gold   1975   *was set up on a*
                                                        plain,
As richely as thei cowde wele ordeyne,
With many moo full goodly to beholde,   *with many more.*
And tentys large, full riche and wele besen),1978
And who so had be thence a myle or twayn),
Vppon) the feld to loke or cast his Ie,
It shuld hym) seme a town or A Citee.   1981

Upon a time the
Sultan went
Vppon a tyme the seasone was fayre,   1982
With his lordes the Sowdon) toke the waye,
Owt of the Cite to take the ayre,
In the feld vppon) a Somerys day,   1985
to see the host, And for to see the Ost in ther arraye ;
Beholdyng them) with countenaunce right stabill,
hym) semyd they were pepill innumerable.   1988

and told them
of the king of
Egypt's demand
Thanne seid he thus vnto them) euerychon),   1989
That were princes and other lordes all,
'In this contre,' quod he, ' ther is come on),
And kyng of kyngges thus he doth hym) calle,   1992
Whiche thing may neuer in my reasone falle ;
ffor ther may now) be suche in dede ne thought,
Butt he that fourmed all this world of nought.   1995

for tribute.
Also he askid tr[i]bute of this land,   1996
Whiche may not be, what case that euer fall.'
The formest ganne to speke, I vnderstonde,
The kyngges sonne of turkey furth with All ;   1999
Sir Abell said, A semely prince, ser abell they do hym) calle,
Vnto the Sowdon) sone he gaue[1] answer',
As these wordes he seid as ye shall here :   2002

the land of
Persia should
pay no tribute.
' As for the land of perse, this will I saye,   2003
It ought to paye noo tribute in noo wise ;
Ne our' enmys shall neuer see the day,
ffor we are strongge I now I yow promys   2006
Too kepe it from) All suche maner seruice ;
We will meet
the Egyptians
in the field. And for to make it good with spere and Sheld,
Goo we to morow and mete them) in the feld.   2009

Do as ye leke, for this is my councell ;   2010
Besechyng yow to be remembryd here,
That whanne the lande of perse hath gevyn) batell,

[1] MS. gaue an.

Of tyme passid before in many yere,   2013
My lord and fader hath ben Banyere,
And in the formest batell for to be
he and his ayeris claymeth it of dewte.   2016

Also to be made constabill of your ost,   2017 Let me be the
And the voward to haue in gouernaunce,   constable of
ffor to Turkey of right it longith most ;   your host,
Beseching yow with vmble obeysaunce,   2020
Of your lordshipe ye list so it Avaunce,
That I may [here] withoute envy or blame
The formest baner in my faders name.'   2023 and standard-
                                                                    bearer.'

Anon with all the Sowdon gaue answere ;   2024 [leaf 11]
'All your desire I graunt, it is but right.'   The Sultan
The kyng hym thankid in full curtes maner,   granted his
Thanne to ther tentys sone they ganne them dight,   desire.
And dressid all ther harnes ouer nyght,
That they myght on the morow withoute faylo
All maner men be redy to Batell.   2030

Whanne it was day, forward they ganne them dresse   At daybreak
In bright harnes these princes euerychone,   they made them
With other dyuerce lordes more and lesse,   ready for batt'e,
Of Dukes and Erles and Barons anon,   2034
Ther helmes garnysshed that they had vppon,
With perlys and dyamauntez of price,
Ther course[r]s trappid in the fresscst wise.   2037

In the Citee through owt in euery strete   2038
Ther was grete noyse of pepill all abought,
To dresse them fourth ther enmys for to mete,
And sone vppon withoute eny dought   2041
ffro the Citee the Sowdon passid owt,   and went out
And rideth streyte to his pavilion,   of the city,
With lordes abought hym in euery rome.   2044

And whanne that they were redy to goo,   2045
And Aħ assemelid in a companye,

60,000 strong.   iij skore thowsand they were withoute moo.
Thanne were ordeyned the wardes by and by ;   2048

The foremost   The formest warde Aħ redy for to gye
ward the king
of Turkey   The kyngꞇ of Turkey had in gouernaunce,
had with   Be very rigħt of his enheritaunce.   2051

8000 knights;   Thre thowsand knygħtes att his demening,   2052
Be side Archers and foote men) that were *ther*,
And As his graunt was atte begynneng,
his sonne *ser* Abeħ he was baneer.   2055
The secunde ward, to certifie yow here,

the king of   Was putte on) to the kyngꞇ of Araby,
Arabia had the
second, with   ij thowsand knygħtez in his companye.   2058
2000;

the third, Sir   The iij^de warde ther in was ser Anasore,   2059
Anasore and
Generydes,   And with hym) was Generydes also,
And Aħ the new made knygħtez they were thore,[1]

with 1500;   And xv hundred men) withoute moo,   2062
Of chosen) men) what euer they shuld do,
Aħ vnder nethe bothe the rule of more[2] and lesse,
Of Anasore and [of] Generydes.   2065

Cherydone was   The prince of Cesare, callid cherydone,   2066
fourth,
he was the iiij^th, aħ in Another ward,
his felisshepe wele be sene echon),

with 1000 knights   A thowsand knygħt[ez] wayteng on) his garde.   2069
waiting on him;
next came the   Thanne came the kyng of Ceseħ afterwarde,
king of Sicily and
8000 knights;   iij thowsand knygħtez in his companye,
With Archers and foote men) by and by.   2072

the king of   Nexst after·hym) came the kyng of Nycomede,   2073
Nicomedia
V thowsand knygħtes, wonder to behold,
ffuħ begely shapen) bothe in lengeth And brede,

---

[1] MS. *yꞯ*.   [2] So MS. *? the rule bothe more.*

As blak as coole, as I befoore haue told,   2076
The vj^to batell to rule it as he wold,   *ruled the sixth battle;*
And as in writeng in fynde¹ remembraunce,
Was putte hooly on to his gouernaunce.   2079

The kyng of Ethiope, with pepill grete,   2080 *the king of Ethiopia had the seventh;*
The vij^te ward he hadd in gouernaunce,
ffull wele purveid his enmys for to mete;
And in the viij^te ward, to saye yow the substaunce,   *the king of Macedon and two others the eighth;*
iij kyng[ez] moo, with all ther ordenaunce,
Of Masedoyne and other kyngez twayne,
With moche peopill to sey yow the certayn).   2086

The ix^te ward the kyng of Capadoce,   2087 *the ninth, the king of Cappadocia;*
With the nowmber of knyghtez iij thowsand,
ffull wele wellyd to werre vppon) ther foys;
The x^te batayll kyng Balam toke on) hond,   2090 *the tenth, king Balam;*
With iij thowsand knyghtez I vnderstonde;
The xj^te ward² therin was zepherus,   *the eleventh, Zephyrus;*
A myghti prince in armys corageus.   2093

The xij^te ward the kyng of Orkenaye,   2094 *the king of Orkney twelfth;*
With grete peopill I say yow sekerly;
The xiij^te, the southly³ for to say,   *the thirteenth, King Phares;*
Kyng² phares with a nobill companye;   2097
The last saue on) the kyng of Barbary.   *the last but one the king of Barbary.*
These iij princes hadde after ther entente
vj thowsand knyghtez in ther poyntement.   2100

The last batell therin the Sowdon) was,   2101 *The Sultan was last of all,*
iij thowsand knyghtez with hym) ther were,
Some of his lande and some of dyuerce place,
And euery man) wele dressid in his geere;   2104
In that batell Darell was Baner,   *and Darell his standard-bearer.*
And as the story seith in euery wise
he was a likely knyght for that Office.   2107

¹ So MS. ? I fynde.   ² MS. was.   ³ So MS. ? southe.

Anon) with all ther Baneres were displayed, 2108

A riall sight it was to behold,
Eche of them) wele horsid and arrayed,
And in ther harnes dressid as they wold, 2111
Ther cote Armers of siluer and of gold ;
And so forward they partid all in feere,
The trompettys blew, it was A Ioye to here. 2114

Now late vs leue them rideng on) the way, 2115
And to this myghti kyng turne we agayn),
Hough he purveith in all that euer he may, .
And in what wise that he may best ordeyne, 2118
Of euery ward to make a capteyn),
ffirst he appoynted in especiall,

hym) self was in the formest of them) all. 2121

Three kynggez were with hym) in companye, 2122
Also he hadde of[1] knyghtes vj. thowsand,
And in nowmber as many by and by,
In euery warde was poynted afore hand, 2125
And by writeng as I vnderstonde ;

Gwynan his sonne, whiche was full dere,
Of his batell he made hym) Banere. 2128

Thanne came ser Amelok, the kyng of ynd, 2129
Whiche lande, god wote, full traytoru[s]ly he wanne,
And vntrewly, the story makith mynde,

Betrayed his prince whiche was a nobill man). 2132
The secunde ward ser Amelok beganne
With meche pepill, to say yow certenly,
ij kynges mo were in his companye. 2135

So forthermore thanne came the kyng Sanyk 2136
Nexst afterward, and with hym) kynggez twayn) ;

A myghti prince, and kyng[2] of Auferyk,[3]

---

[1] MS. haddes f.   [2] MS. kyng he was.   [3] MS. Anscryk.

And fader to the quene of ynde certayn, 2139
The whiche forsoke hir husbond be a trayn:
This prince hadde in his rewle and gouernaunce
The iij^de batel with all the ordenaunce. 2142   had the third battle;

The iiij^te batel to rule and to ordeyne 2143   the king of Thrace the fourth;
Madano¹ hadde it, whiche was kyng of Trace;
And as myn Auctour specifieth certayn
Right yong And fressh a lest man he was. 2146
And in the v^te ther came Barachias,   the fifth, Barachias, king of Europe;
Kyng of Europe, and suche a companye
As euery ward was poynted by and by. 2149

Nexst after hym came Ermones the kyng, 2150   the sixth, king Ermones,
The vj^te Batel to gouerne as he wold,
ffull boustous folk and ill faryng,   with men
With visages fowle, full gresely to beholde, 2153
All of on sorte they were both yong and old,
Ther bakkes and ther belly were soo large,   so big that horses could not carry
Ther was noo hors of them wold bere the charge; 2156   them,

Wherefore they rode on camelys euerychon, 2157   so they rode on camels,
Think wele it was a vounderfull array,
ffor as for spere or swerd they handelid non,
Ther wepons were more stronger, I yow say, 2160   and had weapons (see p. 80) like mattocks, with long helves;
lyke as mattokez Shapyn so were they,
Ther helvys long, that whanne they shuld fight
Ther strokes shuld come with grete wight. 2163

Two kyngez moo were in his company, 2164
Of suche makyng and of on maner kynd.
The vij^te ward the kyng of Assirye,   the seventh, Galad, king of Assyria;
Galad he hight in story, as I fynde, 2167
A prince worthy for to [be] had in mynd;
The viij^te Batel therin was manassen,   the eighth, Manassen;
And vnder hym was his sone ruben. 2170

¹ MS. *Madame.*

the ninth,
Lamadone,
king of Libya;

The kyng of lybie, callid lamadone,   2171
The ix^{te} warde hadde att his leding';

the tenth,
Auferius,

And the x^{te}, the last of euerychone,
Was auferius, the welebelouyd kyng   2174

king of India,

That was of ynd, and ther had his dwellyng
Till he was putte [from] his enheritaunce,
Wherof be fore was made remembraunce.   2177

Two kynges mo were in his poyntement,   2178
With the nowmber of knyghtes accordeng,
Owt of the Reme of Trace with hym) ther were,
To wayte on) hym) ther were [they] well willyng', 2181

who knew not
that he had to
fight against his
son Generydee.

But of on) thing he had no knowlaching',
That his fortune was suche withoute lese
To fight ayenst his sone Generydes :   2184

The last batell was putt on) to his gard,   2185
And for this cawse it was apoyntid so,
Ser Amelok he hadde the secunde ward,
That noo debate shuld be bytwix them) twoo,   2188
Thanne after this ther was no more a doo ;
The men) of armys bothe with spere and sheld,
With grete corage dressid them) in to the feld.   2191

And on) the toder part forward they went ;   2192
Among his men) the Sowdon) came rideng',

The Sultan sent
out 3 knights
to reconnoitre.

And prevely iij knyghtez owt he sent,
Of his enmys to knowe ther demeanyng',   2195
They brought hym) word ayenward *thei* were comyng',
And so they rode ye space of half a nyght,
That euerychone of other hadde a sight.   2198

Thanne afterward thei made noo taryeng',   2199
But furth they goo withoute eny lett,
Wete ye wele ther was a sorowfull encounteryng',

Whanne the batels to geder were mett, 2202 *The battles met.*
Euerychone on other ferly they sette
With grete corage, and trewly for to speke
It was a world to here the sperys breke. 2205

The kyng of kynggez rode on euery side, 2206 *The king of kings*
ffull clene armyd formest of euerychone,
There were butt fewe his strokes wold abide, *[leaf 12]*
So many he on horsid one be one ; 2209 *unhorsed many a one.*
A comly prince he was to loke vppon,
And therwith [all] right good and honorable,
And in the feld a knyght right confortable. 2212

Ser abell was of perse the Banere, 2213 *Sir Abell met him,*
Avaunsid hym and to a kyng ganne ride,
And thorough owt the body he hym bare,
That on his hors he myght not longe abide, 2216
Butt to the grownde he felle and ther he dyed ;
And thanne ser Abell, in a hasty brayde,
Vnto the kyng of kyngges thanne he seide : 2219

' Good ser,' quod he, ' how likith yow this game ?'
With tho wordes the kyng liked full ill,
he thought full wele to quyte hym with y° same,
And ranne to hym with a full eger will, 2223
That from ser Abell downe the baner fell, *but lost his banner in the fight,*
And suche a stroke he hadde, to say yow trew,
That from his hors almost he ther ouer threw. 2226

The kyng his fader sawe the baner down, 2227 *which his father rescued.*
he hastyd hym as fast as euer he myght,
And with an hundered knyghtes of renown
The baner sone they reisid it vppe right ; 2230
Thanne was the batell sore, I yow be hight,
And many slayn ; but or the day was past
The men of perse with drew them atte last. 2233 *The men of Persia withdrew,*

but Generydes
came up and
won the ground
again,

The nexst bateH, whanne thei wist how it was,   2234
Generydes and Anasore in certayn,
They brought ther felishepe bothe more and lesse,
And in a while they wanne the grownd ayen;   2237
Generydes sawe Guynan on the playn,
The kyngges sone, rideng' with spere and sheld ;
he taryd not, butt mette hym in the feld.   2240

fought with
Gwynan,

Gwaynan on to Generides he ranne,   2241
And with [his] spere he brake his sheld on twayne ;
Generides ayenward like a man
With stode his stroke, and smote hym so ageyn,   2244
That from his hors he felle vppon the playn,
And who that euer that was wele payde or wroth,

unhorsed him,

he toke his hors with hym and furth he goth.   2247

Thanne was ther on not ferre owt of yͤ prese,   2248
lyke a harowed he semyd for to be,
To hym Anon thanne seid Generydes,
'Good ser,' quod he, 'doo now sum what for me ;'   2251
' What is your' wiH and pleasure ?' quod he.
' My lorde,' he seid, ' that ye wiH in this nede
Chaunge my SadyH and sett it on this stede.   2254

Whanne ye haue do, take ye my stede therfore.'   2255
Sygrem hym did as Generides hym badde,
he hight so, and to sey yow more
In his demeanyng he was wise and sadde ;   2258
Of bothe partys right grete favour' he hadde,
To gentilmen he was right servisable,
And ther withaH fuH good and companable.   2261

and took his
horse,

Generydes leppe vppe vppon his stede,   2262
A better was not onder nethe the sonne ;
ffor grete suerte in story as I rede,

The kyng of kyngges gave it to his sonne,   2265
Or the batell was eny thing begonne ;
Sygrem was glad of chaungyng of his hors,   *giving his own*
ffor of his owne he gave butt litill fors.   2268 *to Sygrem.*

To hym ąnow thanne seid Generydes,   2269 *He asks Sygrem*
' Sygrem,' quod he, ' do me to vnderstonde   *where Sir*
Ser Amelok, if he be in the preese,   *Amelok is.*
Whiche trayturly hath wonne my faders lande.   2272
ffayne wold I wete if he were here nye hande.'
' Trewly,' he seid, ' now I remembyr me,
Suche one ther is in very certente.   2275

Butt as for yow, I wote not what ye be,   2276
hym knowe I wele trewly, that is noo nay ;   *' I know him*
The first batell saue on ther in is he,   *well ; he is in*
                                                              the first battle
This is the very trougth that I yow saye,   2279 *save one.*
And what ye be, I beseche and praye
To lete me wete the truthe in euery wise,   *Tell me who*
And I shall trewly owe yow my seruice.'   2282 *you are.'*

Generydes thanne gaue hym this answere ;   2283 *Generydes said,*
' Sygrem,' he seid, ' to yow I will not leyne,
I shall yow telle the trouth of this mater,
kyng auferius is my fader in certeyn,   2286 *' Auferius is*
                                                              my father.'
Whiche was of ynd bothe lord and souereyn,
And now is kyng of Trace, as I yow say,
Butt lete this go noo ferther, I yow praye.'   2289

' Kyng auferius,' quod he, ' I knowe hym wele,   2290 *' I know him*
The last batell of all ther in he is,   *well,' replied*
                                                              Sygrem,
As ferre as I canne vnderstonde and fele,
Ser Amelok is not his frende I wis,   2293 *' and Sir Amelok*
                                                              is not his friend.'
And by what reason I will tell yow this ;
The kyng of kynggez partyd them twayn,
Be cause they shuld noo debate begynne certeyn.' 2296

'How shall I
know Sir
Amelok?' said
Generydes.

'How shall I doo,' thanne seid Generydes,   2297
'Of Amelok to haue sum knowlachyng?
ffor hym that I may knowe among the preese,
But if I haue sum redy tokyni[n]g.'   2300
'I shall yow telle,' quod he, ' withoute feyneng,

'His steed is
grey, with a
white head,

his stede is gray withoute layen,
The hede is whight, to say yow for certayn.   2303

For more knowelage to telle yow which is he,   2304

and his arms are
the field gules
[leaf 16, back]
with three bands
of gold.'

his harmes are, who so list to be holde,
The felde of Goulys in very certeynte,
Ther with also iij bandes all of gold.'   2307
And whanne that he Generydes had told
Of Amelok, and hough he shuld hym fynde,
Wete ye wele he was the gladder in hys mynde. 2310

They ride
on together,

Furth on his stede rideth Generydes,   2311
To fynd ser Amelok if that he may,
With hym rideth Sygrem still opeese,
And as they twayne rode spekyng be the waye, 2314

and meet Sir
Amelok in a
valley.

Segrem was ware wher in a valay
Ser Amelok came on rideng A pace,
hym for to rest as for a litill space :   2317

'Loo yender is ser Amelok,' he seid,   2318
' And saving on with hym ther is no moo.'
And with that word Generydes abrayde,
'Now is,' quod he, 'good tyme for me to goo ;'   2321
So furth he ridith till that he came hym too :
The toder sawe hym come with spere and sheld,

They fight.

And furth he gothe and mette hym in the feld. 2324

Amelok breaks in
two Generydes'
shield.

And atte first he stroke Generydes,   2325
And with that stroke he brast his sheld in twayn,
Anone with all he quyte hym dowteles,

And smote his sheld quyte on the playn.   2328   *Generydes cuts*
                                                 away Amelok's
Thanne seid Generides, 'now am I fayn,   *shield.*
Thow shalt not laughe atte me in mokkery,
ffor thow hast lost thy sheld as wele as I.   2331

And as for on thyng I shall the wele ensure,   2332
As for thy sheld thu shalt haue it no more,
ffor myn is broke it may noo more endure,
Be thow right sure I will haue thynne therfore :'   2335
And thanne beganne the batell passing sore,
Ther was non of them shewid favour to a *nother*,
ffor right dedely the tone hatid the toder.   2338

Syr Amelok was wrothe as he might be,   2339
And to Generydes right thus he sayde ;
'I shall yow quyte that thu hast doo to me,'
And smote hym on the hide with suche a brayde,   2342   *They fight on.*
That in hym self he was some what dismayed :
Quod Amelok, 'thu hast I now this day,
Reche me my[1] sheld and thu goo thy waye.'   2345

'Thow getist it not, fals tray*tour* [that] thu art,   2346   *Generydes*
                                               reproaches
Or thu goo ferther thu shalt haue myschaunse,   *Amelok for*
ffor thu hast with thy fals envyous hert   *his treachery.*
Putte my fader from his enheritaunce,   2349
Whiche was his Ioye, his lyfe, and his pleasur,
And in my faders presence thu me smote,[2]
Whiche I haue not forgete yet, god it wote.   2352

And thanne I might not ease my hert in dede,   2353
But now thu shalt repent it or thu goo :'
And with his swerd he smette hym on the hede,   *Sir Amelok*
The helme to brast anon in peces two ;   2356   *is wounded*
his lippys and his noose he smote away also,
Clene from his face, and ther with all full sone,
he bledde so fast that he felle in A swonne.   2359   *and unhorsed,*

               [1] MS. *thy.*   [2] MS. *smette.*

To hym thanne seide Generides anon, 2360
'Whil ere thu bad I shuld reche tho thy sheld,
And now me think thu hast nede of on,
ffor neyther spere ne sheld that thu may weld :' 2363

but rescued And with that word vppeward his hede [he] helde,
Risyng with all to helpe hym self right fayne ;
Generydes thanne smote hym down ageyn, 2366

Hym for to slee was fully his entente. 2367

by his knights. With that anon his knygutes came hym to,
And sette hym on his hors and furth they went,
As soft a pace as y^{el} myght with hym goo, · 2370
Too se hym in that plight they were full woo ;

Generydes took the horse he had won of Amelok, his stede anon thanne toke Generydes,
And led hym furth with hym in to the prese. 2373

And whanne that he was eskepyd trewly, 2374
Sygrem he found anon in contenent,
'My frende,' quod [he], 'I prae yow fethfully
To do my massage after myn entent, 2377

and sent it to Auferius by Sygrem. That ye will take this stede, and hym present
To auferius my lord and fader dere,
And say to hym that I haue wonne hym here 2380

Off Amalok, the traytour most vntrewe ; 2381
And if he aske as for more witnesse,
Who sent to hym and how that I hym knewe,
Telle hym it is his sone Generydes, 2384
And hough that Amelok in all the prese,
Withynne his howse and in his high presence,
ffull cruely smote hym with violence ; 2387

And he ayenward smote hym with his knyff 2388
Thorough the Arme in very certente.'
Sygrem Ayenward seid, '*ser*, be my liff,

I shall do that ye haue comaundyd me, 2391
And take hym this present where euer he be.'
Now goo Sygrem, as fast as ye may spede,
To Auferius to present hym this stede. 2394

And whanne this stede to Auferius was brought, 2395
And wist fro whense he came, thanne was he fayn ;
'Now, good Sygrem, as euer I may do ought
ffor thy pleasur',' quod auferius ayen, 2398
'Of my sonne telle me somme token playn,
hough I may best knowe hym among them all ;'
'Ser,' quod Sygrem, 'with right good will I shall.' 2401

Auferius asked Sygrem some token by which he might know [leaf 13] his son.

Sygrem hym told tokynnes moo thanne on, 2402
his sonne to knowe be right of his office,
What colour was his hors he rode vppon,
And what harmys he bare, and what devise, 2405
All this he told hym in full redy wise ;
kyng auferius ther with he was contente,
And hym rewardid well for his presente.[1] 2408

He told him the colour of his horse and his arms.

As now putte we this mater in respite, 2409
And to Generydes turne we ageyn,
Whiche founde his felawes all most discomfete,
ffor they had fought all the day certeyn ; 2412
Yet whanne they hym sawe thenne were *thei* fayn,
And ganne reioyse whanne they to geder mette,
With knyghtly corage frely on they sette. 2415

Generydes found his fellows almost discomfited.

When they saw him they were glad.

And thanne beganne the batell passing sore ; 2416
They fought alway to geder still opece,
The men of perse were hartid more and more,
All be counfort of Generides : 2419
he styntid not, nor neuer wold he sese,
And with his swerd where that his stroke glynt,
Owt of ther sadill full redely they went. 2422

Every one went down before the stroke of Generydes.

[1] MS. *presence.*

The kyng of kyngges toke good hede [   ],   2423
To hym) he callid Sygrem furth with all anon),

'What knyghte is yender,' quod he, 'canne ye me saye?
That in the feld outrayth euerychone ;   2426
So good a knyght as he me semyth non)
In all the world, but on) thyng I mervell,
My sonnys stede hath he, withoute fayle ;   2429

Where with trewly I am not wele apayed,   2430
Notwithstondeng' a nobyll knyght is he,   '
And that ye knowe right wele, Sygrem,' he sayd,

'Wherefore I wold he were dwellyng with me ;   2433
Of gold and siluer he shall haue plente,
Townys and castelys at his obyseaunce,
And other thinges moo to his plesaunce.'   2436

'Ser,' quod Sygrem, 'trewly it will not be,   2437
he is descendid of an high lenage,
And as fer[1] furth as I canne fele and see,
he waytith after right grete heritage,   2440
ffor with the Sowdon he will take no wage,
And for to telle yow trouthe as in this case,

his trost is to haue fayre Clarionas.'   2443

'Clarionas,' quod he, 'nay, lete be that ;   2444
I take hir for my owen), ser, be the rode,

Whether he will or noo, for wote ye what,
Vppon) his body I will make it good :'   2447
And whanne Sygrem these wordes vnderstode,
ffull sone he went to Generydes,
And told hym) what he seid more or lesse.   2450

Now kyng Belleyn) secheith Generydes   2451
Thorough the ost, to fynde hym) if he maye,
And as he rode a side hand of the prece,

---

[1] MS. *for.*

he sawe where that he rode in [a] valaye;   2454   and finds him in
To hym anow full streyght he toke the waye,   a valley.
And on a high he beganne to crye,
'Turne the,' he seid, 'for tyme it is trewly :   2457

Vppon my stede blanchard thu ridest here,   2458
Butt on my list thu shalt hym sone for goo.'
That word anow Generides ganne here,
he turnyd hym withoute wordes moo.   2461
They toke ther coursis and ranne to geder soo,   They ran
Thanne iche atte other and bothe ther sperys helde,   together and were
But thei were clene onhorsid in the feld.   2464   both anhorsed,

Vppon ther stedis sone thei were ayeyn,   2465   but got up on
And so they fought to geder hand to hand,   their steedis
Ther was noo favour shewid be twix them twayn,   again, and
                                                           fought hand to
Butt strokes grete and sore, I vnderstonde ;   2468   hand.
ij better knyghtes were not in all the land,
ffor long thei fought and neuer wold thei lette,
No yet departe to tyme the ostes mette.[1]   2471

Thanne wax the batell euer more and more,   2472   The battle waxed
As thei resortid on euery side ;   sore.
lordes and knyghtez were hurt right soore,
And many ligging dede with woundes wide ;   2475
lucas ffull sone Manessen had aspied,   Lucas rode at
With sheld and spere he dressid hym full right,   Manessen,
And ranne to hym in all that euer he myght.   2478

The stede[2] was good that lucas rode vppon,   2479
And suche a stroke he gave hym with a spere,
That thorough the harnes and the shulder bon,
Thorough owt his bak and slew hym ther ;   2482   and slew him,
Thanne to the kyng he seid in this maner :
'Take yow here this present or ye goo,
And I shall do my part to send yow moo.'   2485

        [1] MS. mettez.   [2] MS. stede.

Tho wordes toke the kyng in Mokkery,   2486
And made hym redy with spere and sheld,
To ser lucas he ranne full egerly

but was unhorsed by the king, and rescued by Generydes, [leaf 13, back]

And stroke hym fro his hors in to the feld ;   2489
With that anon Generydes beheld
how lucas was owttrayed among' his foys,
And in he came and rescuyd hym att onys.   2492

Streyght to the kyng he rideth for certayn,   2493
And with his swerd he smote hym on the hede,
The helme to brast anon in pecys twayn,
And with that stroke he slewe his hors in dede,   2496

who slew the king's horse.

And so the stede fell vnder nethe hym dede,
hym self also ther with was astoinyd sore,

The king blew his horn,

And blew his horne, to saye yow forthermore.   2499

and a thousand knights came up

Thanne came a thowsaund knyghtez of his ost,   2500
And vppe thei sette hym on a nother stede,
And glad they were, wenyng' they had hym lost,

and carried him off.

And furth owt of the prese with hym they yede.[1]   2503

Then came in the men of higher India, (see p. 60)

Thanne came ther in as fast as thei myght spede,
The buscommest folk, the men of higher ynd,
Of whom before the story makith mend.   2506

Whanne they come in they made rome Alabought,

with weapons out of all measure.

Ther wepons were made owt of all mesur',
ffull ill shapyn with pekys in and owt,
Ther strokes myght no man endure ;   2510

The men of Persia were discomfited,

The men of Perse were att discomfeture,
And whanne the Sowdon hard of that tiding',
he came anon and made no taryng';   2513

Conforting' them in full good maner,   2514
And for ther seruice thankyd them Also :
The prince of Cesare gave hym this answere,

[1] MS. *yode.*

'Now truly, ser,' quod he, 'if it were so   2517
That they were men with whom we haue a do,
We wold not dowte to mete them on be on,
But suerly they be fendez euerychone.   2520

Ther wepons be suche ther may no man abide,   2521
Wherefore this is now myn avise,' quod[1] he,
'Vs to with drawe a liteH owt aside,   *and withdrew towards*
That our enmys perseyue not that we fle.'   2524   *the city,*
The Sowdon saw it wold now other be,   *Mountenor.*
Butt nedis he must geve his assent ther to,
And yet he was fuH loth so for to do.   2527

They drewe softely to the Citee WarH,   2523
The Sowdon blew his horn that thei myght here,
The lordes and the knyghtez of his garde,
Whanne thei it harH anon thei drew hym nyere, 2531
As as they rode to geder aH in feer,
Ther enmys made on them a newe afraye,
That vnnethe myght the Sowdon skape a waye. 2534   *The Sultan barely escaped,*

V. hunderyd of his men he lost also,   2535   *and lost 500 men and 1000 horses.*
And of horsis a thowsand atte lest
Among them AH thei lost withoute moo,
And some lordes and knyghtez of the best ;   2538
The day passid, the sonne drewe to the rest,
And be that tyme his felisshepe and he
Were come to Mountoner the riche Citee.   2541

And of aH this wist not Generides,   2542   *Generydes and Anasore wist not of this, but fought Galad, the king of Assyria,*
Nor anasor, to say yow certeynly,
ffor thei were aHway fightyng stiH opeee
Ayenst Galad the kyng of Asirye ;   2545
And whanne they had knowlage vtterly,
Of the Sowdon and of his distresse,
Thanne were they bothe in right grete hevynesse. 2548

[1] MS. *now q*.

Yer[1] fought thei still and reskew was *ther* non,   2549
Nor non comyng' as ferre as they myght see,
· Ther men almost distressid euerychone,

till their men
were distressed,
and they tried
to retire,
but found the
enemy between
them and the
city.

And many slayne, thenne of necessite   2552
They them withdrewe, and towarde the Citee
They toke the way, and in conclusion
Thanne was the oste be twene them and y° town;   2555

That in no wise they wist not hough to pas,   2556
Ne hough to do they knowe noo *sertente*,
Thanne Anasor' remembred that ther was
A postrene yssuyng' owt of the Citee,   2559
And thederward they drewe to haue entree,
But or they myght in suerte come and goo
Be twix them bothe they had I noughe to do.   2562

Now to the Sowdon lete us turne ageyn,   2563
ffor here peopill what mone that he do make;
Of euery man he enqueryd the certente,
Whiche of his men were ded and which were take;
The Citee made grete sorow for ther sake,
And specially thei made grete hevynes
ffor Anasore and for Generides;   2569

And thought suerly it myght non other be,   2570
Butte thei were bothe [putte] to discomforture.
Thanne sayde Dareil, 'it were full grete pite
Suche ij knyghtez to lese, I yow ensure;'   2573
And furth he goth vppon his aventure,
Beseching' god to councell hym and rede,
ffor he wold fynd hym[2] eyther quyk or dede.   2576

There was a
rumour in the city
that Generydes
and Anasore
were slain.
Clarionas heard

Thanne was a noyse the Citee all along'   2577
That they were slayn, and woo thei were *ther*fore;
Clarionas herd how the tydingez sprong',

---

[1] MS. *Yey*.   [2] MS. *hyn*.

here chere was don), she wept passing sore :   2580 It and wept sore,
Myrabell sawe she wept more and more,
'Madame,' quod she, 'these tydengez that be now,   but Mirabell did not believe the
A wager dare I ley they are not trew :   2583 news.

And if it please yow, for your disporte,   2584
To walk vppo to the towre[1] ther shall ye see
Paraventur that may be your counmfort.'
'I will,' she sayde, 'do as as ye councell me :   2587 [leaf 14]
Comforte or no, or hough that euer it be.'
So furth she went vppo to the towre on) hye,   Clarionas went to the top of
Butt nought she sawe, she wept so wtterly.   2590 the tower, but saw nothing for weeping.

Thanne was Darell come to Generides,   2591 Sir Darell made his way to
And glad thei were, bothe he and Anasor,   Generydes.
ffor thei had long endured counfortles :
Whanne he was come amendid was ther cher,   2594
And att that tyme owt of the prese thei were,
To rest them) self a season) to endure,
Ther eche to other told his aventur.   2597

Clarionas was on) the towre on) hye,   2598 Clarionas on the tower
Of here wepyng she ded hir self refrayn),
And owt vppon) the feld she ganne aspye,
Where Anasore came rideng vppon) the playn) ;   2601 saw Anasore,
By his Armys she knewe hym) for certayn)
That it was he, and ther withall anon)
A grete part of hir hevynesse was goon).   2604

Generides was also in the feld,   2605 but did not know Generydes because
Butt whiche was he she had noo knowlaching,   he had Sir Amelok's shield.
ffor he had on) ser Amelokkez sheld,
With his devise, in very tokenyng   2608
That he it wanne att ther encounteryng,
And so they rode oyther with spere and shield,
Toward town) clarionas them) beheld.   2611

[1] MS. town.

Auferius with 500
knights rode

And as thei rode anon) thei were Aspied   2612
By on) that was with Auferius the kyng,
And in noo wise thanne wold he not abide,
And told his lord withoute more taryeng;   2615
And he anon), leving' AH other thing,
Sent furth knyghtez v. C. in aray,

to meet them.

hym) self also to mete them) on) the waye.   2618

And aH was to withstonde ther passage,   2619
With these knyghtes he rode on) still opece;

The foremost was
Ismael the
Savage,

The formest was Ismael the Savage,
Kyng' Auferius sonne withoute leese,   2622
And very brother onto Generides;

who encountered
Generydes.

Be fore them) aH he came hym) self alone,
Generides was ware therof anon).   2625

He toke his spere And mette hym) in the feld,   2626
They toke ther course and ranne to rownde :
he stroke Generydes vppon) the sheld,
That hors and man) Almost were att grownde,   2629
But vppe he rose anon) both hoole and sounde,
And with his swerd he smote hym) so ageyn),
That with that stroke he brake his sheld on) twayn).

They fought till
Generydes smote

So fought y^el still withoute eny drede,   2633
And neyther of them) wold to other yeld ;
Generydes hym) sette so vppon) the hede,

off Ismael's helm,

That his helme flew quyte in to the feld,   2636
With that anon) Generydes beheld

and saw his
features.

The fetures wele that was in his visage,
Demyng' that they were aH of on) lenage.   2639

And for to haue ther of very knowlaching,   2640
To Ismael he said, in very certente,
'Good ser,' quod he, 'for loue of hevyn) kyng,

Tell me for trougth what maner a man ye be,　　2643　He asked him
And whense ye came, and owt of what contre ?'　　who he was.
' What man I am,' quod Ismael ayeyn,
' And of what kynne I will not layn.　　2646

Kyng auferius trewly my fader is,　　2647　'Auferius is
To say yow sothe, and for to bere noo blame,　　my father,'
And of the Reme of Trace is kyng I wis,　　quoth Ismael.
Ther was I born and brought vppe in the same,　　2650
And Ismael the Savage is myn name ;
Now I haue told yow all withoute leese.'
' Gramercy, frende,' thanne sayd Generydes,　　2653　'Gramercy,
friend,' said
Generydes,
' For we haue fought to long I yow ensure.'　　2654
With that he toke hym in his armys twoo,
' We are broderen,' quod he, ' of on nature,　　'we are brethren.
kyng auferius my fader is also ;　　2657
I may nott tary now, for I must goo,
My felawes hath mervell to see me heer,
Butt here after I shall make yow better chere.'　　2660

Thanne ther was an hevy departeng,　　2661　There was a
hough iche of them made to other mone.　　heavy parting
between them.
Generydes sawe where was thanne comyng
his faders men, wele horsid euerychone,　　2664
And he full hevy butt hym self alone,
And they to many as to his entente,
So furth on was he to his felawes went.[1]　　2667　Generydes went
on to his fellows,

Whanne he was come ther as his felawes were,　　2668
They sawe comyng along in a valay　　and in a valley
A grete peopill, wele dressed in ther geere,　　saw a great people
coming to hinder
To lette hym and his felawes on the waye,　　2671　them with a
Thanne was ther on a knyght in good aray,　　knight at their
head.
Be fore them all avaunsid hym to ride,
Generydes hym had right sone aspyed ;　　2674

[1] MS. *was to his felawes he went.*

Generydes rode
at him, and slew
him.

And furth with all he mette on the playn,   2675
In sight of all the pepill that were ther,
And Atte first he brast his sheld in twayn,
That thorough owt the body ranne the spere ;   2678

Clarionas saw
this, and recog-
nized her lover.

Clarionas demyd that he was ther,
And to hir mayde she sayde full sobyrly,
'What knyght is that that doth so worthyly?'   2681

[leaf 14, back]

'It is your loue,' quod she, 'withoute moo.'   2682
'Now good Mirabell, what is your avise?'
'Trewly,' quod she, 'I trow that it be soo,
Me think it shuld ben he in eny wise ;   2685
The rede pensell I see att his devise,
The whiche in sothe ye dede for hym ordeyn,
Gwynot brought it hym your Cha[m]berleyn.'   2688

'O trouth,' quod she, 'Madame,[1] that is trew ;   2689
Now am I wele remembryd ther vppon,
Butt euermore my sorow doth renewe,
Withoute reskewe to se hym so alone,   2692
Thus shall they be distressid euerychone,
Namely my love, whiche is so good a knyght,
ffor hym is all my mone I yow be hight.   2695

For wele I wote, ther is noo knyght a lyve   2696
That better doith here and in euery place,
And this to say my reson doith me dryve,
ffor I am his while I haue lyffe and space.'   2699
And while she remembryd all this case

Ismael and
Darell meet,

Come Ismael rideng with spere and sheld,
And to Darell he ridith in to the feld.   2702

Bothe to the grounde he bare hors and man,   2703
ffurth with came the ost vppon the playn,
And as ser Darell wold haue Res[k]eu thanne,

[1] ? *Mirabell.*

Ther came a knyght and held hym down Ayeyn, 2706
And with his swerd wold haue Darell slayn,
Butt in the most and in the thikest prese
hym to reskew thanne came Generides. 2709

and Darell would
have been sla'n,
but was saved
by Generydes,

Streight as he cowde to that knyght he rode, 2710
he brake his helme and stroke hym on the heede,
That on his hors no lengger he a bode,
But downe he feH and fast beganne to blede ; 2713
Generydes with hym he toke his stede,
And furth fro them he rode a litiH aside,
And toke it Darell theron for to ride. 2716

and they rode
forth together.

Clarionas beheld this euery dele ; 2717
Quod she ayeyn to MirabeH here mayde,
' The same is he, the whiche I love so weH ;
' Madame,' quod she, ' so haue I alway sayde, 2720
ye nede noo thyng for hym to be dismayde,
Nor let no mo suche thoughtez yow assayle,
ffor it is he withoute eny fayle.' 2723

Now rideth DareH with Generides, 2724
As fuH of thought for his fortune that day,
And as they rode a litiH fro the prese,
kyng Auferius came crossyng them the way, 2727
ffuH clene armyd in riche and good Aray.
DareH anon dressid hym fuH right,
And ranne to hym in aH that euer he myght. 2730

Auferius crossed
their path,

and Darell rode
at him,

Aud one the hede smote Auferius the kyng ; 2731
The helme was sure, or ellys he had hym slayn,
kyng auferius withoute more tarieng
he gave ser DareH another for certayn 2734
Vppon the helme, the fyre thanne sprang owt ayeyn,
And ther withaH, with a fuH soden brayde,
To ser DareH right in this wise he saide : 2737

and smote him
on the head.

Auferius gave
him a blow in
return.

'Old men can smite,' quoth he.
'The [1] yong' knyghtez,' quod he, 'that ben) so prowde,
Old men) canne smyte, wete wole it is trew.'

Generydes heard his voice, and knew it was his father.
Generides hard hough he spake so lowde,
And by the voyce his fader thanne he knewe,   2741
Toward them both anon) he drewe ;
Whanne he was come in full vmble wise
To his fader, he said right in this wise :   2744

'I praye yow, ser, your' hand fro me refrayn),   2745
To the tyme ye knowe my purpose vtterly,
He parted them,
here am I come to departe yow'twayn),
ffor I must loue yow bothe and reason) whye ;   2748
And namely yow alone most specially,
As for this knyght whill my life [2] maye endure,
I shall hym) neuer fayle I yow ensure.'   2751

'What maner a man) be ye thanne,' saide the kyng',
'That putte your' self soo fer[3] furth in the prese ?'
'I shall yow telle,' quod he, ' withoute feyneng' ;
Of Surre am I born) withoute leese,   2755
told his name,
As for my name I hight Generides.'
And ther with all he tared not certayn),
and joined his fellows.
Butt to [4] his felawes furth he goth ayeyn).   2758

Auferius was dismayed.
Kyng' Auferius thanne was sumwhat dismayed,   2759
Be cause that he departid so ayeyn) ;
ffor be the wordes whiche he to hym) saide,
he was his sonne, he knew it for certayn) ;   2762
Yet of the sight of hym) he was full fayn),
As nature wold, and in especiall
That he was wexen) soo goodly a knyght with all. 2765

Now was the batell dureng' still o'pece,   2766
The kynggez ost encresid more and more ;
Said Darell unto Generydes,
Thanne sayd Darell on) to Generides,

[1] ? Ye.   [2] MS. list.   [3] MS. for.   [4] MS. he to.

'ffor your' pleasure we shall repente it sore.'   2769
'ffor hym)[1],' quod he, ' now good tell me wherefore.'
'yes yes,' quod he, ' this is the case,
your' Ice is euer stedfast in on) place.'   2772

'What place is that?' [quod he] ' I prae yow saye ;
As for the kyng', I see hym nott I wise.'
'I mene not that,' quod Darell, ' be this daye,
It is another thing', so haue I blis.   2776
On yonder towre on) highe I see where is
That causith yow these mastereys for to shewe,
Now haue I told yow all with wordes fewe.'   2779

'In sothe,' quod he, ' ye bere me wrong' in hand,   2780
ffor certenly I saugh hir not to nowe ;
Sithe she is ther, as now I vnderstonde,
If I do wele she woll me more allowe.   2783
Now be not wroth, for by licence of yow
Yet onys I will assaye what I canne do.'
'I graunt,' quod Darell, ' late vs goo thertoo.'   2786

Generides, and with hym) ser Darell,   2787
Bothe on) thei rode to knowe what was *ther* vre ;
And with Generides was Natanell,
Beryng' a spere of tymber good and sure ;   2790
Generides ther mette att a venture
The kyng' Ruben, Redy with spere and sheld,
And ther they strake to geder in the feld.   2793

Vppon) the sheld he strake Generides,   2794
And ther with brake his sheld in pecis twayn) :
A mighty man) he was, butt neuer the lesse
Atte same course he smote hym) so ayeyn),   2797
That of his hors he felle vppon) the playn),
With that Generides both fair' and wele
his hors he delyuered on) to Natanell.   2800

¹ ? *myn.*

' For your
pleasure we
shall repent
it sore :

your eye is ever

[leaf 15]

on yonder tower.'

' In sooth,' quoth
Generydes, ' I saw
her not till now.'

They rode on,

and Generydes
met Ruben,

and smote him
from his horse,

which he sent 'I·pray yow, ser,' he saide, ' haue here this stede, 2801
And take ye hym on to my lady der' ;
Me recomaunding' on to hir' goodly hede,
And say to hir that I haue wonne hym here.'   2804
' Well ser,' quod he, ' as towching' this mater,
late me alone now that I knowe your entente,
In all the hast I wull hym to hir present.'   2807

Furth with the steede he went owt of ye prese, 2808
to Clarionas by
Natanell. And streyght he goth on to Clarionas ;
' Madame,' quod he, ' my lord Generides
hym recommaundith lowly to your' grace,   2811
And sent yow here a stede of his purchase
And where that he hadde it to tell yow very playn,
Of kyng' Ruben he wanne hym for certayn.'   2814

She was right
glad. 'Ye be right welcome, Natanell,' quod she,   2815
' Of this I am right gladde and wele content,
And moche gladder to knowe the certente
Of his welefare that hath yow heder sent.'   2818
' Madame,' quod he, ' right now encontynent
I wold that he hym self were with yow here.'
' With me,' quod she, ' so wold I that he were.' 2821

Natanell returned
to Generydes, Thanne Natanell departid furth with all,   2822
And had a token onto Generides ;
In to the feld he goth among' them all,
And founde hym ther aside hand of the prese,   2825
and told him all. And furth with all told hym the [1] hoole processe,
In euery thing' that he hadde done and saide,
Tho was Generides full wele apayed ;   2828

He took courage, And ther with all he toke anon corage,   2829
And to the feld he dressid hym to ride ;
Of yong' and old and euery man of age

[1] MS. all the.

Ther wer butt few his strokes wold abide.   2832   *and few could abide his stroke.*
The kyngges ost drew to the Citez side,
Generides was thanne vppon) the playn,
A while ther to rest hym) *ther* in certayn).   2835

The kyng' of kynggez thanne was in his tente,   2836   *The king of kings*
And of all this he hard no maner thing' ;
he harde a noyse and wist not what it ment,
But furth he goth leving' All other thing',   2839
And toke his hors withoute taryeng',
he blew his horn) that all his men) myght here,   *blew his horn, and his men came about him.*
With that thei come a¹ bought hym) All in feere.   2842

Whanne Darell sawe the kyng' of kyngges ost,   2843   *Darell prayed Generydes to retire into the city.*
Generydes anon) full fayre [he] prayed ;
'ffor love of god that is of myghtez most,
Goo we in to the Citee now,' he sayde ;   2846
'Darell,' quod he, 'wher of be ye dismayd?
I see noo cause, for we shall do right wele
And skape ther handes, doughte ye neuer a dele.'   2849

'I am contente,' quod he, 'that we do so ;   2850   *'I am content,' quoth he.*
As for my part now late vs goo ther on.'
And with hym) was ser Anosore Also ;
his horn) thanne blew Generides anon),   2853
With that ther came A bowte hym) euerychone,
his felasshepe and what that euer he ment,
Thei were redy atte his commaundment.   2856

And furth they dressid hym) in his gere,   2857   *He, Darell, and Anasore have done bravely.*
Generides, Darell, and Anasor',
Might neuer men) doo better on) a day ther,
Thanne they dede ther so fewe pepill as thei were :
Eche of them iij so wele quiete them) ther,
They slew iij knyghtez eu[er]ychone for on),
The remenaunt were putte to flight euerychon).   2863

¹ MS. *an.*

And while they fougĥt to geder in the feld,   2864
The cite sent owt anon) in contenent
iij skore knygĥtez, Armyd witĥ spere And sheld ;
Ther witĥ Generides was wele content :   2867
' lo serys !' quod hee, ' Aftur your own) entent,
The felisszheppe is yourez that yender ye see,
Now may I suerly entre the Citee.'   2870

They took the way to the city. [leaf 15, back]

And whanne they were aĥ to geder mett,   2871
To the Citee they toke the wey fuĥ rigĥt,
And in they went withoute eny lette :

Then was there joy.

Thanne was ther Ioy, I yow be higĥt,   2874
In euery strete si[n]ggyng' and fyres bright ;
And euery creature, botĥ more and lesse,
Gaue a gret lawde onto Generides.   2877

The Sultan anon sent for him and thanked him.

Anon) withaĥ the Sowdon) for hym) sent,   2878
And gaue hym) ther his thank in feythfuĥ wise ;
ffor he perseyuyd wele in his entent,
he hadde hym) do rigĥt wurchipfuĥ seruice :   2881
And ther the Sowdon) made hym) fuĥ promys,
Seyng' his labour' and his grete traveĥ,
That in noo wise he wold hym) neuer fayle.   2884

The king of kings sent for men of craft to

The kyng' of kyngges erly vppe he rose,   2885
And sent for men) of craft in aĥ the hast,
To make engenys after his purpose,

break the walls.

The waĥtis to breke, the Citee for to wast ;   2888
Whanne this was purveyd for thanne atte last,

Ermones said

Kyng' Ermones stode vppe before them) Aĥ,
And to the kyng' he spake in especiaĥ :   2891

' Me think, ser, as after myn) avise,   2892
It nediĥ not to make aĥ this arraye,
To distroye the Cite it is noo grete entrepri[se],

It were better to saue it if ye may :　　　　　2895
ffor yow it were more wurchippe euery waye,
And in your fame the lenger to endur,
To wynne it in the feld I yow ensure.'　　　　2898

'How may that be ?' thanne saide the kyng Ayeyn,
'Your councell is right good, so mote I goo,　　2900
Owt of the town they will nott in certeyn,
What think ye best thanne,' quod he, 'y' we shall doo ?'
'Ser, on my life, ye shall not fynde it soo,
And if ye will enbatell vs euerychone,
Owt of the Citee thei will come anon ;　　.　　2905

I wote my self as wele as eny wight,　　　　　2906
for ther is on that will be all ther gide ;
In all the world is nott A better knyght
Thanne he is on, and better dare Abide.'　　　2909
'Nay,' quod the kyng, 'All that shalbe denyed,
ffor in wurchippe and in knyghtoode sekerly
I knowe hym nott that is so good as I.　　　2912

Notwithstondeng After your good avise,　　　2913
late vs anon goo sett our feld ayeyn,
And wheder they or we shall bere the prise,
Ryght sone we shall haue knowlage in certayn.'　2916
Anon withall thei gaderid on the playn
The kyngez ost, and in conclusion
They hym enbatelid streyght as for the town.　2919

Thanne sayde madan, that was the kyng of Trase,
'Me think ye do right wele to sette this feld,
for ye shall see withynne a litill space,
They will come owt or ellys them yeld.'　　　2923
And whanne thei of the Citee them beheld,
hough sone they were enbatelyd euerychone,
They tared not, butt furth they come Alone,[1]　2926

Margin notes:

It were better to save it.

'They will come anon out of the city.

'Let us go set our field again.'

They of the city came forth

A grete nowmber of men) in good arraye :   2927
Thanne they withoute anon to them) thei hyed,

and made no
more delay.
Right sone thei mette, And made no more delaye,
ffull fressh on) [them] thei sette on) euery side,   2930
Darell anon) kyng' Sanyk had Aspyed,

Darell ran at
King Sanyk,
and broke his
arm in two.
And with his spere he ranne and smote hym) soo,
That with that stroke he brake his arme on) twoo. 2933

Barachias, king
of Europe,
Thanne came rideng' the kyng' barachias,   2934
Of Europe he was lord and Souereyn) ;
Whanne Anasore Aspyed where he was,

was smitten down
by Anasore.
To hym) he ranne and smote hym) for certeyn),   2937
That from) his hors he felle vppon) the playn),
And as he fell his legge was brokyn) soo,
That from) the grownde he myght noo ferther goo. 2940

Thanne the kyng' of Trace putt hym) self in prese, 2941

Madan, the king
of Thrace,
was slain by
Generydes.
Madan he hight so as I vnderstounde,
To hym) anon) thanne ranne Generides,
Right wele armed, a good spere in his hande,   2944
Ther myght no maner harnesse hym) withstonde ;
ffor thoroughowt he strake hym) quyte And clene,
That atte bak the rede pensell was sene ;   2947

And with that stroke he fell and ther he dyed.   2948

The king
of kings
The kyng' of kynggez harkenyd of that case,
he taryd not nor lenger wold' Abide,
Butt rideth furth streyght in to the place   2951
Ther as Madan the kynggez body was,

beheld it with
a heavy cheer.
And it beheld with a full hevy chere,
Complayneng' sore[1] A pitevous thing' to here.   2954

He hadde hym) do right wurchipfull seruice,   2955
And harmones, the kyng' of higher ynde,
That what so euer he dede in eny wise

[1] MS. *sone*.

Thoo ij princes wer' neuer owt of his mynde :   2958
And for be cause they wer' to hym so kynd,
And sware his othe as he was rightwise kyng',
Ther deth he wold avenge for eny thing.   2961

And in this hast he rode in to the feld,   2962   He rode to
Abell that was of perse the Banere,   the field and
                                                               slew Abell,
To hym he Ranne and smote hym thorough y⁰ sheld,   the standard-
                                                               bearer of
ffor thorough owt y⁰ harnes persid y⁰ spere,   2965   Persia.
And afterward he bought that stroke full dere,   [leaf 16]
And with his swerd he smote hym ayeyn,
And slew hym or he passid owt of the playn.   2968

Grete hevynes made his felissheppe all,   2969
Whanne thei perseyued suerly how it was,
And first and formest in especiall,
The dede body they caryed from the place   2972
To the Citee not half a myle of space,
And as the Costom was, after ther gise,
They beryed hym¹ in honorabill wise.   2975

The batell thanne enduryd passing sore,   2976
And many lordes slayn on euery side,
They of the town had fought so long' afore,   They of the
                                                              town rode city-
That thei ne myght noo lenger ther abide,   2979   ward,
And to the Citeewarde furst ganne they ride ;
Yet or they were entered euerychone,
Of them ther were distressid manye on.   2982   and many of
                                                              them were
                                                              distressed.

The Sowdon was as woode as he myght be,   2983   The Sultan
To see his knyghtes stande in suche distresse,   was mad to
                                                              see them.
All full of thought and counfortles was he ;
To hym anon thanne seid Generides,   2986   Generydes said,
'Good ser,' quod he, ' take ye no maner of hevynesse,
Now shynneth the sonne and [now] god sendith showrez,
This day was therys, A nother² shalbe ourez.   2989

        ¹ MS. *them*   ² MS. *And A nother*

'Let us rest a day or two, And late vs rest as for a daye or twayne,   2990
That your pepill may haue refresshing,

and give them battle again.' Thanne we wolle geve them batell new ageyn,
Withoute delaye and lenger taryeng,   2993
And with the grace of god and good gideng;
And trust suerly, ye shall wele vnderstonde,
That we shall haue of them the ouer hande.'   2996

Now they haue refresshid them trewly,   2997
And are redy ther enmys to Assayle,[1]
A thowsand knyghtez in A companye,
And furth they went to geve them new batell,   3000
With grete corage in knyghthode to prevayle ;
And whanne the toder meny them beheld,
Anon they came and mette them in the feld.   3003

And in a valy togederward they went,   3004
The battle then began anew. The batell thanne beganne new ayeyn,
No trewys was taken ne noo poyntement,
Butt strong feightyng and many knyghtez slayn; 3007
Generides, for to sey yow certeyn,
Whom that euer he mette vppon the grene,
ffrom his sadill he wente quyte And clene.   3010

Syr Anasore the knyght, And ser Darell,   3011
And All the toder knyghtez euerychone,
Eche for his parte quyte hym self full wele,
The king's host fled. And of the kynges ost slew many on ;   3014
The remenaunte remevid bak anon,
And as thei fled, the writeng makith mynd,
Ermones, Come Ermones, the kyng of higher ynd,   3017

with his mighty men and their foul weapons, (see p. 60, p. 80,) With myghti men of mervelous makyng,   3018
like as it is rehersid here before ;
Ther wepons fowle and ill faryng,

[1] MS. Assoyle.

Wher with they layde on stroke[s] grete And sore.
Kyng' Ermones, to say yow ferthermore,
Ser Anosore right sone he had Aspied,
And furth with all to hym he ganne ride :   3024   rode at Sir
                                                         Anasore,

With his wepon long' and ill faryng',   3025
he slew his hors and smote hym on tho hede,   slew his horse,
And in tho feld he left hym liggeng',   and left him
                                           lying in the
Demyng' non other butt that he was dede,   3028   field for dead.
With Anosore ther was non other rede,
Butte vppe he rose as god wold geve hym grace,
And to his felawes furth he goth a pase.   3031

Hym to a venge his thought was and his mend,   3032
And sone he was vppon another stede,   Anasore got
                                          another steed,
Streyght he rideth to a knyght of ynde,   and slew a
                                             knight of India.
And with a swerd he cleue a ij his hede,   3035
That in tho feld he felle ther and was dede :
Whanne Ermones wist of this Aventure,   Ermones
A hevy man he was I[1] yow ensur',   3038

And streyght he rideth onto Generides :   3039   rode at
                                                    Generydes,
Butt[2] he anon was ware of his comyng',
And with a naked swerd in to the prese
Ayenst hym full fast he come rideng' ;   3042
As sone as Ermones the kyng'
Sawe that he was withynne his wepons length,
Anon he smote Att hym with all his strength.   3045   and smote
                                                          at him,

His wepon light vppon Generides,   3046
And brast his sheld with all in pecys twayn,   breaking
                                                  his shield.
Also it ranne down quyte thorough the harnes,
A grace of god that he had not ben slayn ;   3049
Ther with Generydes smote hym ayeyn,   Generydes clave
                                          his head to the
Thoroughowt the helme a hye vppon the crest,   breast.
And claue his hede streyte down to the brest.   3052

_____
[1] MS. _h._   [2] MS. _Be._
GENERYDES.   7.

And with that stroke kyng⸱ Ermones was ded ;   3053
ffor hym his knyghtez made grete ordenaunce,
His men
carried him off,
They hym with drew, ther was non other rede,
And fast they hyed them owt of ther distaunce,   3056
Thinkyng⸱ them self owt of good gouernaunce,
[leaf 16, back]
And as they rode togeder complayneng⸱,
and met King
Belen,
Vppon the way they mette Boleyn the kyng⸱ ;   3059

who would have
had them turn,
And fayn he wold haue them turne ayeyn,   3060
Comfortid them in all that euer he myght, ⸱
Butt All that euer he spak it was in vayn ;
With that anon ther answerd hym a knyght,   3063
And as the story seith Otran he hight,
‘ Of our⸱ fortune in euery thyng⸱,’ quod he,
‘ I shall suerly telle yow the certente.   3066

but they said,
‘ In yonder host
is a knight who
is a very fiend,
In yender ost,’ quod he, ‘ ther is a knyght,   3067
he is noo very man, what euer he be,
Butt rather a fende, and that I yow be hight,
Ther is no man alyve that he wolle flee ;   3070
and hath slain
our king.’
Oure kyng⸱ is ded, whiche sore repentith me.
And suche a prince we canne not gete ayeyn,
And he it is suerly that hath hym slayn.’   3073

Belen seeks
Generydes,
Whanne kyng⸱ Bolyn had knowlage of yᵗ case,   3074
A hevy man he was and comforteles,
And furth with all he rideth on a pace,
All in a rage seching⸱ Generides,   3077
And ther they mette togeder in·the prese,
Thanne was the batell all togeder doon,
but they were
parted.
So att that tyme thei were departid sone.   3080

The men of
Persia won
the day.
The men of perce that day were fortenat,   3081
The toder fled as fast as euer thei might,
And in hym self they stode soo desolate ;

Whanne kyng Bolyn saw they were putte to flight,
That in noo wise they wold no lenger fight,
With hym ther was now other poyntement,
Butt lost the feld and rideth to his tent.   3087

Too the Citee rideth Generides,   3088
With knyghtes and with Sqyers many on,
ffor hym was made grete Ioy of more And lesse,
And festis made among them eu[er]ychon.   3091
Thanne to the Sowdon furth he went anon,
Of whom he hadde his thank right specially,
And grete yeftys as he was wele worthy.   3094

Generydes rides
to the city,

and is received
with great joy.

The kyng of kynggez still was in his tent,   3095
And yndly wroth that no man cowde hym plese,
And in hym self he cowde not be content,
Till he had fought with Generides,   3098
They twayn to geder owt of all the prese,
And ther vppon he callid his councell,
That his entent the souner myght prevayle.   3101

The King of
kings was wroth,

and would not
be content till
he fought
with Generydes.

At his callyng his lordes came anon,   3102
And this he sayde, that euery man myght here,
' Now ye be here in present euerychon,
This is,' quod he, ' the effecte of my mater,   3105
It is now a full quarter of a yere,
Oure lyeng her the Sowdon for to wynne,
And att this day we are new to be gynne.   3108

He called his
council.

' We have been
here now a
quarter of a
year,' said he,

' and have to
begin anew.

And yet I wote right wele it lithe in me,   3109
The Sowdon to distroye and all his lande,
Of all maner vitayle I haue plente ;
Notwithstondyng, if he will take on hand   3112
To fynde a knyght, that I may vnderstond
Be right wele born and of high lenage,
To fight with me for all this Eritage,   3115

Let the Sultan
find a knight to
fight with me,

and make an
end of this war.'
And so to make an ende of all this werre   3116
Betwix vs twayne ; and if he wold not so,
I will distroye his land both nyghe and ferre,
his land and hym self, where euer hee goo,   3119
And for the Accompleshment Also,
Be cause I wold that it shuld be endid sone,
Withynne iiij dayes I wold that it were done.'   3122

King lamadon gave answere in this case,   3123
And in his speche he was som what dismayed,
This cowardly his hert and his seruice
Was to the Sowdon, what so euer he sayde ;   3126
Yet not for thy his reasone furth he layde
All opynly ; 'my lordes,' quod he,
' The kyng hath seid right wele as semyth me.'   3129

For this cause he gaue sone his assentt,   3130
That in that space a trety myght be hadde ;
And as he seid all other were content,
Thanne was the kyng of kynggez passing glad,   3133
Three lords were
appointed to go
to the Sultan,
And vppon these iij lordes wise and sadde
A poyntid were to goo on this massage,
Onto the Sowdon and his Baronage.   3136

On of them iij of Corynth [1] was he born,   3137
Callid Sampsone, the story doth expresse ;
The secunde, and his ancetors be forn,
In Damask born, the writeng doth witnesse,   3140
A man of wurchippe and of grete sadnesse ;
The iij[de] was a man, to say yow right,
Of Ethiope, and Ionathas he hight.   3143

Anon these lordes went on ther message,   3144
each with a
branch of olive.
Eche man A brawnche of Olyve in his hande,
In token of pece for ther viage,

[1] MS. *Cornyth.*

Too goo and come saff, as I vnderstonde,   3147
lyke as the custom) was in euery lande ;
So fourth they went withoute more¹ delay,
To the Sowdow) ther errand for to say.   3150   [leaf 17]

And whanne that thei were come to his presence, 3151 They came to
                          the Sultan
Of ther massage they kept noo thyng' in store,   and told him
                          the message,
Butt in all the hast they told hym) the sentence,
like as it is rehersid here before,   3154
In euery maner thing' and summe² what more,
So as the kyng' gave them) in commaundment,
Accordeng' sum what onto his entent ;   3157

The whiche was this, to say yow in substaunce, 3158 and that he
                          should send
That he shuld send his doughter to the kyng',   his daughter to
                          the King.
And by that meane the striff and variaunce
Be twix them) bothe myght the souner haue endyng.³
ffor an answere in ther aycyn) goyng',
Of ther massag' they praed them) to say
In all this mater playnly ye or nay.   3164

Whanne ther massag' was all to geder sayde,   3165
Ther was noo lord nee knyght that gave answer',   The lords were
                          silent and the
Wher with trewly the Sowdow) was dismayde ;   Sultan dismayed.
Generides sawe that, and drew hym) nere :   3168
' Ser, if it like your' goodnes for to here,
I shall for yow,' quod he, ' be in this place,
Be your' licence geve answer in this case.'   3171

And thus he sayde be fore them) eu[er]ychow) :   3172
' Thez massangers they shall wele vnderstonde,
Among' your' knyghtez all that ther is on)
Shall vnder take to Answer' for this lande ;   3175 Generydes
                          undertook to
ffor I my self will take it att ther hand,   answer .or the
                          land.
And here is my glove, this mater to defende,
Withynne iiij dayes therof to make an ende.   3178

¹ MS. *wordes more.*   ² MS. *sunne.*   ³ MS. *an end.*

Generydes
guaranteed that
no dishonour
should befall
Clarionas.

And your' doughter also, Clarionas,　　　　　3179
he shall do hir no maner of villanye,
Nother dishonour, whill I haue liff and space,
And ferthermore I vnderstonde trewly,　　　3182
By ther massage declaryd opynly,
Ther shall now take of hym this enterprise,
Butt he be wele born in eny wise.　　　　　3185

And to that ye shall wele knowe my councell,　3186
Was neuer man herd so moche of me ;
A kyngges sonne I am withoute fayle,
And my moder is a quene in certayn[te] :　　　3189
here afterward ye shall wele know and see,
All though he be a prince of nobyll fame,
To fight with me to hym shalbe noo shame.'　3192

Whanne the Sowdon perseivid his entent,　　　3193
And herd hym wele in all that euer he sayde,
The Sultan was
glad.
Thanne was he gladde and verily well content,
That he was of so good a knyght purveyd ;　　3196
Yet with hym self he was nott wele apayde,
And in his mende repentid hym full sore,
That he so meche had wrongid hym before.　　3199

Whanne these lordes had answere in this wise,　3200
One of the lords
said Generydes
should take
advice before
meddling with
a prince that
was peerless.
One of them sayde on to Generides ;
' It is well don that ye take a good avise,
Or that ye putt your' self so ferre in prese,　　3203
To medyll with a prince that is perles ;
ffor he is knowen in contres ferre and nere.'
Generides anon gave hym answere,　　　　　3206

Generydes said,
' Your king is
a noble knight,
And this he sayde, in presence of them all ;　3207
' As for your' kyng', he is a nobill knyght
I canne wele think, and so men do hym calle ;

Butt my quarell is growndid vppon right, 3210
Whiche gevith me corage for to fight,
And here my trowth I wolle not fayle my day, bet I will not
fall my day.'
My self alone, and so I prae yow saye.' 3213

They toke his glove, And to that prince thei went 3214
With ther answere in euery maner thing:
And of Generides and his entent
ffull playnly thei told onto the kyng: 3217
And whanne that he ther of had knowlaching,
The kyng hym self, withoute eny more, The king
Ayenst that day he purveyd hym therfore. 3220

Too all his ost he gave A speciall charge, 3221 gave his host
charge to remove
two miles away,
Ayenst that day that he shuld fight alone,
They shuld remeve that place ij myle large,
And ther to geder abide euerychon 3224
What euer fall, for reskewe wold he non; for rescue would
he none.
And ther vppon, to folow his entent,
To them he gave a streight commaundment. 3227

The Citesens thanne was not wele apayde, 3228 The citizens were
not pleased,
Be cause Generides to[ke] this in hand :
They love[d] hym so wele, and this they said,
'A better knyght ther is in noo land.' 3231
And whanne Clarionas ded vnderstonde and Clarionas
was full of
thought,
That he shuld take vppon hym this batell,
Thanne was she full of thought and noo mervell. 3234

'Now, good Mirabell, what is best?' quod she, 3235
'What shall I doo? saye me your good avise.'
And said, ' wold god he wold do Aftur me,
Thanne shuld he not take this interprise.' 3238
'Nay, late be that in eny maner wise,
Madame,' quod she, 'for sothe he hath it take,
ffor his wurchippe he may it not for sake. 3241

Nether he will, Madame, I telle yow playn.'   3242
'Now thanne,' quod she, 'me think this is to doon;
I will send hym Gwynot my chaunberleyn,
This rede pensell I will send hym anon;   3245

[leaf 17, back]   And or that he on the batell goon,
ffor esing of my hert I will hym praye,
To speke with me to morow or to day.'   3248

'That is wele doo,' quod she, 'withoute lese.'   3249

and sent for Generydes   Thanne chargyd she hir chaumberleyn to goo :
'hye yow,' quod she, 'onto Generides ;
This rede pensell ye shall bere hym also,   3252
Whiche I myself enbrowdred and no moo :
Pray hym also or he passe the Citee,

to come and speak with her.   In eny wise that he will speke with me.'   3255

On this massage now goth hir chaunberleyn,   3256
And to Generides he takith the waye,
With hir tokyn and all hir errand playn,
In all the hast possible that he may ;   3259
And he also for gate nott for to say,
On hir behalf afore his departeng,
hir for to see leving all other thing.   3262

Generydes was glad of this,   Off that massage Generides was fayn,   3263
And furth with all rewardid hym right well ;
he sent a token on to hir ayeyn,
Bee cause that she shuld vnderstonde and fele,   3266
That he had don his massage euery dele,
And ferthermore he chargid hym to say,

and promised to see her soon.   he wold see hir in all the hast he may.   3269

Now goth Gwynot[1] vnto Clarionas,   3270
And told hir what he had don that day.
Generides, whanne he had tyme and space,

[1] MS. *Gwynan.*

To hir chaunber he toke the redy waye ;   3273   He came to her
                                                                chamber window.
And att a wyndow, sothely for to say,
he spake to hir, right as he wold devise,
Att good leysere in honorabiłł wise.   3276

Whanne he departid ther was grete hevynes,   3277
And as he toke his love in his goyng·
Thanne eche to other made to geder fułł promyse,   Each to other
                                                                made promise
To kepe hym trew aboue ałł other thing·,   3280   to be true.
Now late vs thanne speke of Belen) the kyng,
Whiche att his day thinkyth with spere and sheld
hym self alone to come into the feld.   3283

The iij^{de} morow, as sone as it was day,   3284   On the third
                                                                day King Belen
kyng· Belyn) rose and made hym ałł redy,
his stede morełł trappyd in good arraye,
With his harnes enbrowderyd by and by,   3287
hym self armyd fułł wele and fułł sure[ly],   armed himself,
his helme was wele ordeynyd for the nonys,
Right wele garnysshed with perle & precious stonys.

Kyng· Bellyw) rideth in to the feld alone,   3291   and rode to
                                                                the field.
As it appoynted was betwix them) twayn) ;
his pepiłł were avoydid euerychone,
And ther he taryed stiłł vppon) the playn),   3294
Supposing· wełł ther was no man) certeyn),
Consideryng· his manhod and his myght,
Wold be so bold ayenst hym) to fight.   3297

The tidynggez thorough owt the Cite sprong·,   3298
hough kyng· Bellyn) was armed in the mede,
Generides thought he was passing· long·,   Generydes
                                                                mounted his
And furth anon) was brought Grissełł his stede,   3301   horse Grisell,
A myghti hors and very sure atte nede ,
The Sowdon) gave it hym) in certente,
Whiche no man) shuld haue saue only he.   3304

Hys trappour was made in the fressest wise,   3305
Wrought with peerlys of mervelus makyng,
hym self armyd atte poynte devise,
his helme with stonys had his garnysshyng;   3308
The rede penseH vppon his spere hangyng,
hym to behold and Iuge withoute dought,
A knyght hym semyd for to be right stought.   3311

and all the
people prayed

AH the pepyH that in the Citee were,   3312
Men and women to prayer they them gave,
Besechyng god, with devout maner,

God to speed
him.

To spede hym weH ther contre for to save :   3315
Clarionas, good tidenggez for to haue,
late nee erly she wold nott seese,
Butt nyght And day prayed for Generides.   3318

The Sultan
brought him
to the gate,

The Sowdon brought hym streight on to ye gate, 3319
And in like wise the Citezens euerychon,
And whanne that they had brought hym AH yer at,

and he rode
forth alone,

he toke his leve and furth he rode alone   3322
In to the mede, and ther he founde anon

and found the
King of kings.

The kyng of kynggez vppe and down rideng,
And he anon to hym com waloping.   3325

Whanne kyng Bellyn saw he was comyng,   3326
To hym he rode, and mette hym on the waye,

' Say me sooth,'
quoth Belen,
' whether thou
art a messenger
or nay.'
' I am,' said
Generydes,
' and this is my
message :

' Now say me soth,' quod he, ' withoute feyning,
Wheder art thu a massanger or nay ? '   3329
·' I am,' quod he, ' a massanger I saye ;
This way I take for my right viage
ffro the Sowdon, and this is my massage.   3332

To warre vppon my lord thu dost hym wrong,   3333
he sent the word now, whanne I cam hym fro,

Vold my lord's
ground,

To voyde his grownde and tary not to long,

Vnto thy contre wher thu hast to do :   3336
This thinkith me best, and if thu wilt do so,
Ayeyn) I will goo as a massanger,
And full trewly declare hym) thynne answer'.   3339

And if thu will not follow myn) avise,   3340   [leaf 18]
Thu shalt wele knowe that I am not come on) massage,
Peraventur' thu may¹ repent it twyes,   if not thou
                                                                    mayst repent it.'
That thu hast askid of this lande trevage ;   3343
To kepe it fre and owt of all seruage
I shall my self, as for this landis right,
With goddes grace defende it as a knyght.'   3346

And kyng' Bellyn) whanne his purpose hard,   3347   King Belen
And wherfore that he came in to the feld,
Thanne wex he pale and chaungyd clene his mode,   ·waxed pale ;
hym) self anon) he closed in his sheld ;   3350
Generides his countenaunce behelde,
he tared not butt dressid hym) in his gere,
And in his hande anon) he toke his spere.   3353

Thanne was no more a do butt on they sett,   3354
Anon) they Ranne to geder in the·feld,   they ran together,
The kyng' and he fresshly ther they mette,
And eche of them) smote other on the sheld,   3357   and smote each
                                                                    other with great
With strokez grete, and bothe ther sperys helde,   strokes.
So ther vppon) they tared not certayn),
Butte furth with all they toke ther course ayeyn). 3360

Ther stedys were both Inly good and weight ;   3361
Generides came rounde vppon) the grownde,   In another
                                                                    course Generydes
And brake the kynggez helme before his sight,   brake the King's
The spere went to the vesage quyte and rownde,   3364   helm,
Duryng' his liff it myght be know that wound.
The kyng' ayenward strake Generides   and the King
Vppon) the side, and perisshed the harnes   3367   pierced his
                                                                   harnes

¹ MS. *may it.*

so that the blood ran down.

Vnto the skynne; the blode ranne down therby,   3368
Butt, as god wold, he felt no harme in dede.

He said in mockery,

Thanne saide the kyng sum what in mokkery,
'Maister,' quod he, 'thy side begynne for to blede,
Wherefore this is my councell and my rede,
ffor this mater noo lenger for to stryff,

'Go home again, and escape alive.'

Go home ageyn and thu shalt skape alyve.'   3374

'I know,' quod he, 'that on lyve I may skape,   3375
And so I shall wheder thu wilt or noo,

'The bleeding,' said Generydes, 'is but a jape; think of the wound on your face.'

The bledingge of my side is butt a Iape,
It encreasith my corage to and too;   3378
In thi vesage think on thy wounde also,
The whiche shall neuer a way I the ensure,
Whill that yⁿ art a lyvez creature.'   3381

The King was wrother, and they ran another course;

Thanne was the kyng' wrother, I yow behight;   3382
They toke ther course and ranne to geder new,
And ther the stedis mette with suche a myght

horses and men went down.

Ther hors foundred, and, for to say yow trew,   3385
Bothe hors and man and all yer ouer threw;
They of the Citee sawe that encownteryng',
And hough it was befall euery thing'.   3388

And ferd they were as for Generides,   3389

Clarionas was heavy for Generydes.

ffull hevy was Clarionas thanne also,
And euer more in prayours still opese,
Vnto the tyme she knew it shuld goo.   3392
of that fortune kyng Bellyn was full woo,
So was Generides a bashed¹ also thore,

They rose up,

Butte vppe they rose, to say yow ferthermore,   3395

and without knowing it changed horses, and went at each other with their swords.

And chaungyd horses onto them bothe vnknowyng,²
Wherefore they were full wroth, I yow ensure;
To geder thanne they went with swordes drawe,

¹ MS. and bashed.   ² So MS. ? vnknowe.

And leyde on) strokes owt of all mesure,   3399
Generides sward was passing sure,
And, as the story wele remember canne,
It was a princes callid Iulyan),   3402

Generydes'
sword had
belonged to the
Emperor Julian.

Waiche was sumtyme of Rome the Emperour;   3403
The Sowdon) had it after his deccasse,
And as a tresour' euery day and owre
he kept that sward in grete tendernesse,   3406
And after gaue it on to generides;
So ferthermore, as I this mater feele,
Whanne eche of them) had beten) other wele,   3409

The kyng' of kynggez seid to hym) ayeyn),   3410
'What aylith the to fight for this mater?
A grete foly for the take the payne,
To the it towchith not in no maner;   3413
I councell ther for, while thow art here,
Be come my man), and thu wilt do so
The pese shall sone be twix vs twoo.   3416

The King of
kings said to him.
'Why dost thou
fight thus? It
toucheth thee
not.

Become my man,

I shall also in wurchippe the avaunce,   3417
And largely departe with the also ;
ffor meche better it lith in my puessence,
Thanne in the Sowdon) powre so to do :   3420
And for Clarionas I say also,
Whanne she is myn), here what I say to the,
Att thy pleasure hir shalt thu haue of me.   3423

I will advance
thee,

and when
Clarionas is
mine thou shalt
have her.

And thu wilt not do as I the sayo,   3424
I late the now haue knowlage vterly,
That of my hand here shalt thu dye to daye ;
Troste noo lenger to my curtessy,   3427
I haue entretyd the full Ientelly,
And how thu wilt be rewlid in this case,
Say ye or nay, or ye go owt of this place.'   3430

If not thou shalt
die to-day.'

Thanne furth with all Answered Generides,   3431
'To thy seruice,' quod he, 'if I me bynde,
I so right wele I may sone haue my pece;

But that was neuer enprentid in my mende,   3434
To be vntrew it come me neuer of kynde;
That I haue said and take of my promys,
O trowth I will not breke it in noo wise.   3437

And fortbermore, as for Clarionas,   3438
I vnderstonde thu proferest hir to me,
Whiche is not thyne truly ne neuer was,
And suche a yeft is litill worth parde;   3441
ffor one thing shall I say in certente,
If I hir shall reioyse, so god me save,
Of the playnly hir will I neuer haue.'   3444

Thanne was the kyng mech wrother than before, 3445
And on they went to geder now ayen;
Thanne eyther other layde wonder sore,
Wherof the sownd rebowndid on the playn,   3448
The stede that was the kynggez for certayn
Vnder Generides beganne to fayle,
Whiche hym abasshed sore and noo mervell.   3451

The kynggez stede was alwey good and sure   3452
ffor all his labour, yet onnese he swett;
he saw right wele ye toder myght not dure,
Wherefore on hym right fressly[1] he sett,   3455
The shulders of ther horsez to geder mett;
Generides vppon the feyntid stede,
Streyght to the grownde hors a[nd] man yede.   3458

His swerd ther with ou[t] of his hand it fell,   3459
Butt as god wold he had it sone ayeyn,
he lay not long but riseth fayre and still,

¹ ? fersly.

And furth he goth, to sey yow for certayn,   3462

To kyng Bellyng, And toke hym be the reyne.   *and seized the king's bridle.*

he sporyd his hors and from hym wold haue goo;[1]

'A bide,' quod he, 'thu shalt not skape me soo.   3465

This stede,' he seith, ' hath scruyd the full wele,   3466

The whiche trewly repentith me full soore,

Ayenst my will thu hast hym cuerydele,

Butt now o trowth thu shalt haue hym no more,   3469

This stede is myn, thu wist it wele [be]fore ;   *'This steed is mine, alight anon.'*

A light anon withoute wordes moo,

Or suerly I shall make the or I goo.'   3472

The kyng presid fast away certayn,   3473   *The king pressed away, but Generydes held the rein, and between them the horse fell backward.*

Generides helde still the reane alway ;

And so be twix the striving of them twayn,

The horse reversid bak, and ther he lay.   3476

Generides anon to hym ganne say,

' Not long agoo thu haddist me in this plight,

And now I trost to god I shall the quyte.'   3479

Generides his swarde toke in his hande,   3480   *Generyden took his sword Claryet*

Claryet it hight, the store tellith me so,

A better swerd ther was neuer in noo land.

The kyng arose and wold a gon hym froo,   3483

ffor of his fayling ther he was full woo ;

Generides was noo thyng evill apayde,

And with his swerd full fast on hym he layde.   3486   *and laid on the King full fast,*

The kynges sheld he made a quarter lesse,   3487   *cutting a piece off his shield, and breaking the harness on his knee.*

The swerd is glansid down on his kne,

And ther is[2] brake asonder the harnes,

That all to geder bare a man myght see :   3490

The kyng Bellyn was wrothe as he myght be,   *The King wounded him in the teeth.*

he strake att hym with a full eger will,

And in the tethe he woundid hym full ill.   3493

---

[1] MS. *goon.*   [2] ? *it.*

' Now,' said he,
'I have quit you.'

Thanne seyde the kyng, 'now att all aventur' 3494
I haue the quyte, and ther of am I fayn,
The nexst that I the geve I the ensure,
I will thu vndersto[n]de it for sertayn : 3497
Ne shall thu quyte it me ayeyn.'
With thoo wordes wrothe was Generides,
And to the kyng presid still opese. 3500

Generydes
gave him such
a stroke that
he cut his ear off.

And thanne suche a stroke he gave hym yer 3501
Vppon the helme, the bare visage was sene ;
The swerd was sharpe and ranne down be his ere,
That from the hede he smote it quyte and clene, 3504
And from his swerd it felle vppon the grene :
Thanne [1] was kyng Bellyn astownyd sore,

The King was
abashed.

And in hym self abasshed more and more. 3507

Both were weary,
but their hearts
were strong.

They were full wery bothe, I yow be hight, 3508
Notwithstondeng ther hartys were full strong,
On them ther was no pece of harnys right,
Of plate ne mayle, but all to geder wrong ; 3511
And no wonder, for they foughten long,

The King struck
again at
Generydes,

Yet in his hert for anger and for payn,
The kyng stroke to Generides ayeyn, 3514

and smote him on
the head.

And with his swerd he smote [him] on the hede, 3515
That wher he was he wist not vterly ;
'If thu,' quod he, 'had done after my rede,
Thu shuldest not now haue ben in this parte.' 3518
Generides hym Answeryd trewelly,
'If I noo thyng dede after thynne entent,
Trust me right wele yet did I not repent.' 3521

Generydes in
return smote
him on the same
side where he
was hurt before,

And with that worde he smote hym so ayeyn, 3522
And cleue his hede down and hurt hym [2] sore,
And by fortune it happid so certeyn,

[1] MS. *Thāme*.   [2] MS. *hyn*.

Vppon) that side that he was hurt before :   3525
he bled so meche he myght stond no more,
Butt to the grownde anon) *yer* he felle down),   **and he lay in a swoon.**
And sore for blode he lay still in swoune.   3528   **[leaf 19]**

Generides stode still and hym) be [1] held,   3529
And of the kyng' thanne had he grete pite,
he toke hym) vppe and layde hym) on) his sheld ;
Thanne seid the kyng', softely as it wold be,   3532   **The King said softly, 'Here is my sword,**
'haue here my swerd, I yeld it vppe to the,
As to a knyght the wordes,' [2] he saide,
'In all my lyffe that euer I assayde.   3535

Off all this land I geve vppe my quarell,   3536   **I give up my claim to this land and Clarionas,**
And so I do Clarionas also,
ffor certayn) butt if she loue yow wele
She do no thyng' hir part as she shuld do,   3539
And this I wold require yow or ye goo,
That I myght goo ther as my pepill be,   **and will pass forth to my country.'**
And so to passe furth in to my contre.'   3542

To hym) thanne sayde Generides ayeyn),   3543   **'I grant this request,' said Generydes,**
'All this request I graunt it verely ;'
And vppe he toke hym) in his armys twayn),
And sett hym) on) his stede [3] full Ientely.   3546   **and set him on his steed again.**
So furth he rideth fayre and soberly ;
Whanne his pepill sawe hym) in that maner,   **His people met him with a heavy cheer.**
They mett hym) all with a hevy chere.   3549

Vppon) the playn) restid Generides,   3550   **Generydes rested on the plain,**
Wery and feynte, it was noo synne to saye ;
And whanne he was sum what more att his ease
Toward' the Citee streyght he toke the waye.   3553   **and then went back to the city**
They of the town) knewe wele be his araye
That it was he, and glad thei were eche on),
So furth he came rideng' hym) self alone,   3556

---

[1] MS. *he.*   [2] So MS. *? worthiest.*   [3] MS. *stote.*
GENERYDES.   8

with his two
swords.
The lords all
met him, and
all the people

Towarde the Citee girde with his swerdez twayn :   3557
The lordes all mett hym withoute the town,
And all tho Citezens vppon tho playn,
With mynstrellys of many A dyuerse sownd,   3560

with royal
procession.

Preletys, prestys, with riall precession,
And Childryn syngeng in the fressest wise,
With merthis moo thanne I canne now device.   3563

Clarionas was
nothing behind.

Clarionas she was noo thyng behynd,   3564
All hir counfort was by hir self alone ;
In hir hart she was and in hir mende
As well content as all they euerychone.   3567

They brought
him to the
Sultan, who
gave him great
gifts and thanked
him.

To the Sowdon thanne was he brought anon
Whiche gave hym yeftez grete for his seruice,
And thankid hym in full specially wise.   3570

Anon with all were brought fro dyuerse place,   3571

The best surgeons
that could be
found came to
attend him.

Good sorgeons, the best that cowde be fownde,
And they full sone withynne a litill space,
hym vndertoke to make hym hoole and sounde,   3574
Of euery hurt and eke of euery wounde,
Whiche that he had and so to hym thei saide,
Where with the Sowdon was full wele apayde.   3577

Belen told his
lords he had
given up his
claim to Persia
and Clarionas,

Now kyng Belyn lithe in full hevy case,   3578
And told his lordis stondyng hym before,
Of perce lande and of Clarionas
he hath geve vppe his clayme for euermore :   3581
And ther with all his woundes blede so sore,
his liff cowde no man vnder take certayn,

and died of his
wounds in a
day or two.

And so he dyed withynne a day or twayn.   3584

For hym his pepill made grete hevynes,   3585
Among them self with peteuose complayneng,
And in all goodly hast thei ganne hym dresse,

In to Egipte his body for to bryng, 3588
With grete estate and honour like a kyng;
Whanne that was don with grete solempnite,
The lordes all went home in to ther contre. 3591

His people took his body to Egypt, and the lords went home to their countries.

Now late vs leue them in ther contros all, 3592
In to the tyme thei were sent for ayeyn,
Whiche was not longe, and in especiall
To make Gwynan[1] ther kyng and souereyn, 3595
Whiche was the kyng of kyngges sone certayn,
And so thei were agreed on hym alone,
he for to Reigne vppon them euerychone. 3598

Gwynan, the King's son, succeeded him,

And to sey yow in short conclusion, 3599
Be all the hoole agroment of the lande,
Of Egipte he was kyng and bare the crown,
Thanne to them all seid he, as I wnderstonde, 3602
'Suche maters as my fader toke in hande,
Towchyng the Sowdon and Clarionas,
Ye shall sone wete my plesure in this case. 3605

and told his people that he did not give up his claim to Persia and Clarionas.

As for the land of Perce all maner wayis, 3606
I will pleynly declare yow myn entent,
My lord and fader quyte it in his dayes
Yet for all that I was not of assentt, 3609
Nor noo wise I canne not be content;
And in like wise as for clarionas,
I will not be agreyd, nor neuer was.' 3612

Thanne was ther a man of grete powre, 3613
A knyght that was wele cherisshed with ye kyng,
he was right weel betrost both ferr and necre,
What euer he saide or dede in eny thyng, 3616
A witty man, And subtill in werkyng,
Ser Yuell the Barn, the story seith he hight,
This was his name to say the very right. 3619

There was a subtill knight,

Sir Yvell the Barn,

[1] MS. *Snynan.*

[leaf 19, back]
to whom the
King in secret
told his love for
Clarionas.

In secrete wise the kyng' saide to the knyght,   3620
'I shall yow telle my fortune as it was:
It happyd me,' quod he, ' I had a sight
Vppon) the towre of faire Clarionas,   3623
And here I loue; play[n]ly this is the case:
here to reioyse I wold haue sought the wayes,
Butt I for bare, it in my faders dayes.   3626

' How can I
best obtain
her?'

And now I prae yow telle me your' avise,   3627
hough I myght best to my purpose Attayne.'

The knight said,

The knyght anon) gave answere in this wise:
'To folow your' entent, I wold be fayn)   3630
To putt ther to my diligence and payn),
And in this case I hope to do so wele,
That ye shall haue your' pleasure euery dele.   3633

' I must have
a swift ship
prepared for
seven years,

Butt I must haue A shippe bothe good and wight, 3634
And that it be right swiff vnder a saile;
ffor vij yere it must be redy dight,
With men) I now and plente of vitalle,   3637

and in that time
I shall convey
her to this
country.'

And in that tyme withoute eny fayle,
I shall conveeye hir in to this contree,
And peraventur' souner so may it be.'   3640

With his promys the 'kyng' was wele content,   3641
And thankyd hym) right hertely therfore:

A ship was
provided,

A Shippe was purveyd after his entent,
With all that is rehersid here before,   3644
And as fortune kepith here thanke in store,
And Shewith favour' to suche as ben) full ill,

and the wind
was ready.

Come was the wynde full redy att his will.   3647

He sailed to
the land of
Persia,
and found a
haven

So long' he sayleth as I vnderstonde,   3648
That of the lande of Perse he hadde a sight;
Whanne he came nere a havyn) ther he fownde,

And thederward he toke the way full right :   3651
Whanne thei were in, as fast as euer thei myght,
Ther ancers owt thei cast on euery side,   *where he cast*
ffor ther awhile they cast them to Abide.   3654 *anchor,*

Vppon that havyn ther was a faire Citee,   3655
Whiche stode full fayre vppon the Ryvers side ;
This knyght anon owt of the shippe goth he,
Butt twayn with hym and on to be his gide,   3658 *and landed with*
The remenaunt shuld in the shippe a bide   *two others,*
                                                          and a guide.
A day or twayne, and thanne, in craft[y] wise,   *The rest he*
Go to the town be waye of merchaundise,   3661 *ordered*

To bye and sell as thei see other doo,   3662 *to buy and sell*
Vnto the tyme they hard of hym ayeyn.   *till they heard of*
So gothe he furth withoute wordes moo,   *him again.*
And as he went, he mette vppon the playn   3665 *As he went he*
A man that was right ferr' in age certayn,   *met an old man,*
And all for growe, a pilgrim as he were,   *a palmer,*
Thanne to hym saide the knyght in this maner: 3668

'Fader,' quod he, 'what tyme is of the day?'   3669 *of whom he*
'ffor certayn, ser,' he saide, 'ij after none.'   *asked the time*
Thanne seid the knyght, 'I purpose, if I maye,   *of day.*
This town to se, and whanne I haue don   3672
In to the shippe to come ayeyn right sone.'
Ayen thanne seid the palmer to the knyght,
'That may ye do long er¹ it be nyght.'   3675

'What do yow calle this town?' quod he ayeyn. 3676 *the name of*
'Ser,' quod the palmer, 'Clarionat it hight.'   *the town,*
                                                          Clarionat,
'Now, good fader, yet wold I wete full fayn,
Wher is the Sowdon, tell me very right :   3679 *and where the*
Of his estate fayne wold I haue a sight.'   *Sultan lay.*
'The Sowdon,' he saide, 'ser, belevith me,
he lith att Mountoner the riche Citee.   3682 *'At Mountoner,'*
                                                          said the palmer

¹ MS. *longer.*

'I was there
but lately,
and he made a
feast for a
knight Generydes,

Therin I was but late withoute lese,   3683
And thanne he made a fest I vnderstonde ;
Ther is a knyght callid Generides,
he hath made hym Stiward of all his land ;   3686

who fought
King Bellyn,
and kept this
land from
danger.

With kyng Bellyn he fought hand to hand,
And wanne hym in the feld as ye shall here,
And kept this lande from thraldom[1] and dangere.

He loves also
Clarionas,
the Sultan's
daughter,

That knyght also lovith Clarionas,   3690
The Sowdon is hir fader in certayn,
And suche he dede first seruice in the place,
The love hath lastid still betwix them twayn,   3693

and she loves
him again.'

ffor in like wise she lovith [hym] ayeyn :
And sekerly this is the comon voyse,
In all the courte that he shall hir reioyse.'   3696

Then said the
knight,

Thanne saide the knyght, 'now, fader, I yow prae,
Be cause ye knowe so will this contre,

'Set me in the
way to this city.'

To do so moche as sette me in the way
Whiche were most redyest to the Citee :   3700
And dowte ye not ye shall rewardid be.'
' Wele, ser,' he saide, ' I shall yow tell soo wele,
That of your waye ye shall fayle neuer a dele.   3703

Said the palmer,
' Go by yonder
forest, the
way will bring
you to a plain,

Take hede of yender forest, I yow saye,   3704
ffor ther by must ye goo for eny thing ;
Withouten fayle ther lithe the redy way.
Vnto a goodly playn it[2] will yow bryng,   3707

over which you
mnst travel
four days,
and then come
to the city '

Whiche shall endure yow iiij dayes traveling,
And thanne anon, withoute eny more,
The fayre Citee ye shall see yow before.'   3710

[leaf 20]
The knight
came to the end
of his journey

This knyght furth with rewardid hym right wele, 3711
And furth he gothe [full] streight vppon ye way
As he was taught, and faylid neuer a dele,

---

¹ MS. *thraldon*.   ² MS. *in*.

Till he come to the ende of his Iurnay,   3714
Whiche was atte after none the iiijth day :
And as it was aboughť the oure of three,
Ser Iuell the knyghť came in to the Citee.   3717

on the fourth day,

To the Sowdon) full Streighť he toke the way ;   3718
Whanne he hym) sawe he spake att his device,
' Ser, please it yow,' quod he, ' that I may saye
Wherefore that I am come and [in] what wise ;   3721
The troughť is this to offre my seruice :
Gwynan) the kyng hath bannysshed me his lande,
And for what cause ye shall wele vnderstonde.   3724

and went straight to the Sultan, whom he told his story,

how that Gwynan had banished him

His fader made a clayme to y^{ts} contre,   3725
And I was euer ayenst hym) in that case,
Wherefore the kyng' his sonne now ha[ti]tħ me,
And vtterly hathe putte me from) his grace.   3728
here in this lande his fader slayn) was,
Thanne was I trobolid sore on) euery side, '
In Egipte durst I not lenger abide.'   3731

for opposing his father's claim to Persia.

Ther with the Sowdon) answeryd hym) ayeyn) :   3732
' To my presence ye are will come,' quod he ;
' I must of reasone tender yow certayn),
Sithe ye haue be thus wrongyd for love of me,   3735
In my seruice now dayly shall ye be ;
And if ye haue be trobelyd her before,
Of your pleasure now shall ye haue the more.'   3738

The Sultan answered,

' Since you have been wronged for my sake you shall be in my service.'

So still opece he was ther abideng',   3739
In his seruice purposyng' to endure,
Passyng' Ientill he was in euery thing',
And full pleasaunt to euery creature ;   3742
And all that was don) vnder a coverture,
That what he thoughť ther shuld no man) vnderstonde,
Of his tresone that he had take in hand.   3745

He abode in his service,

and was gentle and pleasant to every one, to cover his treason.

One day the
Sultan was alone
in his garden.
Sir Yvell was
aware,

Vppon a tyme the Sowdon was alone,　　3746
In a garden was walkyng· to and fro,
Ser Iuell Was ware therof anon,
To hym he goth withoute wordes moo.　　3749

and told him
that Generydes

'I must say yow,' quod he, 'a word or twoo ;
Besechyng· yow to kepe my councell,
Whiche shalbe to your honour and [a]vayle.　　3752

Ther is a knyght callid Generides,　　3753
here in your howse, and thus standith ye case ;

plotted to carry
off Clarionas.

Bothe day and nyght he laboryth still opece,
ffrom hense to haue away Clarionas,　　3756
he restith not, butt wayteth tyme and space
To bryng· abought his purpose if· he maye,
This is the very trougth that I yow saye.'　　3759

The Sowdon trostid all that euer he spake :　　3760

The Sultan asked
his advice.

'Tell me,' he said, 'what is your best avise ?'
'Yes, ser,' quod he, ' this wolle I vndertake,
he shall not haue his purpose in noo wise,　　3763
If ye will do as I shall yow deuice ;

' Go hunting
to-morrow,'
said he,

Go to morow on huntyng· for the dere,
Thanne shall ye know the trowth of· this mater.　　3766

' and take
Generydes
with you.

But yow must take with yow Generides,　　3767
Not withstondeng· he will be loth ther too ; ·

He will make
an excuse to
come home,

Whanne he is ther homeward he will hym dresse,
Thanne shall ye se anon what he will do.　　3770
Be myn avise me semyth best also,

but I will stay
and defeat his
purpose.'

That I abide atte home and kepe me close,
Thanne shall he not a tayne to his purpose.'　　3773

The Sultan
assented.

The Sowdon gave his assent therto,　　3774
And furth he goth on huntyng· to the woode,
With hym he toke Generides also,

And suche moo knyghtez as it semyd good ; 3777

And aH sone as ser yueH vnderstode

The Sowdon was wele on warde on his way,

Vn to his shippe IucH he sent withoute delay 3780

One of his men As fast as he cowde, 3781

Comaundyng' them be redy euerychone ;

his ij. squyers he toke them owt Aside,

'helpe that I were Armyd anon, 3784

And in like wise cast your' harnes vppon,

Secrely, that no man yow Aspye,

And that ye be on hors bak aH redy. 3787

Withoute the Cite ther shaH ye abide, 3788

And tary stiH as for a litiH space.'

his hors was ther aH redy for to ride,

And furth he went toward Clarionas, 3791

To hir chaunber ther as hir logging' was :

'Madame,' he seyde, 'my lord, your' fader dere,

To yow hath sent me on a massage her'.' 3794

'What wold my fader ? I prae yow saye,' quod she.

'Madame,' quod he, 'he hath right happy game,

Wherefore in eny wise he wold that ye

Wer [1] ther witH hym, that ye myght haue y° same.'

'Now may I goo,' quod she, 'withoute blame :'

And furth with aH sche answeryd hym agayn,

'Att his pleasure to come I am right fayne.' 3801

Two palfreyes anone were brought owt of y° stable,

In aH the goodly hast that myght be do,

One for hir, another for MirabiH,

Bothe were sadellyd redy for to goo, 3805

And furth they rode withoute wordes moo ;

And as ther couenaunde was in especiaH,

his ij squyers metto hym withoute the waH. 3808

[1] MS. Wher.

Side notes:

As soon as he was gone hunting

Sir Yvell sent one of his men to his ship to

order it to be ready,

and told his two squires to be armed

and wait without the city.

He then went and told Clarionas

that her father had sent for her

to join the hunting.
[leaf 20, back]

She and Mirabell mounted their palfreys and rode

forth on their way.

Thanne on hir way rideth Clarionas,   3809
ffull Innocente was she of y^t in hir thought ;

When they were
two miles from
the town, Mira-
bell suspected
something,

Whanne thei were fro the town ij myle of space,
Mirabell demyd sone that it was nought :   3812
ffro the forest a wayward he them brought,
Thanne Myrabell, prevely as sche myght,

and made her
lady alight.

Made hir lady from hir palferay a light.   3815

Sir Yvell
was wroth.

Where with ser yuell passing wroth he was,   3816
vn perseyuyd be countenaunce or sight :
Thanne said Mirabell onto Clarionas,

'Madam,' said
Mirabell, 'we

'Madame,' quod she, 'this gothe not all aright,   3819
I wote my self as wele as eny wight ;

are betrayed.'

We are be trayde,' quod she, 'I dare well saye,
God wote,' quod she, 'this is noo thyng the way.'

As they sat,
Natanell came
up, chasing
a hart.

And as thei sate to geder complayneng,   3823
Came Natanell as fast as he myght ride,
Chasyng an hart as he come Reynyng ;
A none with all Mirabell had hym aspied,   3826

Mirabell
beckoned
to him,

With hir kerche she bekenyd hym aside,
And he full curtesly left all the chase,
And streight to hir he come ther as she was.   3829

'Natanell, for goddis loue, helpe,' quod she,   3830
'As for my lady here, Clarionas,

and told him
that Sir Yvell
had betrayed
them.

Ser yuell hath betrayed bothe hir and me ;
Sayng suerly that he commaundyd was   3833
Be hir fader to bryng hir to the chase,
Whiche hym thought shuld be hir grete counfort,
To see his huntyng And his disporte.   3836

But now I wote right wele it goth a mys ;   3837

'Go to your
master and tell
him this.'

Wherefore,' quod she, 'I prae you hertyly,
Go to your Maister now and tell hym this,

for thanne he wiħ nott tary sekerly,   3840
And that he come as fast as he may hye ;
Now, good Nataneħ, think wele her vppon.'
' It shaħ be do,' quod he, ' and that anone.'   3843

To the Cite streight he toke the waye,   3844 Natanell went
And brought his maister harnes ther he was,   straight to the city, and fetched his master's armour, and told him all
And told hym ther, withoute more delaye,
Of ser yueħ and of fayre Clarionas,   3847 about Clariouas.
Of her messaventur and how it was,
And whanne Generides had hard hym wele,
A none he lefte his huntyng euery dele.   3850 Generydee left bie hunting.

Iu this seasone was fayre Clarionas[1]   3851
ffuħ of sorow, god wote a wofuħ weight ;
Ser yueħ sawe in what plight that she was,   Sir Yvell tried to comfort
And her comfort in aħ that he myght :   3854 Clarionas by telling her she should be
' Madame,' quod he, ' this wiħ I yow be hight,   married to the
Ye shaħ suerly be weddid to A kyng,   mightiest king
Vnder hevyn the migtiest lyvyng.   3857 under heaven.

Wherefore, madame, be ye noo thyng dismayde, 3858
Aħ these thoughtez late them ouer slide ! '
With that anon, as he these wordes sayde,
Generides come fro the forest side,   3861 Just then Generydee
Aħ clene armyd as fast as he cowde ride,   came out of the forest with
To ser Yueħ streight vppon the felde,   his sword drawn.
his swerd aħ nakyd in his hand he held.   3864

And whanne ser Iueħ saw hym come rideng, 3865 When Sir Yvell
he made good countenaunce, but neuer the lesse   saw him he made good
he was fuħ sore adrede of his comyng,   countenance,
Purposing fully for to make his pece,   3868
And thus he seide on to Generides :   and said,
' Good ser,' quod he, ' be ye no thyng displesid,
ffor in this case your harte shaħ sone be easid. 3871

[1] MS. *Clarianos.*

This is trewly the mater in substance ;   3872

'The king of
Egypt would
have this lady
in marriage,

The kyng' of E[g]ipte, born) of highe lenage,
Wold haue this lady here in gouernaunce,
Desiryng' hir be way of mariage ;   3875

and this is the
cause of my
journey, and
not to displease
the Sultan
or you.

And for this cause now I take this viage :
This is the trougth like now,[1] I yow devise,
Not to displese the Sowdon) in noo wise,   3878

Nor yow, and that ye shall vnderstonde,   3879
ffor that came neuer in my thought certayn) ;

Take the lady,
and I will return
to the city.'

This lady here ye shall in your' hande,
And to the Citee will I turne ayeyn),   3882
Be cause no man) shall haue me in disdayn) ;
And forthermore, of that that I haue sayde
I yow beseche that I be not be wrayed.   3885

It is full late for yow and here also   3886
As for this day to travell more And lesse,

[leaf 21]

Att youre pleasure to morow may ye goo.'

'I am content,'
said Generydes.

'I am content,' thanne seid Generides,   3889
ffull Innocente[2] of all his dobilnesse,
The whiche ser yuell thought in his enteute,

Sir Yvell went
in haste to
the Sultan.

ffor to the Sowdon) hastely he went.   3892

Generydes,
thinking no
harm, made
two lodges,

Generides, withoute wordes moo,   3893
Made a logge as sone as euer he myght :
he made another for hym) self' also,
Thinkyng' noo harme ne malys to' no weight ;   3896

and there
they rested.

And ther they restid still as for that nyght.
Thanne was ser yuell full bold in his maner

Sir Yvell told
the Sultan,

With the Sowdon), and saide as ye shall here :   3899

'Your daughter
and Generydes
are this night
out of the town
on their way.

'Off your' doughter And of' Generides,   3900
ffull trewly shall ye fynde it as I say ;
ffor as this nyght thei are, withoute lesse,

---

[1] MS. *now a*.   [2] MS. *Innocence*.

Out of the town welo onward on yer waye :
And if yo wiH goo ther anon), yo may
So where they bo and I shaH bo your gido.'
'Yes,' quod the Sowdon), 'theder I wiH ride,

And that anon as fast as euer we¹ may,
In socrete wise, no mo but yo and I.'
Now goth forwarꝺ the Sowdon) on) his way,
And ser yueH with hym) fuH secretly,

he first bo sougħt the Sowdon) feithfully,
As for tho cheve guerdon) of his seruice,
ffor to slo Gencrides in eny wise.

The Sowdon) grauntyd hym) for so² to do ;
And as he camo owt of⁴ the forest sido,
ho sawe a logge, and in he went ther to ;
Ser yueH stode withouten) hym) to abide,

And furth with aH tho Sowdon) had aspyed
Withynno the loggo wher lay Gencrides,
In his harnes slepyng' stiH opece.

Hys sward was drawyn), on)³ the grownd it lay,
To slo hym) the Sowdon) had grete pite,
Remembryng' the seruice day by day,
Whiche he had don) in his necessite,

And suche as no man) ded saue only he :
Wherefore he thougħt, bo good and sad avise,
he wold not slo hym) in noo hasty wise.

He toke Away tho sward vppo from) yᵉ ground,
And leyde his owen) ther as tho toder was ;
Butt litiH thenso another loggo he founde,
Ther lay myraboH and fayre Clarionas,

ffuH stedefastly he lokid on) hir face,
To knowe his doughter clerly bo sight,
ffor botho thei sloppe as fast as euer thei mygħt.

---

¹ MS. *ho*.   ² MS. *to so*.   ³ MS. *on on*.

and took up
his daughter
fast asleep as
she was, and

He toke his doughter vppe as she laye,   3935

And furth he bare hir in his armys twayn)

Owt of the logge, she sleppe still alway,

delivered her to
Sir Yvell

And to ser yuell delyueryd hir ayeyn,   3938

And told hym) that Generides was slayn).

Whanne ser Iuell herd of that aventure,

Wote ye wele he was a ioyfull creature.   3941

The Sowdon) went ayeyn to his disporte;   3942

to conduct her
to the city.

Ser Iuell hym) promysed for to goo,

With his doughter ayenward to resorte

Vn to the Citee, ther as she came froo,   3945

But he meant
nothing of
the kind.

Butt sekerly his thought was noo thyng soo :

The Sowdon) wende she had gon) ther she was,

Butt alway he led fayre Clarionas.   3948

Clarionas awoke
and saw how
It was;

Anone with all Clarionas awoke,   3949

And whanne that she perseivid how it was,

she took on sore
and swooned
twice.

ffull of sorow she was and sore on) toke,

That twyes she swounyd in a litill space ;   3952

God wote she stode in full petevous case,

More sorow had noo creature levyng,

for she had leuer a dyed than[1] eny thyng.   3955

He set her on
a palfrey and
led her to the
ship.

On a palfrey he sette Clarionas,   3956

And to the shippe he gideth hir full right ;

Generides, withynne a litill space,

he woke anon) thanne was it dayle light :   3959

When Generydes
awoke, he asked
Mirabell for
Clarionas.

Of Mirabell sone he had a sight,

And first of all he sayde in this maner,

' Where is Clarionas, my lady dere ? '   3962

With thoo wordes Mirabell woke anon) ;   3963

'Alas said
she, 'my lady
is gone by false
treason.

' Alas,' quod she, ' what aventur' is this ?

By false tresone now is my lady goon),

[1] MS. thang.

And ser Iuell I wote it is :   3966   It is Sir Yvell,
Of hym I dremyd all this nyght I wis,
I prae god geve hym sorow now,' she saide,
'ffor this is twyes that he hath vs betrayde.'   3969   he hath betrayed
                   us twice.'

'Butt is she goon ?' thanne saide Generides.   3970
'Yee,' quod Mirabell, 'and that me rewith sore.'
'ffare well,' quod he, 'my comfort and gladnes,   'Farewell,'
                           quoth he,
ffare well my ioye for now and euermore ;   3973   'my comfort
                           and joy for
What think ye best that I shall doo yerfore ?'   evermore.
'This is the best,' quod she, 'that I canne saye,   What think you
                           best to do ?'
Go after them as fast as euer ye may,   3976   'Go after them,'.
                   said she,

And if it fortune that he may be take,   3977
ffor erthely good or eny fayre promes,
                           [leaf 21, back]
Do make hym sure what couenaunte that he make.'
'Yes,' hardly thanne seid Generides.   3980
'To the Sowdon,' quod sche, 'I will me dresse,   'and I will go
                           to the Sultan,
And tell hym trewly, as sone as euer I may,
ffor he will trost the wordes that I saye.'   3983   for he will trust
                   my words.';

Generides thanne armyd hym anon,   3984   Generydes then
                       armed himself,
Aftur ser Iuell to folow on the chase ;
he sought after his sword and it was goon,
he founde another lying in the place,   3987   and found the
                       Sultan's sword,
The Sowdons swerd he wist wele that it was :
To myrabell he seide in this maner,
'My lord the Sowdon suerly hath ben here :   3990

Where with I am comfortid verely,   3991   which comforted
                       him.
ffor of my parte [he] demyd not amys,
And if he had, I say yow sekerly,
he wold haue slayn me here, I wote wele this.'   3994
'Right as ye say,' quod she, 'me think it is :
I will telle hym [the] trougth whanne I hym see,
ffor I will seche hym wher euer that he be.'   3997

Then quoth he,
' Tell Natanell to
come after me.'

'Thanne,' quod he, 'Mirabell, I yow prae,   3998
Byd Natanell anon for eny thing'
Come after me as fast as euer he may.'
'It shall be do,' quod she, 'withoute fey[n]ing': 4001
he be your spede that is our hevyn kyng',
Whanne ye are goo I will not long abide,
ffor to my lord the Sowdon I will ryde.'   4004

Generydes
follows Yvell,

Generides is in his way rideng'   4005
After Iuell, to take hym if he may.
Mirabell thanne made noo taryeng',

and Mirabell
goes to the
Sultan,

Butt to the Sowdon she toke the waye,   4008
To tell hym all the trougth of here affraye,

but the Sultan
knew all before,

But or she came the Sowdon knewe it wele,
ffor ther came on and told hym euery dele,   4011

Whiche mette ser yuell and Clarionas :   4012

and was sore
astounded.
He rides to the
place where he
found Generydes,

Where with the Sowdon was astownyd sore,
And furth with all he rideth in to the place,
Ther as he founde Generides before,   4015
Of that fortune to harkyn forthermore ;
This musyng' in his thougth more and lesse,

and met Mirabell
on the way,

he mette Mirabell in grete hevynes.   4018

Be hir semlante he thought it shuld be she,   4019
And this to hir full soberly he sayde ;
'Telle me, where is my dougñter now?' seith he ;
And ther withall she was gretly dismayde,   4022

who told him
how Clarionas
was betrayed
at first,

' ffor certeyn, ser,' quod she, ' she is betrayed ;
Ser yuell seid that ye had for hir sent,
And brougth fro yow a streyt comaundment.   4025

And in this wise away with hir he rode,   4026
ffull vntrewly, and be a subtill trayne ;
Vppon tho way wo hovyd and a boode.

Generides thanne reskewid hir ayeyn,　　　　4029 and how
Generydes
rescued her,
Thanne was the day passid in certayn,
And nere nyght, wherefore he thought it best
Ther to abide as for oñ nyghtez rest.　　　　4032

'As for Generides this dare I now saye,　　　　4033
he was neuer that man, I yow ensure,
To dishonour your doughter be eny way,
Nor neuer while his liff may endure ;　　　　4036
But whels he sleppe this cursyd creature　　　　and how,
while he slept,
Sir Yvell had
carried her off.
ffull trayturly with hir is goo ;
ffull wele I woote it is he and no moo.'　　　　4039

To here answerd the Sowdon in this wise ;　　　　4040 The Sultan
answered,
'It is full true
'Ye say full trew, it may now other be,
With his fayre wordes, full of flatrise,
he hath deseyuyd now bothe yow and me,　　　　4043 he hath deceived
us both.
But where is
Generydes ?'<br>'Truly,' said she,
'he is gone
after this knight.'
Butt where is now Generides ?' quod he ;
'Trewly,' quod she, ' ser, he hath take the waye
Aftur this knyght, and thus he bad me say.'　　　　4046

'What think ye best,' quod he, ' that I shall doo ?'
' ffor sothe,' quod she, ' this is now myn avise ;
Aftur ser yuell Generides is goo,
To take hym if he canne in eny wise ;　　　　4050
And as for yow to take the enterprise,
It shall nede if his liff may endure,
he will do moche ther to I yow ensure.'　　　　4053

And as thei spake to geder he and she,　　　　4054 As they spake
together
Natanell
rode up.
Came Natanell as fast as he cowde ride ;
Myrabell sone perseyuyd it was he,
ffull ertely she prayde hym to abide :　　　　4057
Anow withall he reynyd his hors aside,
Thanne seid he this to Mirabell, ' I yow prae,
What is your will now pleasit yow to say.'　　　　4060

GENERYDES.　　　　9

[leaf 22]
Mirabell gave
him Generydes'
message.

'[M]ynne owyn) lady,' quod she, ' Clarionas,   4061
Ser yueH now aycyn) with here is gone,
Whils we were bothe on) sleppe this is yᵉ case,
Generides is after aH alone,   4064
And wold that ye shuld follow hym) anone.'
'Maystres,' quod he, ' now trost me verily,
To hym) I wiH as fast as I canne highe.'   4067

Natanell rides
after his master;
Now NataueH, in aH the hast he may,   4068
Is rideng¹ after now Generides ;
the Sultan and
Mirabell return
to the city,
MyrabeH with the Sowdon) take the way,
And to the Citee ward¹ the Sowdon) ganne hym) dresse,
Complayneng¹ sore in right grete hevynes ;
and Clarionas
by this time is
going on board
with Sir Yvell.
And by that tyme ser yueH redy was,
Takyng¹ the shippe with fayre Clarionas.   4074

When they were
under sail
Generydes
came up.
It was not long¹ or thei were vnder saylc,   4075
And by that tyme come was Generides ;
Ser yueH knewe hym) wele withoute fayle,
By his stature and by his likenesse,   4078
And these wordes he sayde to hym) expresse ;
' It is too late,'
said Yvell.
'Gcnerides,' quod he, ' I telle the playn),
Thou comyst to late to haue hir now ageyn).   4081

Thow slepist to long¹, and I woke the while   4082
To spede this mater after my device,
My purpose was the fully to be gile,
With the Sowdon) whanne I was in seruice ;   4085
I sette not be the thretyng¹ in noo wise,
' Thou hast
lost her.'
And vterly this wolle I saye the more,
ffro this day furth thu hast lost her yerfore.'   4088

Generydes was
sore grieved,
Generides thanne was agrevid sore,   4089
ffor thoo wordes were saide in mokkery,
And in hym) self abasshed more and more,

Butt att that tyme ther was noo remedy :   4092   but there was
                                                                    no remedy.
Clarionas be held hym verily,   Clarionas
                                                                    saw him,
his countenance was all togeder doon,   and fell down
                                                                    in a swoon,
Anone with all ther she fylle down in swoune.   4095

Syr yuell sawe she made suche hevynes,   4096
And with hir self she was not all aright ;
ffor as the story doth witnesse,
xv tymes she swounyd in his sight :   4099
he hir comfortid in all that euer he myght ;   Sir Yvell tried
                                                                    to comfort her,
To turne hir hart he dede his besy payne,
And all for nought his labour was in vayne.   4102   but to no
                                                                    purpose.

Generides the porte goth all a long,   4103   Generydes
                                                                    went all along
To seke a shippe streight be the havyns side ;   the port to
                                                                    seek a ship,
Att last he saw a galy fayre and strong
lay atte rode, which was both large and wide,   4106
And men I nowe therin for to gide ;   and found a
                                                                    galley with
The maister of all was ther present,   master and men.
Generides anon to hym he went.   4109

'Owt of what cost come ye, I prae yow say,   4110   He asked
                                                                    them of what
Or what contre,' quod he, ' telle me the right.'   coast they came.
The maister thought anon be his array,
Be cause he was armyd and like a knyght,   4113
he was a man of powre and of myght,
Wherefore in sothe he was sumwhat dismayde,   The master
                                                                    was afraid,
And to Generides right thus he saide.   4116

' Sir, be not ye displeasid now,' quod he,   4117
' Be cause I haue of yow noo knowlachyng,
Owt of danger I wold be and in surete.'
' Surete,' quod he, ' drede yow no maner thyng';   4120   but Generydes
                                                                    reassured him,
On your part ther is now other desireng,
Butt I haue a mater now to begynne,
And I wold fayn haue your councell therin.'   4123   and asked
                                                                    his advice.

'My counsel,
sir, is but simple,'
he said.
'My councell is but symple, ser,' he seide ;   4124
'Butt as I canne I shall say myn) avice :
In this havyn) this galy now is layde,
I shall yow tell wherefore and in wha[t] wise ;   4127

'I come from
Syria, where
King Auferius
lieth.
I come fro Surre and fro those partis,
Kyng' Auferius hath it in mariage,
And ther he lith with all his Baronage.   4130

I was with
100 ships on
the way to
India to win
A hunderyd shippes I lift ther Also,   4131
With them) I was in company certayn),
And toward ynd they purpose them) to goo,

Auferius his
right again.
To wynne kyng' auferius right ageyn),   4134
And of his sonnys, to say yow trew and playn),

To one of
his sons, Ismaell
the Savage,
A likely knyght on) And of mannys age,
The whiche is callid Ismaell the Savage.   4137

the king has
given Thrace ;
The kyng' his fader hym) hath gevyn) fre   4138
The Reme of Trace, to rule it in his hand ;
And ferthermore, in very certente,
He hath a broder as I vnderstonde,   4141

the other,
Generydes, a
good knight,
As good a knyght as is in eny lande,
And as it is seide I telle yow very right,
And for certayn) Generides he hight.   4144

After decoasse of auferius the kyng',   4145
shall have Syria
and India ;
He shall haue Surre in his owne demeyn,[1]
And all the Reme of ynd withoute feyning',
If fortune will that he it gete aycyn) ;   4148

and my errand
is to seek him.
In to this contre was myn) erande playn)
hym) for to seche, and as I vnderstonde
Withynne few dayes he was here in this land.   4151

And if ye knowe wher that I may hym) fynde,   4152
Let me know
where I may
find him.'
[leaf 22, back]
Now lete me wete, I prae yow hartely.'
Generides remembryd in his mynd.

[1] MS. demenyng.

he was not wonte hym self to be wreye ; 4155
Yet this to hym he seid full soberly,
' My frend,' quod he, ' ye shall knowe my councell, Generydes said,
I am the same withoute eny fayle. 4158 ' I am the same,

Generides I hight, this is noo nay, 4159 my name is
kyng auferius my fader is certayn ; Generydes,
Butt I am a carefull man this day, but I am full of
By fortune suche before was neuer sene, 4162 care to-day, for
By a subtill and false compassing trayn, my lord's
Clarionas, my lordis doughter dere, daughter
Vntrewly is betrayed as ye shall here. 4165 Clarionas is
untruly
betrayed.

It is but late sithe she was vnder sayle, 4166
A knyght of Egipte, callid ser yuell, A knight of
With here is gone away withoute fayle.' Egypt is gone
Thanne the maister seid, ' woll ye do well ? 4169 with her.'
This galy lith not here to by ne selle ;
Do now be myn avice, and hardely The master said,
With goddes grace ye shall fynde remedy. 4172 ' Do now by my
advice ;

This galy shalbe redy for to goo, 4173 this galley shall
If ye will come ye shall hym ouer take.' be ready to go,
'Now,' quod Generides, ' late it be soo, and we will
I prae yow hartly for cristis sake.' overtake him.'
And furth with all he did it redy make, 4176 ' Now,' quoth
In all the hast possible that¹ he may, Generydes,
To shippe he goth withoute more delay. 4179 'let it be so.'

And whanne they were all redy for to goo, 4180 When they were
Came Natanell onto the havyns side, ready to go,
his Maisters hors he brought with hym Also ; Natanell came
And whanne Generides hym had aspyed, 4183 with his master's
he prayde the maister sumwhat to Abide,
full wele content he was of his comang, horse, and was
Anone thei putt ther horses to shippyng. 4186 taken on board.

¹ MS. *that that.*

The master and
Generydes
sailed on,

Now is the Maister and Generides   4187
Vppon) the see, and sayle beganne to make,
And in here viage sailed still opece,

and if the wind
had not begun
to slacken,
Sir Yvell would
have been taken,
but he landed
with Clarionas,

Till atte last the wynde beganne to slake,   4190
And ellis in very trougth they had be take ;
Butt afterward, withynne a litill space,
Syr yuell londyd with Clarionas.   4193

And thanne anon), as fast as euer he myght,   4194

and hasted on to
King Gwynan

Thei hastid them) forward of ther Iurnay ;
Ser yuell gidyd hir the way full right,
ffor he had knowen) the contre many A day ;   4197
To kyng' Guynan he toke the redy way,
To his palys ther as his abideng' was,

to a city called
Egidias.

In a Cite callid Egidias.   4200

Four hours after,
Generydes landed
with the others

Not long' after[1] the space of ourez fewe,   4201
The galy landyd with Generides ;

in the guise of
merchants.

In gise of mercaundez thei dede them) shewe,
ffull craftely in All ther besynes,   4204
Not like no men) of warre but all of pece,
So to gide them) thei wer' well apayde,
To harkyn) tidynges what these pepill saide.   4207

The king was
glad when
he heard of
Clarionas,

And whanne the tidynges came onto the kyng'   4208
Of ser yuell and fayre Clarionas,
A gladder man) was ther non) leving',
Nor might not be more ioyfull thanne he was :   4211
The Citee made grete festis in euery place,

and his knights
went to meet
her, himself
following.

his knyghtes went to mete here on) the way,
hym) self come after in full good Arraye.   4214

He sent for his
lords to come
to his marriage,

And for his lordes furth with all he sent,   4215
They for to come onto the mariage,
And to folowe the effecte of his entente,

---

[1] MS. *after after.*

To the Citee came Al his Baronage : 4218

And as it is the custom) and vsage

Al way for princes shortly to devico,

The ffest was made in right solempne wise, 4221 and the feast was made,

And lastid long, my Auctour seith expresse ; 4222 and lasted long.

Another custome was in that contre It was the custom during the feast that

Of old vsage, the writong doth witnesse,

What tyme that eny kyng weddid shuld be, 4225

Duryng tho tyme of that solempnite,

The kyng and she shuld neuer togeder mete, the king and his bride should

To tyme tho fest were done And full complete. 4228 not meet.

Thanne seid the Maister onto Generides, 4229 The master said to Generydes,

'Now it is wisdome to do be good avice,

ffor by manhood[1] suerly or by prow[e]se

Yow shal spede your mater in noo wise ; 4232

ffor your entente I shal a craft devise 'I shall devise a craft that you may gain your

With goddes grace, and if it fortune wele, end.

That ye shal haue your purpose euery dele. 4235

I haue A thing shal lye vppon) your face, 4236 You shall put something on

That ye shal seme a mesel [in] certayn), your face which shall make you

Butt dought ye not withynne a litil space, seem a leper,

Whanne euer ye list it shal a voyde ayeyn), 4239

And your visage to be as fayre And playn),

As wele coloured and ther with also clene, '

With onys wasshyng as it had neuer ben). 4242

And forthermore ye must chaunge your Array 4243 and you must change your clothes

With sum pore man), and take ye his clothing, with some poor man.

And bere with yow sum tokyn) that she may

Of your persone haue redy knowlaching ; 4246 [leaf 23]

And from here pales as she is comyng, Take with you some token by

Bothe to and froo ther must ye haue A place, which she may know you,

Now do as wele as god will geve you grace ; 4249

---

[1] MS. mandhood.

and she will
ordain some
way to speak
with you.

And, well I woote, som way she will ordeyn)   4250
That she may speke you[1] atte your own device,
And as ye canne accorde betwix you twayne,
This wold I that ye did be myne avise;   4253

Bid Natanell
be ready to
meet you with
your horse.'

Bid Natanell in eny maner wise,
That he be redy and in especiall,
To mete yow with your hors what euer fall.'   4256

So Generydes
did,
and changed
his clothes with
a beggar,

Generides dede after his councell,   4257
And with a begger he chaungyd his wede,
The pore man) thought it was for his availe,
And glad he was, for he ther of had nede.   4260
Thanne seide Generides, 'so god yow spede,
Whanne were ye atte court I pray yow saye.'

who told him
he had been
at court,

'Trewly,' quod he, 'I come fro thense to day;   4263

and seen the
queen,

And ther I sawe the quene in riche araye,   4264
But as me semyth by here countenance,

but that she
looked unhappy
as she came
from the temple.

And as she came from) the tempill by ye waye,
She likyd not that riall ordenaunce;   2467
Me think ther was some cause of displesaunce,
Butt me ought not to speke therof in dede.'
'Now goo, fader, and Ihu be thy spede.'   4270

Now Generydes
goes to the court

Now goth Generides furth, I vnderstonde,   4271
Vn to the courte, his clothis all to Rent;

with his cup
and clapper
in his hand,

holdyng his cuppe, his claper in his hande,
And on) his face he layde this oyntement,   4274
To bryng abought the effecte of his entent;

and stood in a
place near the
temple where
she should pass.

And ther anon) he purveyd hym) a place,
Withoute the tempill ther as she shuld pase.   4277

He put a ring
on his finger,

Whanne he had restid hym) he putte a ryng   4278
On his fynger, be cause she shuld it see,
And fro the tempill as she is comyng,

[1] MS. yom.

Thorough owt the prese anon to hir com he,   4281
And Askyd Almes for seynt charite,
The ryng vppon his fynger sone she knewe;
'I shall,' thought she, 'here sum tidynggez newe.' 4284

and as she came from the temple he asked alma. She knew the ring,

Thanne seid the quene, 'good man, whense be ye?'
'Madame,' quod he, 'o trougth I shall yow say;
In ynd I was goten in very certente,
In surre I was born, this is no nay;   4288
Now come I owt of perse the redy way,
And ther I was brought vppe, I telle yow playn,
Sone¹ I was first att mannys age [certayn].   4291

and asked whence he was. 'Madam,' said he, 'I was gotten in India, and born in Syria, and now I come from Persia, where I was brought up.'

Ye are a lady born of that contree,   4292
God hath me visite as his creature,
Besechyng yow your almes man to be.'
The quene Answeryd with countenaunce demure, 4295
'Of myn Almes,' quod she, 'ye shall be sure.'
And furth with all, withoute taryeng,
She bad he shuld be brought to hir loggyng.   4298

She ordered him to be brought to her lodging.

To hir chaunbyr right sone he was conueyed,   4299
And ther he spake with hir hym self alone;
'Madame,' quod he, 'be ye noo thing dismayde,
Thoughe my visage be lothe to loke vppon,   4302
With onys wasshyng it will away anone,
And trost that I say withoute othe,
I am your trew seruaunt Generides in sothe.'   4305

He was conveyed to her chamber, and spoke with her alone. 'Madam,' quoth he, 'be not dismayed,

'Generides!' quod she, 'nay that is not so,   4306
It is to me a wonder thing to here.'
'Madame,' he saide, 'ye shall wete or ye goo,
Plese it yow to see a ryng that I haue here,   4309
The whiche I had of yow, my lady dere;
And though² I seme a mesell in your sight,
It is but counterfete,³ I yow be hight.'   4312

and though I seem a leper it is but counterfeit.'

¹ So MS. ? Sene.   ² MS. thought.   ³ MS. coumterfcte.

'This ryng',' quod she, 'I know it veryly,   4313
Butt of your persone yet I mervell more.'

He had with
him a water
with which he
washed his face,
and he was
as fair as ever.
When she saw
it she took him
in her arms.

With hym he had a water ther redy,
And from his face he wessh away it thore,   4316
he was as faire as euer he was be fore,
And whanne she sawe his vesage fayre and clene,
She toke hym in hir Armys as I wene ;   4319

She was soo glad, she had noo worde to saye. 4320

'Madam,' said
he, 'appoint
some ready
place,

'Madame,' quod he, 'in sothe this is the case,
If ye will now for sake all this arraye,
And that ye list apoynte some redy place,   4323

and Natanell
and I will meet
you.

Bothe Natanell and I, be goddes grace,
With hors and harnes noo thing shall be lette
To mete yow ther, what our ye will sett.   4326

There is a ship
ready to sail.'

Ther is a shippe All redy for to sayle,   4327
A bideng still opece of my comyng.'

'Generydes,'
quoth she,

'Generides,' quod she, 'I haue mervell
. That ye putt dought in eny thing   4330

'though he
were king of
ten realms,

As to meward, for though he were a kyng
Of reames x, And so fourth to endure,

I would go
with you.

yet wold I goo with yow, I yow ensure.   4333

And for to spede this mater to purpose,   4334

You and Natanel
must hide in
my garden to-
night early.'

In my garden Att nyght sone must ye be,
Bothe Natanell and ye, and kepe yow close,
Treis and busshes full thikke yer shall yow se, 4337
To kepe yow secrete in, and as for me
I will be ther, trost me in feithfull wise,

[leaf 23, back]

Betwix the day and nyght, I yow promys.'   4340

Generydes joined
Natanell in
the forest,
put off his rags,

Generides owt of the Castell went   4341
To Natanell, whiche in the forest lay,
Ther he dede of his ragyd garment,

his dissho, his claper, and aH he cast awaye,   4344
And harnesid hym aH now aycyn in his array :   *and armed himself again, and then waited in the garden.*
To the garden he toke the waye [att nyght],
And tared ther as he had hir be hight.   4347

Thanne Clarionas is now in grete musyng,   4348
And in this case be thinkith hir fuH strayte,
hir purpose craftely abought to bryng,
And vterly hir seasone for to wayte ;   4351
Atto last she founde one of hir consaite   *Clarionas found a laundress to whom she told her plan.*
To whom she told here councell aH in fere,
And in certayne she was a lavendere.   4354

To here thanne sayde fayre Clarionas,   4355
'Ye are,' quod she, 'a woman that is to trost   *'You are a woman to be trusted,' said she.*
Of eny one that is withynne the place,
Of my councell fayne wold I that ye wist.'   4358
'Att your pleasure, Madame, what *euer* ye list.'
Quod she agcyn, 'withoute wordes moo,
That lith in me I wiH be glad to do.'   4361

'Ye say right wele, and as it semyth me,'   4362
Quod she onto the lavender thanne aycyn,
'I am a straunger here in this contre,   *'I am a stranger here,*
This is my mater aH togeder playn ;   4365
The kyng, whiche is my lord and souereyn,   *and my heart is set on the king my lord.*
On hym my hert is sette, I yow be hight,
That I for gete hym not neyther day ne nyght ;   4368

And most I drede of eny maner thing,   4369
That I to hym am noo thing in this case,
Butt be the sterrys,' quod she, 'and be my connyng,   *I wish by the stars to stand always in his favour.*
Where euer he goo or ride in eny place,   4372
I trost to god to stond so in his grace,
And in his favour lengest to endure,
Of eny other lovyng creature.   4375

You and I must go into my garden when the stars are up;

In to my gardeyn) yow and I must goo, 4376
Whanne sterrys are vppe and whan) it is very nyght,
Butt I must surely be disgised soo
That I may goo vnknowen) to eny wight, 4379

I will wear your kirtle, and each of us must bear a truss on our heads.'

Your' kirtill will I were be cause of light,
And iche of vs a trusse vppon) oure hede,
This is trewly my councell and my rede.' 4382

The laundress answered, 'I will keep your counsel.'

Thanne Answeryd the lavender ayeyn), 4383
Seid [she], 'Madame, your' seruaunt will I be,
And all your' councell kepe and layn),
I trost ther shall no fawte be founde in me, 4386
haue here my hande for a surete ;
And trostith wele that at I shall saye,
ffor erthely good I will not yow bewraye.' 4389

She went to her house and brought a kirtle

And so fourth withoute wordis eny moo, 4390
And to hir house as fast as euer she myght
She went, and brought ayeyn) with hir also
A kirtill, like as she be fore hight. 4393
Whanne the day was passid and it was nyght,

which the queen put on, leaving her rich array.

The quene dede on) hir kirtill fayre and well,
here riche aray she left it euery dele ; 4396

Her clothes were well tucked up,

And tokkyd vppe she was well fro the grounde, 4397
Before hir eyne a kerche hanging' side,
Ther trusses on) ther hedes all redy bounde,

and forth they went, 'Stop, stop,' said the laundress, 'your white legs will betray us.'

And furth thei went, them nede non) other gide ; 4400
Thanne saide the lavender, 'abide, abide,
This white leggys,' quod she, 'I woote it wele,
They wolle shende oure purpose euery dele.' 4403

She washed Clarionas's legs with ashes and water, and

'Ye, wote ye what,' quod she, 'that ye shall do? 4404
Bryng' me water, and thanne late me alone,
A Coppe of Aisshes ye must bryng' Also,

Where with my leggys shalbe wasshid anone, 4407
That All the white I warant shalbe gon) ;'
Right thus she dede in like wise as I saye,
And to the gardeyn) right thus she toke the waye. 4410

she and Clarionas went on to the garden.

Thorough owt the hall bothe to geder gan) goo, 4411
As no thyng' were, full sofft And demure,
Thorough out the courte they toke the way Also,
And atto gate thei motto att aventure 4414
With ser yuell, that cursid creature ;
She hard hym) speke, and knewe hym) be y° voyse,
To me[te] hym) ther was none other choyse. 4417

At the gate they met Sir Yvell.

Whanne she perscivid well that it was he, 4418
A bak she drew and was full ill apayde.
Thanne came he hir nere to knowe the certente,
What that she was ; ' Whom) haue yow here ?' he scid.
' Me think,' quod he, ' it is a praty mayde ;
I cast here for to se what euer fall :'
And vppe he lift here kerchewe furth with all. 4424

The queen was afraid and drew back.

' Whom have you here ?' said he, and lifted up her kerchief.

She was so ferde hir truse was in falling', 4425
With that the lavender putt hym) abak aye,
' Ye are to blame,' quod she, ' be hevyn) kyng';
Now late my mayde alone, ser, I yow praye, 4428
We must hast bo[the] as moche as euer we maye,
These are the quenez clothes, I tell you playn),
And she must haue them) all to morow aycyn).' 4431

The laundress put him back, saying ' Let my maid alone, sir, we must make haste; these are the queen's clothes.'

' Yet woll I wete,' quod he, ' withoute fayle, 4432
ffrom whense she came, and what she is,' quod he.
' Now, good ser,' quod she, ' what shall it availe
To make iche man) to speke of yow and me ?
Yet and ye will be rewlid well,' quod she, 4435
' ffor your' entente and after myn) avise,
Ye shall speke with hir att your' owyn) device. 4438

' I will know,' quoth he, ' from whence she came.'
[leaf 24]

This is the mater in short conclusion,   4439
I am hir maystres and here gouernour;

'Her father is
a merchaunt of
this town,
and there is a
knight who
woos her for
his paramour,
so her friends
put her with me
for safety.

hir fader is a merchaunt of this town.
Ther is a knyght hir wowith euery owre,   4442
Not for to wedde butt for his paramour;
hir frendis wold haue hir in suerte,
And for that cause she is now here with me.   4445

Not withstondyng, withoute wordes moo,   4446

Go to my house,
and wait there,

Go to myn house and tary ther,' quod she,
'Till I haue washt, and this moche woll I doo;
Whanne I come home I shall bryng hir with me,

and you shall
see her at your
pleasure.'

And att your pleasur ther shall ye hir see,
And speke with hir, ther shall noman sey nay.'
'I graunt,' quod he, 'will ye do as ye saye?'   4452

He goes
to her house,

He left them ther, and on he goth a pase   4453
Vnto hir howse as fast as euer he may:

and the laundress
and Clarionas
go into the
garden,

The lavander with Clarionas
In to the garden all another way.   4456
Whanne thei were ther yer trussez down thei lay;
'Now, faire Madame,' seide the lavender,
'Do now sum good for spede of this mater.'   4459

where they
see Natanell,

Thanne in to the gardeyn came Natanell,   4460
Clarionas full sone had hym aspied;
'Where is your maister?' quod she, 'will ye me tell?'

who tells them
Generydes is
close at hand.

'Madame,' he saide, 'her be the gardeyn side,   4463
Att your comyng ther he will abide,
And euery thing is redy to your entente.'
Thanne was Clarionas right wele content.   4466

The laundress
wishes her-
self hence,

The lavender thanne was some what dismayde;   4467
'I wold,' quod she, 'I hadde be hense this nyght,
ffor we do noo thyng here as ye haue sayde,

Noyther in noo wise like as ye be hight;   4470
Madame,' quod she, 'this goth not all aright;'
'Now be not wrothe,' thanne seid Clarionas,   but Clarionas
tells her that
'And I shall tell yow trougth of all the case.'   4473

To hir' anon) thanne Answerd the lavender,   4474
'As for my part,' quod she, 'this shall I saye,
I wolle not here noo thyng' of this mater,
ffor me likith noo thyng' in this arraye,   4477
I will calle after helpe some maner way!' ·
'Nay, god defende it,' quod Clarionas,
'That ye shall inpert me so in this case;   4480

I haue your' faythe and promys in my hand,   4481
That ye shall kepe my councell secretly;
If ye do this, ye shall wele vnderstonde,   If she does not
keep faith she
will repent
it sore;
Ye shall repente it sore as wele as I,   4484
Me think ye were moche better certaynly
To be rewlid as I shall yow councell,
And it shall suerly be to youre avaylo: 4487

To knowe the very trougth of this case,   4488
I shall declare it all [at] aventure;
Ther is a knyght not ferre owt of this place,   that there is a
knight whom
she loves,
I loue hym) best of eny creature,   4491
And of his loue ayenward I am sure;
Right sone I wote he will be here with me,   and who will
take her to her
own country.
And streight with hym) I will goo in to my contre.

Wherefore I councell yow leue all this fare,   4495   She advises
her to come
with them.
And come with me, it shall be for your best,
here shall ye leve in sorow and in care,
I canne not thynk that ye shall leve in rest,   4498
And I suerly will make yow this behest,
If ye will take the payn) me for to plese,
I shall o trowgth make yow right wele At ease.'   4501

The laundress thought that as she had deceived Sir Yuell this would be the best thing to do.

The lavender be thought hir in hir mynd,   4502
That she disseyuyd ser yueH be a trayn),
And if so[1] were that she abode be hynd,
She were vndone for euer in certayn) ;   4505
Thanne seid she to Clarionas ayeyn),
' ffor your plesure, madame, I am contente,
With you to go att your commaundment.'   4508

Off hir Answere Clarionas was fayn),   4509
And ellys she had gon) all womanles,
Whiche had not ben) hir honour in certayn),
And as thei went to geder stiH opese,   4512
Generydes came to the garden.
In to the garden) came Generides,
And atte first he wist not whiche was she :
' Where are ye now? fayre lady myn),' quod he.   4515

Now what nedith long processe of y[is] mater?   4516
and took up Clarionas behind him.
In like manner Natanell took the laundress.
She was sette vppe behynde Generides,
And NataneH sette vppe the lavendere
vppon) his hors, and furth they ganne them) dresse.
AH this while was ser yueH stiH opese,
Euer wayteng whanne the lavender shuld bryng
That she promysed att hir departeng.   4522

Butt as it hath be sayde full long agoo,   4523
Some bete the bussh and some the byrdes take,
And wheder that I be on) of thoo or noo,
[leaf 24, back]
I me reporte onto the letterys blake,   4526
And reasone wiH it may not be forsake,
he that entendith villany of shame,
It is no synne to quyte hym) with the same.   4529

Meanwhile Sir Yuell was waiting at the laundress's house till he thought something was wrong.
Syr IueH thought she taryed passyng long,   4530
And vppe he rose and furth he goth alone,
In his conseite he demyd that it was wrong,

              [1] MS. sore.

And to tho quenys chaumber he is furth gon ;   4533   He went to the
                                                                         queen's chamber
' Where is the queno ?' quod he, ' telle me anon.'
' It is not long,' they sayde, ' sithe she was here,   and heard she
                                                                         had been with the
And with hir also spake the lavander.'   4536   laundress.

Whanne he hard that his hert was all away,   4537   Then he wist
                                                                         well it was not
thanne wist he wele it was not all a right,   all right.
' This lavender,' quod he, ' this is noo naye,
hath don all this, that most vnhappy wight.   4540
Butt I shall do my powre and my myght
hyn for to take, and if I happyn wele
full sore thei shall repent it euery dele.'   4543

He armyd hym and left all other thing,   4544   He armed himself
And furth he goth in all the hast he myght ;
he and his page, withoute more taryeng,
After Generides toke the way full right,   4547   and rode after
                                                                         Generydes.
And att the last, of hym he had a sight,
Clarionas thanne cast hir yee a side,   Clarionas saw
                                                                         him coming,
And ser yuell full sone she had Aspyde.   4550

Thanne to Generides full sone she saide,   4551   and said to
                                                                         Generydes,
' yonder comyth your mortall enmy,[1]   ' Yonder is your
                                                                         mortal enemy.
The whiche full oft hath made me affrayde,
Now may ye wele ordeyne a remedy ;   4554
Wherefore,' quod sho, ' I prae yow hartely,
That what some euer he say be his promys
late hym not skape your handis in noo wise.'   4557   Let him not
                                                                         escape.'

To here answeryd Generides ayeyn,   4558   ' Be not afraid,'
                                                                         said Generydes.
' Be ye noo thyng a ferde as in this case ;
Or we departe,' quod he, ' he shall be fayn
his quarell vppe to yelde, be goddis grace.'   4561
With that anon alight Clarionas ;   Clarionas
                                                                         alighted.
Generides anon hym dressid in his gere,
And Natanell was redy with his spere.   4564

---

[1] MS. *elmy.*

Sir Yuell and
Generydes meet,

Syr yuell ranne onto Generides,   4565
Thorough owt the sheld he smote hym [in] certayn),
Butt for all that he skapid daungerles,
And furth with all ranne to hym ayeyn),   4568
That with his spere he brast his sheld on twayn),

and Yuell is
wounded,

And in his body he woundid hym so sore,
That down) he fello, endure myght he no more.   4571

and yields up
his horse to
Natanell.

Hys stede he delyueryd to Natanell,   4572
A myghti hors and called passing wight;
'I wold,' quod he, 'this hors were cherisshid wele,·
ffor he is sure and good, I yow behight.'   4575
Generides adown) from) his hors alight,
Ser yuell sawe it wold now) other be,
And vppe he rose and knelid on) his kne.   4578

He begs mercy
of Generydes,

Thanne seid he thus, 'mercy, Generides,   4579
I haue affendid yow, I will no more ;'

but Clarionas
warned him not
to trust him
again.

Clarionas cryed alway still opece,
'Though he speke fayre, trost hym) not therfore ;   4582
And if ye do ye shall repente[1] it sore :
Remembre wele he hath desseyuyd yow twyes,
Shall he neuer be trew, I yow promys.'   4585

Generides remembryd hym) ther one,   4586
She sayde hym) trew, he knewe it verily ;
With that Clarionas aspyed anon),
Ser yuell held a knyffe in his hande secretly ;   4589

'He will slay you,
he hath a knife in
his hand.'

'By ware,' quod she, and ganne hym) to Aspye,
'he will sle yow, ye may wele vnderstonde,
A knyff all way he kepith in his hande.'   4592

He stabbed
Generydes in
the thigh,

He smote generides in to the thye,   4593
And he was not gretly hurt, it was his yre ;
his purpose was to sle hym) vterly,

[1] MS. repentid.

with fals tresone vnder a coverture :   4596
Thanne Generides thought on hym to be sure,
And with his swerd he clefe his hede on twoo,   *and he in return*
That neuer after spake he wordes moo.   4599 *cleft his head in two.*

Thanne vppon his stede lept generides,   4600
Be hynd hym was sett Clarionas his lady dere,
And Nataneƚƚ aƚƚ redy ganne hym dresse,
Vppon an hors beforn the lavendere,   4603 *So they all got on horseback again and rode on.*
And soo thei rode togeder aƚƚ in feer',
Owt of ther onmys handes they were sure,
Euerychone talkyng' of ther aventure.   4606

In this meane tyme the body of the knyght   4607
his page anon vppon his hors it layde,
And to the courte[1] he went ayeyn fuƚƚ right.
Whanne it was knowen the kyng' was sore dismayd,   *The king was*
'Now haue I lost my wor[l]dly Ioye,' he seid :   *sore dismayed when he heard*
Grete thought he toke and way[led] more And more,
Wher with the courte[1] was trobelyd very sore.   4613

And how it was of aƚƚ that aventur',   4614 *of the adventure from the page of Sir Yuell.*
Thanne to the kyng' he told aƚƚ the hoole processe,
'Ther is,' quod he, 'no levyng creature
So dere to hir as is Generides ;   4617
Whiche in long' tyme hath dured stiƚƚ opese,
This is the trougth I say yow for certayn.   4619

.   .   .   .

[*A leaf has been here cut out of the MS., containing* 187 *lines. The catchwords of the next line are,* 'And he it is suerly.']

.   .   .   .

'And it obeye with humble reuerence,   4620   [leaf 25]
I[n] yow only is aƚƚ my feithfuƚƚ trest ;
I am your' child, demeane me as ye list.'   4622

[1] MS. contre.

She was glad
for Generydes,
but when she
thought of his
departure
her joy turned
to heaviness.

Right gladde she was as for Generides,   4623
But whanne she thought of his departeng,
hir ioy was turnyd in to hevynes,
yet therof she made now opyn tokenning,   4626
By countenaunce or by other thing,
Butt alway kept it close in hir entente,
And to hir chaunber furth with she went.   4629

She lay on her
bed in despair,

Down on hir bed she felle[1] and ther she laye ;   4630
Mirabell had mervell what it was,
'Madame,' she seid, 'what is this new affraye ?   4632
What mysfortune[2] ? and hough be fell this case ?'
To here anon Answerd Clarionas,
'This is,' quod she, 'come to me a late,
ye may wele saye I am vnfortunate.'   4636

'Vnfortunate,' quod she, 'that is not soo ;   4637
I canne wele think it is your owyn conseite.'
'Nay,' quod Clarionas, 'so mote I goo,

and told Mirabell
that Generydes
had deceived her

I doo none other but myn owen deth Awayte,   4640
Generides hath done me this disseite,
My fader hath geve hym half his eritage,
And me also ther with in mariage.   4643

In saying that he
would go to
India and be
made king,
and then come
again.

In to the reame of ynd now will he goo,   4644
And ther he seith that he shalbe a kyng,
Thanne will he come ayeyn whanne that is do,
And so make an ende of our weddyng :   4647
But wele I wote all this is butt feyning,
he is purveyd of some new Acquentaunce,
Whiche I canne think is more to his plesaunce.'   4650

'Leave these
fancies,' saith
Mirabell.

Thanne seid Mirabell, 'Good Madame,' quod she, 4651
'ffor goddes loue leve all these fantesies,
ffor this I knowe in very certente,

<hr>

[1] MS. lay.   [2] MS. my fortune.

ye shaH not fynde it thus, I yow promes ;   4654
Wene ye that he wiH departe from your seruice
And vtterly refuse yow now euerydele ?
Nay, Madame, I know his trougth soo wele.'   4657   'I know his truth so well.'

To hir anon thanne answerd Clarionas ;   4658
' Ye make yow sure of euery maner thing.
I warante yow,' quod she, ' as in this case,
That I haue seid ye shaH fynde noo lesing ;   4661
he will wedde me, he seith, whanne he is a kyng,
In grete estate and wurchippe many wayes,
And aH these are butt triffolys and delayes.'   4664

So lay she stiH in right grete hevynes :   4665   Clarionas lay still in great heaviness,
MirabeH thanne owt of hir chaunber went ;
In hir goyng she mette Generides,
And told hym aH hir ladyes entent,   4668   and then Mirabell brought
' ye must come now,' quod she, ' or AH is shent,
ffor she canne think non other sekerly,
Butt that ye haue for sake hir vtterly.'   4671

' For sake,' quod he, ' aye, benedicite,   4672   Generydes
Why wiH she me mystrost in eny wise ?
Trewly MirabeH,' quod he, ' As for me,
My hert his heris, my trowth and my ceruice,   4675   to her
It grevith me fuH sore suche fantesyce,
ffor be that lord that formyd me of nowght,
Other to wedde came neuer in my thought.'   4678

' AH that,' quod she, ' I haue told here fuH playn,
Yet takith she noo credence what I say,
Ther is noo bote butte ye must come certayn,
And that anon as fast as euer ye may.'   4682
' I come,' quod he, ' withoute more delay ;'
So with MirabeH furth he went anon,
And to Clarionas streight he is goon.   4685

chamber.

In to hir chaunber furth he goth a pace,   4686
Of his comyng' full redely she knewe ;
'What do yow here ?' thanne seid Clarionas,

She taunted him
with his untruth.

'Of all knyghtes,' quod she, ' the most vntrew ;   4689
Your fayre behest all now may I rewe,
Your beyng' here is to my grete displesaunce,
Goo now away onto your old Acqueyntaunce.   4692

' Sir Amelok hath
a fair daughter

Syr Amelok hath a doughter certayn),   4693
Whiche is right fayre and lucidas she hight,

and the peace
will soon be made
between you.'

The pece is sone made betwix yow twayn),
ffor to the chaunge your hert is wonder light ;   4696
I say for me, ther was no maner wight
That loved yow better thanne I dede before ;
All that is doo, for now I will nomore.'   4699

Whanne she hadde sayde that pleasid hir to say, 4700

At this Generydes
fell down in a
swoon.

Thanne was Generides a wofull man) :
Anone he felle in swouneng' and ther he laye,
All discolored in vesage, pale and wanne,   4703
And furth with remembre she beganne
What man) he was, and also what seruice,
That he hir fader dede in euery wise,   4706

With right good will he was redy alway :   4707
Mirabell saide, 'what maner thing' is this ?
Now certeynly ye are to blame, I saye ;
ffor wele I wote in hym) ye demyd amys :   4710
yet atte last,'[1] quod she, ' ye shuld hym) kysse.'

[leaf 25, back]

Thanne seid Clarionas, ' sith it is soo,
If that may do hym) good, it shalbe doo   4713

With all myn) hert,' quod she, ' what euer fall ;' 4714
To se hym) soo she was right sore dismayde.

Clarionas kisses

Ther as he lay she kyst hym) furth withall,

[1] ? lest.

And he ther witħ aħ sodenly abrayde,　　　4717　him, and he
recovers,
like as a man had ben soro affrayde ;
' Madame,' quod he, ' now pleaso it yow to hero
What I shaħ say as towchyng this mater.　　　4720

As for my parte ther is noo creature,　　　4721　and all was
forgiven.
That wiħ do more your honour to avaunce,
And o my trowtħ it was I neuer sure,
Vnto this our of now none Acqueyntance,　　　4724
In that ther is noo cause of displesaunce,
I hauo ben alway trow in myn entent,
And of aħ this god wote I am fuħ innocent.　　　4727

Whanne he had seid so trewly and so playn,　　　4728
In euerything as towchyng this mater :
' Aħ is for geve,' quod she, ' betwix vs twayn,
And late vs stiħ be frendis as we were.'　　　4731
' Ther to I graunt,' quod he, ' with rigħt good chero
To endure ; ' so witħ good contenuaunce
Iche to other made thei fuħ assuraunce.　　　4734

Vppon this thanne he toke his leve for to goo,　　　4735　He took his leave
of the Sultan,
Of the Sowdon and of fayro Clarionas ;　　　and of Clarionas,
Witħ hir he left a litiħ doggo also,　　　and left with her
a little dog.
Whiche went witħ hir a bougħt in euery placo,　　　4738
In here consoite a greto Ieweħ it was ;
So toward yud Gonerides is gon,
With hym the new made knygħtes euerychone.　　　4741

To Surre camo Gonerides and his knygħtes a pace,
Ther was tho ost of auferius y* kyng,　　　The army of
Auferius was at
In a Cito whicho was callid Damas,　　　Damas when
Gonerydee came
Theder thoi camo withouto more taryeng :　　　4745　with his knights.
Grete ioye mado aħ the ost of ther comyng,
And of aħ other namyd in the prese,
They were most ioyfuħ of Gonerides.　　　4748

To the shippe they went in all the hast y^{ei} myght,
And as thei wold desire thei had the wynd ;
Vppon̅ the see thei toke ther course full right,
That sone thei were vppon̅ the cost of ynde,   4752
Right fayre havenys all redy ganne thei fynd,
And sone thei landyd, shortly for to say,
All atte ther ease, was no man̅ seid nay.   4755

ffurth one thei went, and made noo taryeng,   4756
The Cryes were made in euery good village,
All thoo that wold obey the rightwise kyng
Shuld haue ther lyves and ther heritage ;   4759
And euery man̅ to haue his avauntage,
A moneth day to take avisement,
This was the kynggez own̅ poyntement.   4762

Furth with his ost kyng auferius is gon̅,   4763
And many lordes in his companye,
The townys and the castelys euerychon̅
Euer as he went he wanne them̅ by and by,   4766
Save one, whiche was full stronge and myghty,
And as the story makith remembraunce,
Wold not be wonne withoute grete ordenaunce : 4769

And Vice it hight, whiche is a fayre Cite ;   4770
Ser Amelok fro thense a litill he lay,
And of auferius comyng wist not he
No maner o thing, ne of all that Arraye ;   4773
Thanne was ther on̅ that had hast in his way,
And ser Amelok Anon̅ he ganne hym̅ dresse,
Whiche with a knyght was playeng Att chesse. 4776

'What tyme is now to play Atte Chesse?' quod he,
'Thu byddest thy felaw chese, I vnderstonde ;
Butt for certeyn̅ I saye chek mate to the,

Kyng Auferius is here withynne tho land, 4780 for Auferius and Generydes are here.'
Townys and Castelys are yelde to his hand,
With hym is come Generides also,
Take hede be tyme or all is goo.' 4783

Syr Amelok, whanne he tho tydenges hard, 4784 Sir Amelok was beside himself for rage.
A wrother man yet saw he neuer non,
And as a man beside hem self he farde,
These tydengys came so hastely vppon ; 4787
Ther with he sent his lettres owt anon, He sent out his letters
All men to come and in hir best arraye,
Euery man to make as many as they may 4790

The townnys and the Castellys on be on, 4791 and victualled his towns and castles,
he sett them vnder rule and gouernaunce,
And made them to be vitaylid euerychon
With stuff of pepill And of ordenaunce ; 4794
And specially in his remembraunce, especially Vice.
And in his mende the fayre Cite of Vice,
To make it strong in eny maner awise. 4797

And so he ded in All that euer he myght ; 4798
Withynne ij myle thanne was the kyngges ost, Auferius was two miles off,
And ther was on that gidid them full right,
Whiche somtyme kept tho forest in the cost, 4801
And brought tidengges whanne the Cite was lost, [leaf 26]
The same forster suerly was ther gide, led by the faithful forester.
ffull wele he knew the wayes on euery side. 4804

Whanne tho ost was come before ye town, 4805 When he came before the town
he sett his felde and made no more delay ;
Whanne that was do, the kyng rode vppe and down,
Beholding wele the grownde in euery way, 4808
And thanne he sette the pepill in his arraye, he set his people in array in 20 ranks, 1000 in each.
A xx. Rankys trewly for to accompt,
And iche of them A Ml men affronte. 4811

They of the town were ware,

They of the town were ware of y^{er} comyng',   4812
And toke good hede hough they made ther feld ;
Among' them) was noo lenger abideng',
But furth they dressid them) with spere and sheld 4815
Owt of the town), that myght a wepon) weld,
And ther thei made a feld vppon) the playn),

and mustered 15,000 strong.

xv thowsand to say yow for certayn).   4818

The battles met,

It was not long' or bothe the battellez mett,   4819
And on that side of Auferius the kyng'
Generides full fresshly on they sett,
And was the first of that encounteryng',   4822
ffull wele horsyd att his likyng',

and Generydes bore down Ananyell,

And with a spere, the story can) yow tell,
he bare down) a knyght callid Ananyell,   4825

brother to Sir Amelok.

And broder to ser Amelok he was ;   4826
A semely knyght, a man) of grete powre,
Generides toke Natanell[1] his stede,
And hym) he wold a taken) prisoner,   4829
Thanne was ther of his felisshepe soo nere,
That saw thei hough his stede was gon)
So furth with all they reskewe hym) anon).   4832

He had a sworn brother called Sir Amysell,

He had a felaw that callid was ser Amysell,   4833
his sworn) broder he was in sothfastnes ;
Anone with all ranne to hym) ser Darell,
And hym) vnhorsyd ther in all the prese,   4836
And in like wise so ded Generides,
ffurth on he goth and yer as the prese was most,

whom Darell unhorsed.

Syr Darell toke the stede and led hym) to ye ost. 4839

The other party were wroth.

The toder part avaunce them) anone   4840
And wrothe thei were yer men) were so outrayed,

King Lamedon was there,

kyng lamedon) was ther, and formest of euerychon),

---

[1] So MS. for *Ananyell*.

And aH for love of lucidas tho mayde,   4843
Tho whicho was endly fayre, us it was sayde,
Of aH hir manerys callid trew and p[l]ayne,
Ser Amelok hir fader was certayn :   4846

Serenides hir moder was Also,   4847
And aH sho was of another dissposicion)
As ye haue hard, withoute worles moo,
VnWurchipfuH of hir condicion),   4850
like as tho story makith mencion),
And so furth on, to say yow forther more,
Anone beganne the bateH passing sore.   4853

Syr Amelok in the myddes of tho playn) 4854
Ranne to A knyght, and smoto hym) with his spere
Thorough owt the brest, and slew hym) in certayn).
Thanne he toke[1] tho kyng in this maner, 4857
'Be my councceH take ye this present here,
And so departe and ellys I yow behight,
ye shaH haue more long or it be nyght.' 4860

Thanne who was wrothe but Auferius y[e] kyng ? 4861
With a spere he ranne in to the prese
ffuH egerly, and atte first metyng
he slew tho kyng Sanyk withoute lese, 4864
Tho whiche was fader onto Serenydes,
kyng of Auforyk, the story makith mynd,
As here before in writeng may ye fynde. 4867

IIys sonne was ther and saw hym) wher he laye, 4868
Ser ysores he hight, to say yow fuH trew,
Thanne to ser Amelok this ganne he saye,
'Woo worth the tyme tha[t] euer I the knewe ! 4871
Thy cursyd lyff,' quod he, 'and most vntrew,
Thy hatefuH hart, and thy mysgouernaunce
hath browgth abowt this onhappy chaunse.' 4874

[1] ? told.

With 1000
knights he bore
his father to
town

Syr ysores, as sone as it myght be,   4875
Made certayn̄ knygħtes bere his fader to town̄,
And with A Mł knygħtes in his company ;
And ałł they made grete lamentacion̄ :   4878
The prestis mett hym̄ with A procession̄,[1]
And of the Citee many a creature,

to his sepulture.

Rigħt so they brougħt hym̄ to his sepulture.   4881

Serenydes
saw them,

Quod Serenydes, 'beholde them̄ eu[er]ychon̄ ;'   4882
And what it ment she wold a wist fayn̄ :
And so among̍ ałł other was one,
'Madame,' quod he, 'the sothe I wiłł not layn̄ ;   4885
The kyng̍ your̍ fader ded is for certayn̄,
his knygħtes yender bere hym̄ on his sheld,
kyng̍ Auferius hath slayn̄ hym̄ in the feld.'   4888

and when she
wist how it was
she was a woful
creature.
She took Lucidas
apart, and said,

And whanne Serenydes wist hough it was,   4889
wete ye wele she was a wofułł creature ;
She toke aparte the mayden̄ lucidas,
'Doughter,' quod she, 'now am I very sure,   4892

'My joy is gone.

My Ioy is gon̄, And Ałł good aventure ;

[leaf 26, back]

I mygħt rigħt wele A knowen̄ Ałł this before,
I haue deseruyd it if it were more.   4895

This is all come
for my untruth to

For myn̄ on̄ trowth ałł this come too [me],   4896
For more vntrew I trow ther was neuer non̄ ;
A better prince was neuer born̄,' quod she,
'In ałł this world thanne I was sure of on̄,   4899
And vtterly for euer he is now gone,
Vppon̄ his grace it botith not to wayte,
ffor I shałł neuer stonde in his conseite.   4902

Auferius.'

Kyng̍ auferius it is in certayn̄,   4903
To whom̄ I weddid was be mariage,
I toke a new whiche sore repentith me,

---

[1] MS. *precession*.

It hath and wiH turne me to grete damage ; 4906
And doughter myn), now ye be yong' of age,
haue this in mynde, bothe now and euery owre,
late noo thyng' move yow to your' dishonour.' 4909

In this meane tyme that she complayned soo, 4910
The batcH lasted alway stiH opece,
Moche pepyH hurt and many slayn) Also ;
ffuH egerly thanne came rideng' ser ysores, 4913
And witH a spere ranne to Generides,
And witH grete corage aH redy to fight,
To avenge his faders detH if that he myght. 4916

The battle went on meanwhile,

and Sir Ysores ran at Generydes to avenge his father.

Generides fuH suerly hym) beheld, 4917
hym) for to mete anone he ganne hym) dresse,
And ther they ranne to geder in the feld :
The toder knygHt, callid ser ysores, 4920
vppon) the shelde he smote Generides ;
And with [the] stroke his stede came on) so rounde,
That hors and man) were almost cast to grownd. 4923

He struck him, and nearly brought him down.

Generides recoueryd vppe than) ayeyn), 4924
Thinkyng suerly to quyte hym) to for on),
And with his swerd he brast his sheld on) twayn):
The swerde poynte ranne onto the shulder boon), 4927
Sore hurt he was, and reskewse was yer non),
Nor non) comyng', wherefore ser ysores
Anon) he yelded hym) onto Generides, 4930

Generydes in turn cut him down with his sword,

and took him prisoner.

And furtH with aH delyueryd hym) his swerd. 4931
To hym) thanne seide Generides ayeyn),
'What man) be ye that I haue here conquerred?'[1]
'I am,' he seid, 'to say yow for certayn), 4934
The kynggez sone that here to day was slayn) ;
And eyre to his landes withoute lese,
My suster is the quene Serenydes.' 4937

'What man be ye?' he asked. 'I am son to the king who was slain to-day,

and Serenydes is my sister.'

[1] MS. conquerred here.

'I know her well,'
quoth he,

'Serenydes,' q*uo*d he, 'I knowe here well ;   4938
This warre beganne noo creature but she,

'she is crop and
root of the war.

ffor she is croppe and rote and eu*er*y dele,
yet as for your persone ye shall goo fre,   4941

Tell her I am he
that she would
have destroyed.'

And say to Serenydes that I am he
Whiche she wold haue distroyed eu*er* more ;
And now I trowe she wolle repent it sore.'   4944

Sir Ysores was
sore wounded,

Sore wondid Was s*er* ysores in dede,   4945
And sore for bled that vnnethe myght he stonde,

and Generydes
held him up
on his horse,

Might had he non to kepe hym on his stede,
Butt as Generides put to his hande ;   4948
Whereby a man myght knowe and vnderstonde

like a noble
knight.

A noble knyght and full of prow[es]se,
his enmy so to helpe in his distresse.   4951

To the Cite goth now s*er* ysores,   4952
Rideng alone soft and an easy pace ;

Serenydes saw
him from the
wall.

Vppon the wall stode Serenydes,
And saw hym come and callid lucidas ;   4955
'God wote,' q*uo*d she, 'I stonde in an hevy case,
I se my broder woundid passing sore,
My hevynes encreasith more and more.'   4958

Ther anon the mayde lucidas   4959
Comfortid hir in all that eu*er* she myght ;

Sir Ysores
dismounted in
great pain,

Ser ysores be that tyme come was,
And with grete payne down of his hors light ;   4962

and told her
what Generydes
had said.

To his suster he toke the way full right,
Rehersyng eu*er*y word bothe more and lesse,
Whiche he shuld telle hir fro Generides.   4965

And whanne Serenydes wist hym so nere,   4966
God wote she was a wofull creature,
withoute eny comfort or eny man*er* chere,

Trostyng⁴ vppon noo better aventure,   4969
ffor of his frendshippe cowde she not be sure.
And so furth on to telle yow ferthermore,
Aħ way the bateħ lastid passing⁴ sore.   4972

Off euery side grete pepiħ were slayn,   4973 Many people were slain on each side.
And moche grounde of ser Amelok¹ thei wanne;
Ser Dareħ with a spere vppon the playn   Sir Darell overthrew Ioatan,
Come rideng⁴ on, and to an erle he ranne,   4976
Born in europe, his name was Ioatan,
And in serteyn, be writeng⁴ as I knowe,
Both hors with the Erle was ouer throwe.   4979

Syr Dareħ toke with hym his stede;   4980 and took his horse,
With that anon his knyghtes were redy,
hym to reskew thei made hasty spede;
A long⁴ the Citee Dareħ rode by and by,   4983 and as he rode along the city he saw a maiden on a tower,
Vppon² A towre ther with he cast his yee,
And [on] that towre he sawe a mayde sittyng⁴,
Right Inly fayre she was to his semyng⁴.   4986 right fair as he thought.

And thanne he callid Sygrem furth with aħ,   4987 Then he called Sygrem, [leaf 27]
'Segrem,' he saide, 'now for the loue of me,
Of on thyng telle me in especiaħ,
A gentilwoman that I yonder see,   4990 and asked who she was. 'To tell the truth
What that she is, sey me the certente;'
'Ser,' quod Sygrem, 'the soth I wiħ not layn,   she is the daughter of Sir
Ser Amelok is hir fader in certayn;   4993 Amelok.'

And she is callid good in euery place,   4994
Of hir maners soft and eke demure.'
Thanne saide Dareħ, 'trewly this is the case,   'She shall have my service,'
My seruice she shaħ haue I yow ensure,   4997 quoth Darell,
ffor me thinkith hir a goodly creature;
And yet I drede Generides therfore,   'but I fear Generydes.'
lest he ther with will be displeasid sore.'   5000

¹ MS. *Amelek*.   ² MS. *A rppon*.

'Doubt not,'
said Sygrem,

'Syr,' quod Sygrem, 'dought not in this case,   5001
If he loue not hir fader by noo maner waye,

'for he doth not
hate her.'

In trowth yet hate[t]h he not lucydas.
'Why, Who is that?' quod he, 'I prae yow say.' 5004
    It is the mayde,' quod he, 'ye sawe to day,
And if ye will I shall a token bere
To hir anon, and bryng a trew answere.'   5007

'That I beseche yow hartely,' he saide ;   5008

Darell then gave
him a ring to
carry to Lucidas,

And ther with all he delyueryd hym a ryng,
'Goo now,' quod he, ' to lucydas that mayde,
With this tokyn and make noo taryeng,   5011
And do your massage wele in euery thing.'
Whanne he hadde told hym all his erand playn,

and went back
to the field,

In to the feld he returnyd hym ageyn,   5014

And in the thikkest prece of all the place   5015

and unhorsed
Ananyell,
who was uncle
to Lucidas.
She saw it,

he bare down Ananyell, hors and all,
The whiche was vnkyll onto lucydas ;
She saw all that stondeng vppon the wall,   5018
Thanne thought she this, what thing yᵗ euer fall
Shall noman think but that I do very right,
Though I besette my loue on suche a knyght.   5021

and asked her
mother,
'Which is
Generydes?
I think it is he
with the black
steed.

Thanne sayde she to hir moder in this wise ;   5022
'wote ye whiche is generides?' quod she :
'As ferre furth as I canne device,
his stede is blak, me think the same is he ;   5025
A noble knyght is he, in very certente :
And o thing shall I telle yow that is trew,
Myn owen vnkill now he ouer threw.   5028

But there is
another knight
on a white steed.'

Ther is,' quod she, 'another knyght also,   5029
his stede is whight, this wote I for certayn,
In all the ost suerly ther is no moo,

That in knyghtwoode Are like to then) twayn).' 5032
Thanne to hir answerd Serenydes ayeyn),
'Ah that is sothe,' she saide, 'and as for me,
Yett of then) bothe I wote not whiche is he. 5035

'I know not which of the two he is,' said Serenydes.

But as for hyn)·namyd first of ah, 5036
I shah declare yow trewly myn) entent,
With that ther myght be made a pece fenyah,
And bothe partes beyng' of on) assent, 5039
Whiche in this case were full conuenient,
And if it myght be soo thanne wold I fayn)
The mariage were made betwix yow twayn).' 5042

'But the first you named I would gladly see married to you when peace is made.'

In this mene while that she these wordes seid, 5043
Come Sygrem vppe and founde then) sittyng';
Whanne she hyn) sawe thanne was she wele apayd:
'Sygrem,' she saide, 'canne ye teHe me eny thing',
Whiche are the knyghtes of auferius the kyng'?'
'Ye, ye, madame,' [quod he] 'soo mote I goo,
I know Generides and other moo. 5049

Meanwhile Sygrem came up,

and she asked him of the king's knights.

And if ye wiH haue knowlache whiche is he, 5050
he wiH come here anon) be fore your sight,
his stede is white, this is the certente;
With hyn) ther is also, I yow be hight, 5053
Another man) whiche is a worthy knyght;
his stede is blak, and therto Wight and good,
hyn) self also is come of right noble blode. 5056

'Generides is he with the white steed,

but there is a knight on a black one,

Hys fader is a man) of grete estate, 5057
And p[r]ince of Cesare by his enheritaunce,
A famose man), and alway fortenate
In euery thing' his honour shuld Avaunce; 5060
Now haue I told yow aH the circumstaunce.'
'What is the knyghtes name?' quod she ayeyn);
'Ser DareH he hight,' quod he, 'this is certayn).' 5063

son of the prince of Cesare,

Sir Darell.'

<table>
<tr><td>Lucidas blushed
a little,</td><td>Whanne lucidas had hard hym euery dele,</td><td>5064</td></tr>
<tr><td></td><td>Anon she wex a litiil rede with all,</td><td></td></tr>
<tr><td>and Serenydes
pretended not
to notice.</td><td>Serenydes perseyuyd it full wele,</td><td></td></tr>
<tr><td></td><td>She let as though she knew noo thyng At All,</td><td>5067</td></tr>
<tr><td></td><td>And ther with all she rose vp fro the wall ;</td><td></td></tr>
<tr><td>As they were
going, Sygrem
whispered
Lucydas,</td><td>And as thei [1] were remevyng fro the place,</td><td></td></tr>
<tr><td></td><td>ffull sustely [2] Sygrem callid lucydas,</td><td>5070</td></tr>
<tr><td>and gave her
the ring.</td><td>And furth with all delyueryd hir the ryng,</td><td>5071</td></tr>
<tr><td></td><td>Wherwith in sothe she was right wele apayde,</td><td></td></tr>
<tr><td>She hesitated
about taking it</td><td>Yet made she danger in the reseyuyng,</td><td></td></tr>
<tr><td></td><td>Of his massage she was sumwhat dismayde,</td><td>5074</td></tr>
<tr><td></td><td>And soberly to Sygrem thus she saide :</td><td></td></tr>
<tr><td></td><td>' Ryng ne Writeng, as I remember canne,</td><td></td></tr>
<tr><td></td><td>I neuer yet reseyuyd of noo gentilman :</td><td>5077</td></tr>
<tr><td>[leaf 27, back]</td><td>Butt this I trost, in his grete gentilnes,</td><td>5078</td></tr>
<tr><td></td><td>That his desire suerly and his entent</td><td></td></tr>
<tr><td></td><td>Is only me yn honour to encrease,</td><td></td></tr>
<tr><td></td><td>And in that wise this ryng that he me sent,</td><td>5081</td></tr>
<tr><td></td><td>It to reseyue I am right wele content.'</td><td></td></tr>
<tr><td>but did so,</td><td>And so she toke the ryng in this maner,</td><td></td></tr>
<tr><td>and gave him
another,</td><td>And gave Segrym another for to bere.</td><td>5084</td></tr>
<tr><td>which Sygrem</td><td>Now is Sygrem departid on his way</td><td>5085</td></tr>
<tr><td></td><td>ffrom lucidas, his erande for to do,</td><td></td></tr>
<tr><td></td><td>In to the feld as fast as euer he may,</td><td></td></tr>
<tr><td>carried to Darell,</td><td>To ser Darell withoute wordes eny moo,</td><td>5088</td></tr>
<tr><td></td><td>his tokyn ther he delyueryd to hym Also ;</td><td></td></tr>
<tr><td></td><td>Whanne he it had he was right wele apayde,</td><td></td></tr>
<tr><td></td><td>And to Sygrem full curtesly he sayde ;</td><td>5091</td></tr>
<tr><td>who thanked him,</td><td>' Ser,' quod he, ' I thank yow right hertely</td><td>5092</td></tr>
<tr><td></td><td>Of your good will and trew seruice,</td><td></td></tr>
<tr><td></td><td>And one thyng I yow ensure verily,</td><td></td></tr>
</table>

[1] MS. ther.   [2] ? softely.

The first stede that I wynne in eny wise,   5095

It shalbe your', and that I yow promes ;

So furth he gothe in to the feld anow,

And rode a course onto kyng' lamedon).   5098

and promised him
the first horse he
should win.

He rode at King
Lamedon,

Anone thei mette to geder in the feld,   5099

Ther with ser Darell saw his lady fre,

he smote kyng' lamedon) vppon) the sheld,

And suche a stroke he gave hym) with a spere,   5102

That hors and man) bothe atto grownde were ;

And ther kyng' lamedon) his stede he lost,

Ser Darell hym) toke and led hym) to his ost   5105

and brought
horse and man
to the ground.

Callyng' anon) to his remembraunce,   5106

What full promys he had made before,

Vnto Sygrem for his trew attendaunce,

That he shuld be rewardid wele therfore,   5109

And to Sygrem, I say yow forthermore,

he gave that stede withoute more taryeng',

Tho whiche he wanne of lamedon) the kyng'.   5112

The horse he
gave to Sygrem.

Vppon) the towre on) highe stode lucidas,   5113

And saw all this to hir grete plesaunce ;

Serenydes perseivid hough it was,

She seide noo word, nor made no contenaunce.   5116

And so furth on, to tell yow the substaunce,

The batell still endure[d] to And fro,

Moche pepyll slayn) And Alway moo And moo.   5119

Lucidas saw all
this, to her great
delight.

Kyng' lamedon), of whom) ye hard me speke,   5120

Was sette all now appon) anothe[r][1] stede,

To that entent he wold hym) hym) self A wreke,

And to Generides he ranne in dede ;   5123

Ther hors came on) with suche a spede,

And sothely, atte first encownteryng',

Generides strake lamedon) the kyng'   5126

King Lamedon
mounted another
horse and rode
at Generydes,

who smote him

[1] MS. originally *A stede*, but *anothe[r]* is written above.

to the brain, so that he fell dead.	Thorough the hede streyght in to the brayn);　5127
	The kyng' was dede withynne a litiH space,
	ffor hym) was made grete hevynes certayn),
	And for to teH yow certayn) as it was,　5130
	Whanne he was dede they stode in hevy case ;
His side then fled to the city.	Thei lost the feld, and fled atte last
	In to the Citee, and shette the gatez fast.　5133

They without pitched their tents,	Thanne thei withoute the tentys vppe yᵉˡ pight,　5134
	Eche after other streight abowt the town),
	In aH the hast possibiH that thei myght ;
	And first of AH, the kynges pavilion)　5137
	Set for the kyng' and ther vppon) a crown) ;
and set up engines to break down the walls.	Engyins grete were purveyd for the nonys,
	To breke the waHys with casting' of stonys.　5140

While they besieged the city	And whiH that thei besegid the Cite,　5141
	These lordes and these knyghtes euerychone,
the news came to Gwynan that Generydes was gone to India,	Ther cam tidengys in very certente,
	Vnto Guynan the kyng' be many on),　5144
	hough in to ynde Generides is gon),
	With meche people and many a nobyH knyght
	To helpe the kyng' his fader in his right.　5147

so he resolved to invade Persia, and avenge his father's death, and get Clarionas.	Thanne in to perse purposith he to goo,　5148
	his faders deth to venge if [1] that he myght,
	And of Clarionas he thought also,
	hir to haue he thought it was his right,　5151
	he made a massinger redy day and nyght
He sent to Sir Amelok,	Vnto ser Amelok, And hye hym) fast
	Streyght in to ynde in AH the possible hast.　5154

bidding him hold out, and he would come to his rescue.	' Goo now to Amelok, and byd hym) kepe hym) close,
	That in noo wise he stere not to And fro,
	And kepe hym) owt of daunger of his foys,

[1] MS. *of.*

ffor with myn ost streight to perse I will goo,　　5158
To wynne the Sowdon and his land Also ;
ffro thense I will into ynd without fey[n]ing,
And reskew hym from Auferius the kyng.'　　5161

Now goth the massenger on his viage　　5162
Streight in to ynd, withoute more taryeng,
And to ser Amelok seide his message,
Whiche likid hym right wele in euery thyng,　　5165
And very glad he was of his comyng :
Grete chere also made quene Serenydes,
ffor she purposid wele to leve in pece.　　5168

Than furth with all quod she to lucidas,　　5169
' Telle me, doughter, of very frendlehede,
What Sygrem seid, and what his massage was,
And as longith to my womanhede,'　　5172
With thoo wordes she wexe a litill rede ;
' Madame,' quod she, ' if it please yow to here,
I shall tell yow the trowth of this mater.　　5175

There is a knyght of good and noble fame,　　5176
In very trowth hath sent me here a ryng,
ffor noo slaunder ne hurt onto my name,
Butt to wurchippe in all his demeaneng,　　5179
And myn honour above all other thing,
This is his will and his desire certayn.'
Thanne seid Serenydes to hir ayeyn,　　5182

' What is the knyghtes name ? now tell it me.'　　5183
' Trewly, Madame,' quod she, ' ser Darell he high[t],
And of Cesare the prince sonne is he,[1]
Of his handis callid a noble knyght,　　.　　5186
And ayre to his lande, I yow be hight ;
Now haue I told yow all the circumstaunce,
I prae yow take it to no displeasaunce.'　　5189

────

¹ MS. *he is*.

The messenger
came to Sir
Amelok,

[leaf 28]
who was glad
of his coming.

Serenydes asks
Lucidas what
Sygrem said.

She blushed,
and told her of

Sir Darell and
his ring.

'Therof,' quod she, 'dowte ye neuer a dele,   5190
Butt my conseite wiH I telle yow playne,

' If he love you,'
said Serenydes,
' let him get

If it be so that he love yow so weH,
ye shaH right sone haue knowlage in sertayne,   5193
your pleasur to perfourme he wiH be fayn.;
Send for Sygrem,' quod she, 'that he may goo
To ser DareH your erand for to do.   5196

And as he owith yow feith and trew seruice,   5197
That of Generides he wiH purchase

a gold ring
from Generydes
which Clarionas
gave him.

A ryng of gold, in eny maner wise,
Whiche he in perse had of Clarionas ;   5200
Why and wherefore I shaH teH you ye cause,

I have a sick
friend

I haue a frende, a fuH seke creature,
Grete payn of ache aHway he doth endure.   5203

who has been told
in a vision that it
will make him
whole.'

And by a vision it come hym too,   5204
he shhuld be hoole if he the ryng myght haue ;
And for certayn it were grete pite also,
That he soo soone were dolvyn in his grave,   5207
If suche a ryng myght hym socour And save.
ffor the whiche doughter I yow require,
Send for Sygrem and tender this mater.'   5210

To hir anon Answerd lucidas ayeyn,   5211
Whiche in this mater was fuH Innocente ;
'Madame,' quod she, 'I wiH putt to my payn,
In that I canne to folow your entente.'   5214

Lucidas sent
Sygrem to Sir
Darell to borrow
the ring.

Sygrem anon on this massage was sent,
And to ser DareH dede his erande soo,
The ryng to borow withoute wordes moo.   5217

Sir Darell thought
nothing amiss,

As for ser DareH he thought noo thyng Amys,   5218
Nor he that brought the ryng, but wote ye what ?
ffuH ofte it hath be seide, and trew it is,

ffalshede and trougth is euer atte debate : 5221

And yet Sygrem was allway fortenate ;

ffor lucidas, whanne he brought hir the ryng,

Gave hym a mantell of hir owne weryng. 5224

nor Sygrem, to whom Lucidas gave a mantle when he brought the ring.

Serenides perseivid be the ryng, 5225

hir prayour was obseruyd and obeyde,

And furth with all withoute more taryeng,

She callid lucidas, and this she saide ; 5228

'Doughter,' quod she, 'I am right wele apayde,

ffor now I wote ye haue chose you a man,

That will please yow in all that euer he canne. 5231

Serenydes was well pleased,

And fayre doughter,' quod she, 'this I yow prae, 5232

As late me see the facyon of that ryng.'

'Madame,' quod she, 'ye wote right wele alway,

I haue not disobeyde yow in noo thing ;' 5235

And from a lose anon ther as it hyng,

Be cause she wold in no wise her displese,

She toke the ryng onto Serenydes. 5238

and begged to see the ring, which Lucidas gave np to her.

Whanne she it hadde thanne was she wele content,

And callid furth on of hir Acqueyntaunce,

Suche on as wold do after hir entent,

And brought vppe was vnder hir gouernaunce, 5242

A man that cowde hym self right wele avaunce,

And born he was, the story seith the same,

In Ethiope, and Gusare was his name. 5245

She then called one of her acquaintance,

Gusare,

Ther with all right this to hym she sayde ; 5246

'On my massage,' quod she, 'now must ye goo

ffurth in to perse, and this may not be nayde,

And ye shall bere with you this ryng Also.' 5249

'Madame,' quod he, 'your pleasure for to doo,

I wold be glad in eny maner wise,

To ryde or goo ye shall haue my seruice.' 5252

and sent him to Persia, to carry the ring to Clarionas,

'Gusare,' quod she, 'in sothe this is the case,   5253
[leaf 29, back] haue here a ryng' and kepe it still opece,
To the tyme that ye come onto Clarionas,
ffor she it gave on to Generides ;   5256
that she might
break the love
between her and
Generydes. The love of them) is grete, but,[1] neuer the lese,
I wold ther were a variaunce full fayn),
So that the love were broke betwix them) twayn). 5259

By this meane my pece I may purchase,   5260
And other wise I trow it will not be,
If ye do wele your' labour' in this case,
ffor your' rewarde yow shall wele know and se,   5263
That ye shall haue A cause to praye for me.'
'Madame,' quod he, 'this shall be don) right wele,
In this mater dowte ye neuer a dele.'   5266

Falshede and gile is now togeder mett,   5267
In A persone to awayte ther Avauntage.
vppon) han) hors [Gusare][2] hym) self was sett,
When Gusare
came to Persia
he met a poor
palmer, And rideth into perse on) his massage.   5270
Whanne he come ther he mett in his viage
A pore palmer, goth in sympill gise ;
To hym) anon) he sayde right in this wise :   5273

and asked him
where the Sultan
was.
'At Mountoner,'
said he, 'Now good fader, what contre come ye fro ?'   5274
'ffro Mountoner,' quod he, 'the redy waye.'
'Good ser,' quod he, 'now or ye ferther goo,
Where lith,' he seide, 'the Sowdon) ? I yow praye.'
'I left hym) ther,' quod he, 'as yesterday ;
A grete people surely with hym) ther was,
'with Clarionas.' And his doughter also, fayre Clarionas.'   5280

'And where is
Generydes?'
'He is gone to
India to maintain
his father's right.' 'Where is now hir love, Generides ?'   5281
'he is furth into ynd,' quod he, 'certayn) ;
his faderys right to maynteyne and encrese,

MS. *but it.*   [2] *om.* MS.

ffor ther shaH he be lord and souereyn.'   5284
'ffader,' quod he, 'of on) thyng' yet ageyn),
This wold I vnderstonde in myne entent,
What token) he gave hir whanne he went?'   5287   'What token did
                                                                   he leave with
                                                                   her?'

'In sothe,' quod he, 'that canne I tell some dele;   5288
Whanne he departid owt of the Citee,
With hir he left, I am remembryd wele,
A lityH dogge, and ther ye may hym) see.'   5291   'A little dog,'
'ffader,' he seide, 'do now sum what for me;   said the palmer.
we ij wolle chaunge our' clothyng' or we goo.'   They change
Quod the palmer, 'I gree me wele therto.'   5294   clothes,

Now is Gusare weH onward on) his way,   5295   and Gusare came
And gave the palmer money largely;
To mountoner he came the redy way,   to Mountoner,
Ther was brought tydengez sekerly,   5298   and heard of
That Gwynan was enteryd certaynly   Gwynan's
                                                                   invasion.
Into the lande of perse withoute eny delay,
ffor to make a feld and wynne it by bateH.   5301

And so furth on) to say yow ferthermore,   5302
Gusare is now as besy as he may,
To do that he had promys[ed] before;
And as the palmer went in his Arraye,   5305
So goth Gusare, and toke the [redy] way
Into A tempiH, wheare as the Sowdon) was,   He goes to a
                                                                   temple where the
With hym) ther was also Clarionas.   5308   Sultan and
                                                                   Clarionas were,

On his fynger the ryng' anon) he sett,   5309   and puts the
                                                                   ring on his finger,
And in the temple purveid hym) A place
                                                                   and posted
Among' the prese, for no man) wold' he let   himself so that
That he mygHt stonde before clarionas;   5312   Clarionas might
                                                                   see him.
And ther he stode as for a certeyn) space,
The ryng' vppon) his fynger for to shewe,
She sawe the ryng' and saide butt wordez fewe.   5315   When she saw
                                                                   the ring

Yet in hir self she was gretly dismayde,   5316

she changed
countenance.
Mirabell observed
it,
and asked the
cause.

And ther with aH she chaungyd countenaunce ;
MyrabyH sawe it wele, and this she saide,
'Madame, ye haue som) cawse of displesaunce ;   5319
I prae yow, teH me what is your grevaunce.'
'That shaH ye knowe,' quod she, 'withoute fayle,
And wele I wote therof ye wiH merveH.   5322

'I saw a palmer
in the press,
with a ring on
his finger,
which I gave to
Generydes.'

I saw a palmer stondeng in the prese,   5323
On) his finger,' quod she, 'ther is a ryng,
The whiche I gave,' quod she, ' onto Generides,
And to non) other creature that is levyng.'   5326
'Madame,' quod she, 'that is a wonder thing,
yet for AH that dismay yow neuer a dele,
ye shaH se aH this shalbe rigħt weH ;   5329

'I will bring
him to your
chamber,'
said Mirabell ;

For I myself wiH speke witħ hym),' quod she ;   5330
'To your chaumber I shaH hym) bryng anon),
Ther shaH yow fele and knowe the certente,
In very trougtħ if it be so or noo.'   5333
So her vppon) MirabeH is gon),
And taryd not, but as hir commandement was,

and the palmer
came,

She brougħt the palmer vnto Clarionas.   5336

Whanne he hir sawe, he knelyd on) his kne,   5337
'Madame,' quod he, 'take ye not in disdayne
Of on) fortune, whiche wiH non other be,

and told her that
Generydes was
married to
Lucydas

ffor in this case to yow I wiH be playn) ;   5340
Generides is weddid in certeyn),
It passitħ not a fourthnyght sithe it was,
To Amelokkez doughter lucydas.   5343

[leaf 29]
against his will,

It was ayenst his wiH in euery thing,   5344
The cause was suche that he mygħt not say nay,
his fader chargyd hym) on his blissyng,

That pece myght be apoyntid for alway,   5347   to make peace.
If y⁰ trost not the wordes that I say,
here is a ryng⁺ whiche he sent yow be me,   'Here is the ring
                                                                 you gave him.
ye gave it hym) in very certente.   5350

And ferthermore also he chargid me,   5351   And he charged
                                                                 me to let you
To late you wete and suerly vnderstonde,
That ye may now stonde att your⁺ liberte,   know that you
                                                                 were free to wed.'
To wedde where euer ye will in eny lande.'   5354
Whanne she herd that noo lenger myght she stond,
Butt downe she felle swoninge for very payn) ;   Clarionas fell
                                                                 down in a swoon.
Mirabell ranne and toke hir vppe ageyn),   5357

Comfortyng⁺ hir in all that euer she myght,   5358
And whanne that she was recoueryd vp ayeyn),   When she
                                                                 recovered
To hym) that brought the ryng⁺ she went right,
And in noo wise she cowde not hir refrayn),   5361
And smote the ryng⁺ owt of his handes twayn) ;   she smote the ring
                                                                 out of Gusare's
All sodenly the ryng⁺ from) hym) was gone,   hands,
With that Mirabell toke it uppe anon),   5364   and Mirabell
                                                                 picked it up.

And putte the ryng⁺ in full sure kepyng⁺.   5365
Thanne saide Gusare onto Clarionas,
'Madame,' quod he, 'I haue forgete a thing⁺,
Whiche I shuld say as I commaundid was,   5368
Ye haue a litill dog⁺, this is the case ;   Gusare then asked
                                                                 for the dog,
My charge was this to tell yow euery dele,
In eny wise that ye shuld kepe hym) wele.'   5371

'As for the dog⁺,' quod she, 'here it ys ;   5372
I will noo lenger kepe it sekerly,
Nor no thing⁺ that I may knowe was his.'
To hym) she threw the dog⁺ full hastely,   5375   which Clarionas
                                                                threw to him,
With that Mirabell kaught it sodenly ;   but Mirabell
                                                                caught it.
'Thow shalt nomore,' quod she, 'come in his way,
ffor lucidas with the shall neuer playe,   5378

And I wilt haue the att myn) owen) devicc.'   5379
Whanne Gusare saw that ther was non other[1] way,
he toke his leue anon) in hasty wise,

Gusare then
returned to
India,
And so departid vppon) his Iurnay,   5382
Ayeyn) to ynd as fast as euer he may.

and Clarionas to
her chamber,
Clarionas is to the chaunber gone,
With syghys dcpe and thoughtes many on),   5385

a woful woman.
A wofuH woman) fuH of hevynes,   5386
Generides alway now remembryng',
Complayneng' gretly of his vnstabilnes,
Of wheche he was not gilty in noo thyng';   5389

Mirabell thought
And so Myrabett alway demyng'
Of this mater to vnderstonde it wele,

there was treason.
That it was do be treson) euery dele.   5392

When the Sultan
heard of it
he came to
his daughter's
chamber,
And whanne the Sowdon) hard of y[is] array,   5393
And hough his doughter toke suche a hevynes,
To hir chaunber he toke the redy waye,
As nature wold and also gentilnes,   5396
And fond hir in hir bed in grete distresse ;

and asked what
was amiss.
'Doughter,' quod he, 'ther is some thing' amys,
What euer it be now teH me what it is.'   5399

'My lord,'
quoth she,
'Generydes
is false,
'My lord,' quod she, 'plese it yow to vnderstonde,
ye gaue me onys onto Generides
In mariage, with half your' lande ;
Now is he false alas, an[d] cawseles   5403
With hym) ser Amelok hath made his pece,
And trewly accordid in euery case,

and married to
Lucidas.'
ffor he is weddid vnto lucidas.'   5406

'This aventure,' quod he, ' is passing' new,   5407
And as me think a very wonder thing';

'But is it true?'
Butt wote ye verily that it is trew?'

[1] MS. eyer.

'Ye, ye, my lord,' quod she, 'withoute feyning'; 5410
And ferthermore he sent me here a ryng',
That I gave hym in very certente,
Where by I wote it may now other be.'   5413

To his doughter the Sowdon gave answer',   5414
'Who wold,' quod he, 'have thought in suche a knyght,
That he wold be ontrew in this mater?
A grete merveH to here, I yow be hight,   5417
ffor this is do [a]yenst aH maner right,
And if he shew yow suche onkyndnes,
yet for aH that take ye noo hevynes,   5420

For I wiH purvey for yow another waye,   5421
And moche better as after myn entent;
kyng Gwynan wold be glad, I dare weH say,
That he and I shuld make apoy[nte]ment   5424
Betwix yow twayne, and if ye wiH assent,
That mariage, I cowde wele vnderstonde,
ShaH bryng' a fyniaH pece in to this land.'   5427

Clarionas seide neuer a worde ageyn,   5428
The whiche MirabeH liked neuer a dele;
To the Sowdon than spake she wordes playn,
'My lord,' quod she, 'as ferre as I canne fele,   5431
In this mater I canne think but wele;
And weH I wote that he is suche a knyght,
he wiH not breke that he hath onys behight.'   5434

'Now, good MirabeH,' quod Clarionas,   5435
'ye wote right wele he sent me here a ryng'.'
'In very trought, madame, and trew it is;
Butt this I wote as wele as eny thing',   5438
AH that he saide,' quod she, 'it is lesyng'.'
The Sowdon toke good hede of þᵗ she saide,
Of hir wordes he was right wele apayde.   5441

'Yea, yea, my lord, here is the ring;

It cannot be otherwise.'

The Sultan marvelled that Generydes should be so untrue,

but, said he,

'Gwynan will be glad,

and if you will assent,

we may make a final peace.'

Clarionas said never a word, but Mirabell told the Sultan

[leaf 29, back]

it was all false.

The Sultan took heed of her words, and was well pleased.

'What think yow best, Mirabell?' thanne quod he,
'That shuld be do as towchyng this mater?'
'Trewly,' quod she, 'the best that I canne se,

late me go furth and be the messanger;   5445
And whanne I come ayeyn thanne shall ye here
The very trougth, and trew as it is
Doo as ye list, for this is myn avise I wis.   5448

Iff I shall goo, of one thing I yow praye,   5449
That I may haue a surance or I passe,
The mariage to putte in delay

Betwix my lady here, Clarionas,   5452
And kyng Gwynan, rehersid here in this case,
And att my comyng home ye shall wele know
All other maner tidynges as I trow.'   5455

Too hir desire the Sowdon seid not nay,   5456
And furth with gave hir license for to goo;
In to the reame of ynde she toke hir way,

With hir ther went ij squyers and noo mo,   5459
Save ij pages to kepe ther horses also,
On hir Iurnay to kepe the way full right,
In All the hast possible that she myght.   5462

Now I shall telle yow hough befelle ye case;   5463

Generides was dremyd in his sleppe,
hym thought the Sowdon and Clarionas
Come hand in hand, and she with sighys depe   5466
Complayned sore, and first beganne to wepe,
And thanne anon the Sowdon to hym spake,
'Awake,' quod he, 'Generides awake!   5469

Thy promys is not kept that thow behight,   5470
And namely to my doughter and to me,

ffor thu hast take, ayenst all maner right,

Another wiff in very certente,   5473   another wife.
By tresone colour' vnder a suerte.'
Thanne seid Clarionas, 'geve me my ring',   'Give me my
ffor suerly I wiłł haue Gwynan the kyng'.'   5476   ring,' said
                                                                   Clarionas,
                                                                   'for I will marry
                                                                   Gwynan.'

After ałł this hym) thought Gwynan y⁰ kyng'   5477   After this, he
In to Egipte shuld lede Clarionas :   thought that
                                                                   Gwynan led her
Thanne came Mirabełł as she was goyng',   into Eygpt,
And toke hir from) him) as hir fortune was ;   5480   but Mirabell
                                                                   took her from
he awoke and of this soden) case,   him.
To Darełł and to Natanełł ałł in fere,   When he awoke
Of his dremys he told them) the mater.   5483   he told Darell
                                                                   and Natanell.

Syr Darełł, as sone as he hard of y⁰ ryng',   5484   As soon as Darell
his hart anon) mysgave hym) furth with ałł,   heard of the ring,
                                                                   his heart mis-
hym) thought som) tresone was ymagenyng,[1]   gave him,
And fayn) he wold haue wist what was fałł ;   5487
Vppon) Sygrem anon) he beganne to calle,   and he called
Whanne he was come he told hen) mor And lesse,   Sygre.u,
Of ałł the dreme of Generides.   5490

' Now, good Sygrem, I prao yow goo,' quod hee,   5491   and sent him
' To lucidas and speke for the ryng',   to Lucidas to
                                                                   get the ring
Besechyng' hir that she wiłł send it me,   again.
As euer I may do for hir eny thing'.'   5494
' Ser,' quod Sygrem, ' I say withoute feyning',
I wiłł do your' massage and see what she wiłł say,
And bryng' ayeyn) the ryng' if that ye may.'   5497

Thanne went Sygrem the way to lucidas,   5498   Sygrem went
ffrom) ser Darełł to telle his erande playn),   to Lucides.
In euery thyng' rehersid here the case,
And specially to haue the ryng' Ayeyn),   5501
It was his desire and his comyng' certayn).
Vppon) this anon) she gave an answere,
' I shałł,' quod she, ' speke for this mater.'   5504

[1] MS. ymagenyd.

and she to her mother,
To hir moder anon) with aH she gothe,   5505
And tenderly she prayde here for the ryng',
Butt lucidas wheder she was lefe or lothe,

but could not get it,
She cowde not haue it for no maner thyng',   5508
So partyd she and gretly complayneng',
Rigĥt grete vnkyndnes she thougĥt also,
That vnder trost she shuld be seruyd so.   5511

And whanne she sawe it wold non) other be,   5512
and went her way back to Sygrem.
ffuH hevilly she went hir way ayeyn),
'I shaH telle yow the trowth, Sygrem,' quod she,
This ryng' wiH nott be goten) for certayn,[1]   5515
I haue botĥ lost my labour' and payn),
'There is some treason, I pro-mise you,
And wele I wote it is not aH a rigĥt,
ffor some tresone ther is I yow behigĥt.   5518

And aH I trow be for Generides,   5519
and DareH will bear the blame.
I canne weH think that DareH shaH bere yᵉ name
Of this vnhappy werk, yet neuer the lese
Rigĥt wele I wote that he is not to blame ;   5522
And I suppose ye wiH reporte the same :
Butt this I prae yow hartely,' quod she,
But tell him
'Do my message as sone as ye hym) see,   5525

And say I send hym) word this in sertayn) ;   5526
that Gwynan is gone to Persia to destroy the Sultan and his land.
Gwynan the kyng' is gon), I vnderstonde,
ffourth in to perse, and his erande is playn),
The Sowdon) to distroye and his land :   5529
It to perfourme he hatĥ made fuH covenaunt.
Beg him to get leave to go to [leaf 30] Persia,
Now, good Sygrem, I prae yow say hym̄ soo,
And that he gete hym) licence for to goo   5532

Furtĥ in to perse withoute more taryeng',   5533
where he will hear tidings of the ring,
And say hym) suerly this is myn) avice,
Ther shaH he here some tidynges of the ryng',

[1] MS. certente.

And whoo that take on hym that enterprise, 5536
hougħ it was brougħt abought, and in what wise,
And he most dele witħ aH so sekerly,

but he must deal secretly.'

That no man knowe it save he and ye and I.' 5539

Now gotħ Sygrem, and noo thyng welł apayd, 5540

Sygrem meets Dareli,

he mette ser DareH rideng on the playn,
And told hym aH that lucidas had seide;

and tells him all that Lucidas had said.

hougħ he had lost his labour and his payn, 5543
And hougħ the ryng wold not be goten ageyn;
Whanne he had hard aH this yan was he wrotħ,

As soon as he heard all,

And to Generides anon he gothe. 5546

'I pray yow, ser, now geve me leve,' quod he, 5547

he asked Generydes leave to go into Persia

'ffurtħ into perse I purpose me[1] to goo,
hougħ it is ther to knowe the certente,

to see if his dream were true.

ffor I am alway trobolyd to and to; 5550
ffor your dremys rigħt I drede also.'
Generides ther of was wele apayde,
'Goo on your way, in goddis name,' he seide, 5553

'Go on your way in God's name,

'As fast as euer ye may, and com ayeyn, 5554
Owt of that lande sum tidyngez wold I here;
I pray yow, dareH, bryng me word sertayn,

and bring me some tidings of Clarionas.'

And of Clarionas my lady dere.' 5557
'That shaH not be for gete in noo maner.'
Ser dareH toke his leve, and went his way
Into the lande of perse, as I yow saye. 5560

Now is Gusare, that most on happy wigħt, 5561

Gusare is now come out of Persia,

Out of the lande of perce com[2] into ynd,
ffuH fast seching, in aH that euer he mygħt,
The redy way Generides to fynde, 5564
Witħ new contrivid falshede hym to blynd,

and goes straight with a new lie to Generydes,

In aH the hast to seche hym furth he went,
And atte [last] he founde hym in his tent. 5567

---

[1] MS. ne.   [2] MS. is com.

'My lord,' quod he, 'fro perse now am I come,   5568
ffro the Sowdon with tidynges y^t bo there,
ffor I wiłł tełł yow playnle ałł and som,

that Clarionas
is married to
Gwynan.

Gwynan the kyng is ther with grete powre,   5571
They ben accordid ałł bothe in on maner,
The pece is made and cryed in euery place,
The kyng is weddid on to Clarionas.   5574

These tydingez sendith yow ser Anasore ;   5575
Anoder erand haue I for to do,

The dog which
Clarionas sent,

A litiłł dog Clarionas hath ther,
She bad I shuld bryng hym with me Also,   5578
Butte be the tyme I shuld part And goo,
Thanne shuld I haue brought it with me verily,

he had had taken
from him.

And it was taken ayeyn from me sodenly.'   5581

Generides hard wele ałł that he seide,   5582

Generydes was
sore abashed,

And in hym self he was abasshed sore,
Thanne furth with ałł the message[r] he prayde ;

and asked when
the wedding was.

'Good ser,' quod he, 'yet telle me ferthermore,   5585
Whanne she was weddid and hough [long] before,
Of your departeng sey me the certente.'
'Ther of I shałł tełł yow the trouthe,' quod he ;   5588

'I come fro thense apoynted as thei were,   5589

'The same day
that I left,'
said Gusare.

The same day thei were weddid fułł sekyrly ;
My hast was suche that I myght not be ther,
To see the rewle and it was trewly.'   5592
Generides toke it fułł hevily,
In petuose wise complayneng euer in on,
Thanne Natanełł comfortid hym Anon.   5595

Now let us speak
of Mirabell.

Off Mirabełł now late vs speke a while,   5596
Whiche is reden, in ałł that euer she may,
Into the reme of ynd fułł many A myle ;

Whanne she came nygħ the ende of hir Iurnay,   5599   When she came near the end of her journey she met Darell,
Ther mette she witħ DareH vppoɲ the waye,
A ferde she was in very certente,
ffor Atte first she wist not yat it was he.[1]   5602

Whanne she hyɲ sawe she was righṫ wele apayde, 5603   and was well pleased.
And herd hym speke thanne very glad was she ;
' hougħ dotħ my lord, the Sowdoɲ, now ?' he said,   ' How doth my lord ?' said he,
' And my lady Clarionas,' quod he,   5606   ' and is my lady Clarionas married ?'
' Is she weddid ? teH me the very certente.'
' Weddid ?' quod she, ' nay, nay, I yow ensure,   ' No,' said Mirabell,
Nor neuer wilbe to noɲ erthely creature,   5609   ' and never will

Save only on to my lord Generides,   5610   except to Generydes.
In whoɲ suerly is aH hir fyence,
ffor this I canne yow teH in sothfastnes,
ffuH seldom is he owt of hir remembraunce,   5613
And as for eny new[2] founden Acqueyntaunce,
Ther is noo suche, I saye yow feithfully,
ffor wele I wote she had moche lever dye   5616   She would rather die.

Butt now I prae yow telle me,' quod she,   5617   And now tell me, is Generydes married ?'
' Generides is he weddid, or noo ?'
' Nay,' quod DareH, ' for certayɲ levitħ me,   ' Nay,' said Darell,
It came neuer in his thought so for to do ;   5620   ' It never came into his thought.
And for to say the very trowtħ Also,
ffor hyɲ I dare wele answere in this case,
he wiH noɲ other but fayre Clarionas,'   5623   He will have none but Clarionas.'

' The pece is not appoynted thanne,' quod she,   5624   [leaf 30, back] ' Then the peace is not made between Sir Amelok and him?'
' Of ser Amelok and of Generides ?'
' Nay,' quod DareH, ' trewly it wiH not be ;   ' Nay,' quoth Darell.
holde oɲ your' way,' quod she, ' stiH opece,   5627   ' Hold on your way,' said she,
And sette my lady[3] more in hartes ease ;   ' and set my lady at rest,
ffor oɲ thyng' shaH I say yow that is sure,
Ye shaH fynde hir a wofuH creature.'   5630   for you will find her a woful creature.'

---

[1] MS. *she*.   [2] MS. *now*.   [3] MS. *lorde*.

'I will,' said
Darell,
'In all the haste
I can.
Generydes is
now sad for his
dream.'

'In all the hast,' quod Darell, 'that I canne,   5631
To hir I will withoute eny more;
Generides is now an hevy man,
As for a dreme whiche trobelyd hym full sore,   5634
No thyng' so meche sith he was boore;
And wenyng' in his dreme, this is y⁰ case,
kyng' Gwynan had weddid clarionas.   5637

The Sowdon was agreyd well therto,   5638
All hym thought was trew in euery thing',
Now may ye tell hym it is noo thyng' soo,
And putt Away all this Imagenyng'.'   5641

They parted,

he for Persia,
she for India,
to seek
Generydes.

Thanne departid thei and noo taryeng',
he went to perse and she went to ynd,
The redy way Generides to fynde.   5644

Whanne she cam yer, into y⁰ ost she went,   5645
Generides to seche she ded here payn,

She found him
in his tent with
the false Gusare,

Atte last she founde hym in his tente,
And ther she founde that false Gusare ageyn,   5648
The massenger, wherof she was full fayne;
And bothe here squyers furth with all she prayde,
'lay on handes on that false theff,' she saide.   5651

Whanne he hir saw he drew hym owt aside,   5652
hir comyng' theder likid hym full ill;
Mirabell thanne anon hym had asspyde,

whom she seized
by the head.
One that knew
her wish
hit him a blow
that put him
beyond the help
of doctors.

She toke hym be the hede and held hym still,   5655
Thanne on that knewe hir purpose and will,
he smote Gusare so harde vppon the cheke,
That leche craft hym nede non other seeke.   5658

And ther he dyed withynne a litill stounde,   5659

Generydes
wondered what
it meant,

Generides had mervell what it ment;
As he came owt Mirabell ther he founde;

And as sche was comyng inward to his tent, 5662
Of hir he was full gladde in his entente,
And seid, 'mayde Mirabell, benedicite;
What thyng hath brought yow into this contre?' 5665

and asked
Mirabell what
had brought
her thither.

'I shall,' quod sche, 'telle yow the mater playn, 5666
And of my comyng heder all the case;
This fals traytour that here this day was slayn, 5669
he came and told to my lady Clarionas,
That ye were weddid onto lucidas,
And on his fynger ther he brought a ryng, 5672
Whiche sche gave yow Att your both departyng.

She told him
all Gusars's
treason,

and all about
the ring

For all his bost from hym I toke the ryng, 5673
My lady it forsoke, sche was so wroth;
The litill dog sche toke that he shuld bryng;
Butt as for that,' quod sche, 'I hadde them both : 5676
Now haue I told yow hough the mater goth.'
And he hir thankyd right curtesly,
And hir rewardid as sche was worthy. 5679

and the dog,

'As for the ryng,' quod sche, 'loo here it is ;' 5680
And furth with all delyueryd hym the ryng.
Generides knowe wele that it was his ;
'This ryng,' quod he, 'Darell had in kepyng : 5683
Wherefore,' quod he, 'me think it is a wonder thyng,
his trouth I knowe and haue don many a day,
The fawte is not in hym I dare wele say. 5686

and gave him
back the ring.

Now, fayre myrabell, go to hir ayeyn, 5687
ffor this I canne vnderstonde and fele,
Sche will not leve noo tidyngez in sertayn,
Butt if she here yow speke, this wote I well ; 5690
And yet Darell will tell hir euery dele,
Yet will she geve noo credence I am sure,
Butt ye be ther, ellys to noo creature. 5693

'Go to her again,
fair Mirabell,

and tell her how
unkind she is to
mistrust me.'

And ferthermore I prae yow telle hir this,   5694
Me to mystroste trewly she is vnkynd,
ffor o thing' shall I say, and trew it is,
Vntrew to hir she shall me neuer fynde,   5697
And this I will remembre in my mende
Eche creature of nature hym) delitith,
That on) good turne another quytith.'   5700

At this Mirabell
took her leave.

With these wordes Mirabell ganne to smyle,   5701
hir leve she toke, and furth she goth hir waye ;
Of ser Darell now late vs speke a while,
Whiche hastith hym) as fast as euer he may,   5704
So ferre fourth he was on) his¹ Iurnay,

Sir Darell came
to Mountoner,

That into the land of perse aryvid he,
And came to Mountoner the fayre Citee.   5707

and went straight
to Clarionas.

Full streyght he went onto Clarionas,   5708
And to her chaunber toke the redy waye,
he knockyd softely as the maner was,
Thanne came a mayde and this to hym) gan) say ; 5711

Her maid would
not admit him,

'Go fro the dore,' quod she, 'ser, I yow praye,
My lady had noo rest of all this nyght,
Nor slept not to now, I yow be hight.'   5714

Full fast he prayde, but neuer the neer he was, ·5715

[leaf 31]

And whanne he sawe it wold non) oyer wise be,

but he called
upon Clarionas,

he callyd alow vppon) Clarionas ;
'Madame,' quod he, 'please yow for to see ;   5718
I am Darell, now speke a word with me.'

who heard,
and said to the
maid,
'Open the door.'

Thanne spake Clarionas onto the mayde,
'Goo vpon) the chaumber dore,' she saide.   5721

Then Darell
came in,

Thanne Darell came in and knelid on) his kne,   5722
And thus he saide onto fayre Clarionas,
'ffrom) ynd I come to this contre,

¹ MS. hir.

Generides commaundith hym on to your grace ; 5725 and told her all about Generydes.
As for my comyng now this is the case,
Off yow he hath be dremyd passing sore,
Whiche dayly hym noyeth more and more.' 5728

Thanne he told hir the mater hough it was, 5729
She hard hym speke all his entente to fele ;
'lete be these wordes,' quod Clarionas, She professed at first not to
'This that ye say is lesyng euery dele, 5732 believe him.
Suppose ye not I vnderstonde yow wele ;
Generides, this is the mater playn), 'It is plain,' said she,
To lucydas is weddid for certeyn). 5735 'that Generydes is married to Lucidas.

To hir it is this message shuld be do, 5736 This message should be to her.'
And not to me, for I haue not to dow with all.'
'Now good madame,' [quod he,] 'why say yow soo ?
My message is to yow in especiall, 5739
Now please it yow onto your mynd to call,
hough good, hough trew he was to yow alwaye,
And yet is he the same this dare I say. 5742

Off lucidas,' quod he, 'ye may be sure, 5743 Darell then told of his own love for Lucidas,
ffor I shall tell yow trough withoute feyning,
I love hir best of eny creature ;
She sent to me, noo malyce supposyng, 5746 and how the ring had been obtained.
By hir moderys subtile ymagening,
The ryng to borow of Generides,
Seying she had a frende in grete distresse. 5749

The ryng, she said, wold make hym hoole ayeyn, 5750
And for that cause I sent it lucidas ;
Now wote ye wele, it was but for a trayn
Serenydes it had, this is the case ; 5753
That false Gusare the messanger he was,
ffor yow and for Generides also,
To make a variaunce betwix yow bo.[1] 5756

[1] MS. *bothe.*

This is,' quod he, 'the trowth that I have seide,   5757
And putt me to what othe that ye list.'
In here conseite thanne was she weH apayde,
'To you,' quod she, 'now haue I noo mystrost.'   5760
'.Trewly, Madame,' quod he, 'and I had it wist,
That ye shuld me mystrost in my message,
I had not A take vppon me this viage.'   5763

With that she became friendly,

With that she made hym very frendly chere,   5764
And whanne the Sowdon wist of his comyng,
To hir he went som tidynggez for to here,

and the Sultan welcomed Sir Darell,

And gave ser DareH anone his welcomyng;   5767
'What tidynges now,' quod he, 'do yow bryng?'
'ffor certayn, ser,' he seide, 'suche as thei be,
To yow I wiH declare the very certente.   5770

who told him that Parentyne was closely besieged,

The Sege is leyde to parentyne,' quod he,   5771
'A grete dele nerrer thanne it was before,
TĥE gates ar aH shett of that Citee,
And of vitayle thei haue but easy store,   5774
Nor non may haue, to say yow ferthermore;
So streyte them kepitĥ auferius the kyng,
That owt thei may not for noo maner thing.   5777

and that Generydee was at Vice.

Generides lithe atte Citee of vice,   5778
Whiche is the strongetĥ Citee of aH the land;
he hatĥ besegyd it in suche a wise,
That thei may not skape I vnderstonde,   5781
The contre hoole obeyetĥ to his hand.'
The Sowdon hard hym wele, and this he seid,
'Of these tidynges I am rigĥt wele apayde;   5784

'I would he were here,' said the Sultan, 'for Gwynan is in the land,

Butt now I wold he were here witĥ me,   5785
TeH hym so, DareH, in eny maner wise.
Gwynan the kyng is now in this contre,

And to my land he doth grete preiudice,   5788
Therfore haue I nede of his seruice.'   and I have need
'Ser,' quod Darell, 'as fast as I canne goo,   of his service.'
In all the hast your crande shalbe doo.'   5791

Syr Darell toke his leve and went his way,   5792   Sir Darell took
Whiche euer hath be founde both good and trew ;   his leave,
Mirabell is homeward in hir Iurnay,
Ser Darell and she mette togeder now,   5795   and met Mirabell
Echeon told suche tidynggez as thei cowde,   coming home-
Betwix them was noo lenger abideng,   ward.
Butt furth they rode withoute more taryeng.   5798

Ser Amelok came owt of the Citee of vice,   5799   Sir Amelok heard
With sertayn of his pepill furth he went,   that Generydes
ffor it was told hym in credibill[1] wise,   lay sick,
Generides lay seke in his own tent,   5802   and came out of
Whiche boldith hym the more in his entent ;   the city.
yet were thei blynd in that opynyon,
ffor he was rideng owt before the town.   5805

Now is ser Darell come ayeyn to ynd,   5806   [leaf 31, back]
And furth withall into the feld he went,   Sir Darell rode
ffull fast rideng Generides to fynde,   over the field in
And furth withall he sought hym in to ye tent,   5809   search of
To telle hym all the effecte of his entent,   Generydes,
Butt ther he founde non erthely creature,
So furth he rode seching his aventure ;   5812

And with a Duke of Ethiope he mette,   5813   and met with
Vppon a courser crossyng hym the way ;   a duke of
Eche vppon other ferly on they sett,   Ethiopia,
And or thei partid, shortly for to say,   5816
The duke was slayn and in the feld he lay :   whom he slew.
Whanne lucidas hym saw thanne was she fayn,   Lucidas saw this
And glad she was of his comyng ageyn.   5819   and was glad.

[1] MS. credilbill.

Generides thought wele that it was he,   5820
And furth with all came rideng apace,
'Darell,' he seid, 'right welcom be ye,
What tydinges bryng yow fro Clarionas?'   5823
'To telle yow,' quod he, 'I haue noo space,
Goo now on and take your seasone as¹ it is ;
ffor all is well, ther is noo thyng Amysse.'   5826

Full wele apayde thaunc was Generides,   5827
And in his mynd reioysid passing wele,
In to the feld he rode among the prece,
And in his way he mette ananyell,   5830
A manly knyght, the story canne yow tell,
A wise man and sadde in euery case,
And broder onto ser Amelok he was.   5833

Anon thei ranne togeder in the feld   5834
With sperys sharpe, and made no more delay ;
he smote Generides vppon the sheld,
The sheld to brast and fro hym fell away ;   5837
And as his grace and fortune was that day,
The spere ranne down by generides side,
And ellys withoute fayle ther had he dyed.   5840

And furth with all² or they departid yer,   5841
Generides thanne smote hym so ayeyn,
That thorough owt the body ranne the spere,
And with that stroke Ananyell was slayn,   5844
Down from his hors he felle vppon the playn ;
And whanne ser Amelok saw all the case,
ffor his broder an hevy man he was,   5847

And to ser Darell he ranne with spere & sheld ;   5848
Thanne lucydas was sory in hir hert,
To see them twayn togeder in ye feld,

¹ MS. *at.*   ² MS. *all all.*

Side notes:

Generydes rode to meet him,

and asked news of Clarionas.

'All is well,' said Darell.

Generydes was well pleased,

and rode into the press, and met with Ananyell,

the brother of Amelok.

He narrowly escaped his spear,

but struck him dead in return.

Sir Amelok saw this,

and ran at Sir Darell.

And fast sho praydo that thei myght sone departe,
like as nature required for hir part :
Butt bote was non) to pray ne for to trete,
And bothe thei mette anon) with speris grote.   5854

Full long' thei fought, to say yow ferthermore,   5855
And longer wold haue dow as by ther will
Vnder them) bothe ther stedys feynted sore,
That bothe togeder to the grownde ganne yᵈ fall, 5858
Ser Dareli in tho feld ther lay he still,
The preso was suche he myght not gete away,
Butt still defendid hym) ther as he lay.   5861

They fought till their horses fell under them.

The crowd was so great, Sir Darell could not get away.

Syr amelok was holpyn) att his nede,   5862
his knyghtes came and fechid hym) anon) ;
Sone after that ser Dareli was on) his stede,
With that Generides came rideng on),   5865
They made hym) rome among' them) euerychone,
And where that euer he rode in eny side,
Ther was non) in tho feld wold hym) abide.   5868

At length Generydes came up, and they made room for him.

Tho dede body vppon) a sheld they layde,   5869
Toward the Citee thei caried it anon) ;
Ser amelokkez men) were so dismayde,
To the Citee thei fled his pepili euerychon),   5872
And yet ther were distroyed many on),
And or thei myght gete the Citee, this is sertayn),
An C knyghtes were take and slayn).   5875

Ananyell's body was carried to the city,

Whanne thei were in thei shette ye gates fast,   5876
Ananyell thei beried furth with all ;
Thanne afterward in all tho possible hast,
Too knyghtes thei sent echone in generall,   5879
This was the message in especiall,
ffull tenderly Generides for to praye,
To graunt them) truse for ij monethis day,   5882

and buried.

Two knights were sent to Generydes to ask for two months' truce,

His knyghtes for to bery euerychone.   5883

he grauntid them) and was right wele apayde,
Ser Darell thanne he callid furth anow),
And Natanell Also, and this he saide ;   5886
' The trewse is now appoyntid and prevyed
Betwix the Cite and Me ij monethys day,
And now I will goo see Clarionas I say.   5889

Wherefore, Darell, I prae yow now,' quod he,   5890
' That ye will do so moche as take the payn),
To rewle these men), that hir be vnder me,
In my absence as lord and cheff³ capteyn),   5893
Or ought it be long⁴ I will be here ayayn),
And if ther fortune eny hasty nede,
Thanne will I come as fast as I may spede.   5896

Off⁴ knyghtes And squyers that be here,   5897
Of them) will I haue A C and no moo ;
ffull secretly,' he seid, ' in all maner,

I wold they were warnyd with me to goo ;   5900
And say to Sygrem that he come also
In eny wise, that he may be my gide,
ffull wele he knowith the wayes on) euery side.'   5903

In this meane tyme thanne was come home ayeyn)
Mirabell on) to fayre Clarionas ;
She saide, ' Madame, Generides for certayn)
hym recomaundid onto your' good grace   5907
In humble wise, and as for lucidas,
hir for to wedde came neuer in his thoght ;
The messenger is slayn) that the tidynges broght.

And so furth on) she told all the hole processe,   5911
hough that she founde Generides sertayn),
All discomfortid in right greto hevynes ;

Thanne saide Clariouas to hir ayeyn,   5914
'Moche thank to yow for your labour' a[nd] payn.'
And thus I leve them bothe in hartys case,
And ferthermore I will speke of Generides.   5917

Now toward perse rideth Generides,   5918   As Generydes
Takyng' his viage in the evyn tide,   was riding
And of his[1] Iurnay wold he neuer sese,   towards Persia
Till he came ther wher he shuld abide ;   5921
With hym ther went Sygrem to be his gide,
Costyng' the contre many dyuers way,
And so came he in to perse the redy waye.   5924

The contre was distroyed in that tide,   5925
And as he rode vppon the way,
A lady he sawe rideng' be a forest side,   he saw a lady
Grete hast she had on hir Iurnay,   5928   by a forest side,
To hir he rode withoute more delay,
Whanne she hym saw come toward hir so fast,   and rode after
        her.
Away fro hem she fledde in all the hast.   5931   She fled,

With hir ther were xviij. in company,   5932
Generides rode after hir so fast,
And on his way so fast he ganne hym hye,
he ouer toke the lady atte last ;   5935   but he overtook
        her,
'Madame,' he seid, ' be ye noo thyng' agast,   and told her no
        one should do
Why ride ye thus and in so hasty wise ?   her harm.
Ther shall no man do yow harme o warantise.'   5938

'In trowth I am a wedow, ser,' quod she,   5939   'I am a widow,
        said she, 'and
'The Sowdon is myn vncle in certayn ;   the Sultan is my
        uncle.
kyng' Gwynan wold that I weddid shuld be   King Gwynan
        wishes to marry
To his Cosyn, and me he wold constreyne   5942   me to his cousin,
        but I will not,
So for to do ; this is the mater playn :   and therefore am
        fleeing to
And thus fro hym in all the hast I went,   Mountoner.'
Because I wold not folow his entent.   5945

[1] MS. *hus.*

Too Mounton*er* now I witt take my way,   5946
And with myn vnkitt ther I witt abide,
ffor here I leve in drede and in affray.'

' Madam,' quoth
he, ' I pray you
be our guide to
Gwynan.'
'Madame,' qu*o*d he, 'I p*ra*e god be your gide,   5949
After kyng Gwynan I purpose me to ryde,
ffayne I wold knowe the way and not to mys.'
'I shatt yow tell,' qu*o*d she, 'where that he is.   5952

' He is here in a
castle a mile or
two off,
In a castett here be a forest side,   5953
ffrom hens it passith not a myle or twayne,
hold on your way streight as ye ride,
And ther ye shatt hym fynde, this is certayn,   5956
waiting for the
king of Spain,
A bideng ther Otran the kyng of spayne,
Whiche comyth the kyng to helpe I vnderstonde,
To warre vppon my vncle and his lande.'   5959

'Now, Madame,' thanne seid Generides,   5960
'What pepytt hath he ther? I p*ra*e yow say.'
'Trewly,' qu*o*d she, 'as ferre as I canne gesse,
with 200 men,
he passith not CC men this day,   5963
And Chosen men they be in good arraye,
he is noo thyng a drede in certente,
and every day he
goes hunting.'
ffor eu*er*y day on huntyng rideth he.'   5966

'Madame,' qu*o*d he, 'thanne I beseche yow this,   5967
That it may plese yow do so meche for me,
Whanne ye be ther as your vncle is,
That I to hym may recomaundid be,   5970
A knyght of Surre gladly wold hym see,
Butt now I may not come, the cause is soo,
ffor I witt seche the kyng where eu*er* he goo.'   5973

The lady went on
to Mountoner,
Too Mountoner the lady toke the waye,   5974
And to the forest Generides is gon,
And whanne it was ferre past on the day,

In a buschement he layde his men echo on,   5977
And thanne he callid Sygrem furth anon;
'Sygrem,' quod he, 'afore all other thyng,
I prae yow wete where lith Gwynan the kyng. 5980

Off his demeanyng I wold wete also,   5981
And with my felisshepe I will abide.'
'Ser,' quod Segyrem, 'anon it shalbe doo;
Att your commaundment now I will ride, 5984
And bryng yow worde her be the forest side.'
Now goth Segrym, withoute more taryeng,
To monperson, and ther he founde the kyng. 5987

The town was fast by the castell wher he lay, 5988
Thorough owt the town he went among ye prese,
And whanne that he had Aspyed all yer array,
Agayn he came vnto Generides; 5991
'I shall yow telle,' quod he, 'that is noo leese,
I left them ther att dyner cuerychon,
And to this forest he will come anon. 5994

Armyd thei be eche on atte poynte device, 5995
here will thei hunte I say yow verily;
Butt this I councell yow be myn avise,
Whanne yow them se late them go by and by, 5998
Till thei be passid thanne may ye them askry.
And this suerly if ye do after me,
Betwix them and the Castell shall ye be. 6001

And ferthermore,' as my Auctor doth write, 6002
'Gwynan if ye will [know] whereuer he be,
his owne Array is all togeder white,
hors and harnes and so is non but he, 6005
his spere also is white, that ye shall see,
Now haue I sayde, do as ye semes best,
here will he come anon in to this forest.' 6008

Side notes: and Generydes laid his men in ambush, and sent Sygrem to find where Gwynan was. He found him at Monperson, and came and told Generydes [leaf 32, back] they were all at dinner, and were coming out to hunt. Gwynan dressed all in white.

The king rode out, Anon) vppon) [on] huntyng⸲ rode the kyng⸲,   6009
                    Generides was ware therof anon),

and Generydes kept his men quiet till they were all past, No noyse was made nor ther was noo steryng⸲,
                    To tyme the kyng⸲ and aH his men) were goon);   6012
                    And whanne that thei were passid euerychon),

when he called to them to turn. Generides anon) hym) ganne Askerye,
                    And bad them) ' turne, for tyme it is trewly.'   6015

The king turned his horse, With that the kyng⸲ his hors he turnyd then),   6016
                    And to his knygHtes aH thanne he saye,
                    ' Serys, now is tyme to shewe that we be men),
                    ffor yender folk will lette vs of our⸲ way.'   6019
                    Anone thei mette them) withoute more delay,

and in the first encounter lost 20 of his knights, And atte first encounteryng⸲ certayn),
                    kyng⸲ Gwynan had xx. of his knygthes slayn) :   6022

and 15 were taken. And xv more were taken) furtH with aH,   6023
                    Where witH the kyng⸲ was greuyd passyng⸲ sore,
                    And sware his othe what euer shuld hym) falle,
                    he wold⸲ suerly avenge hym) therfore,   6026

In revenge the king slew Lucas, And in that hete, to say yow ferthermore,
                    Anon) he ranne to lucas witH a spere,
                    And bare hym) thorougH and slewe hym) ther.   6029

                    Whanne he was dede ther was grete hevynes,   6030
and Generydes was full sad thereat, remembering all his love and kindness. And witH Generides was fuH hevy chere,
                    Remembryng⸲ the grete love and kyndnes,
                    Whiche he had shewid to hym) in aH maner ;   6033
                    And specially whanne he was prisoner,
                    And by his meane the Sowdon) gave hym) grace,
                    Whanne he so long⸲ lay in prisone for Clarionas.   6036

He then ran at Gwynan, And for by cause kyng⸲ Gwynan had hym) slayn),   6037
                    To go vn quyte he thougHt noo wurchippe in,
                    And witH his spere ranne toward hym) ageyn),

Thanne was ther on of the kynggez kynne,   6040

but one of his
kin came between,

Betwene them bothe his wurchippe for to wynne,
And with a spere in myddes of the prese,
ffurth with all he ranne vnto Generides.   6043

And bothe thei motte to geder in the feld,   6044
And for to tell yow all the mater playn,
Generides stroke hym thorough the sheld

and was pierced
by the spear.

Owt atte bak, and slow hym for certeyn;   6047
And whanne ther felawes were take And slayn,

At this the king's
men drew back,
and scattered
themselves,

A bak thei drewe, and sperkelyd her and yer,
Thanne was the kyng full wrothe in his maner,   6050

And blew his horn to geder them to bryng,   6051
ffull sory he was to se them goo so wide;
Thanne seid Sampson these wordes to ye kyng,
Off Cornyssh was he born, and of that side;   6054
'It is noo tyme here for vs to Abide,
Drawe to your Castellward, and that anon,
ffor here we do butt lese oure men euerychon.'   6057

Too monpersone the kyng with drew hym yaw,   6058

The king
withdrew to
Monperson,
pursued by
Generydes.

Generides hym folowid in the chase;
'Syr,' quod Sygrem, 'thus shall yow lese your men,
And wery them, withynne a short space: 6061
Butt this me think better in this case;
Gete yow be fore, this wold I yow avise,

'Get between
him and the
town,' said
Sygrem.

Betwix hym and the town in eny wise.'   6064

Generides dede after Sygrems councell,   6065
And to blanchard his stede he saide,

Generydes called
upon his steed
Blanchard,

'Blanchard,' quod he, 'thow dost me neuer fayle,
Nor vppon the I was neuer ovtrayde.'   6068
With these wordes thoughtfull in A brayde
A nother way he rode, and in a while

and outstripped
Gwynan by half
a mile.

he was be fore the kyng welle half a myle.   6071

He crossed
his path,

And whanne the kyng' perscivid that it was he,   6072
Adrede he was, And litill wold he say ;
And verily he thought not hym for to Asse,
Nor hym to mete he thought no more y^t day :   6075
Generides thanne crossid hym the way ;

and told him
he should go
no further,
except he did
battle for
Clariouas.

'This way,' quod he, 'thu shalt noo ferther pas,
Or thu do armys for fayre Clarionas.'   6078

The kyng' sawe well he myght now oyer way,   6079
Nor to the town he myght not ride in pece ;
Anon he dressid hym in his arraye,

[leaf 38]

And thanne he turnyd vnto Generides :   6082

At the first
encounter both
their spears
broke,

Ther mette thei bothe withoute the prese,
And shortly the processe for to make,
Atte first encounteryng' bothe ther sperys brake.   6085

and they went
to work with
their swords.

With yer swerdes to geder thei went,   6086
And layde euerychone on other strokes grete,

The sparks flew
from them,

The fyre sparkelid and fro the harneys glynt ;
Betwix them twayne it was noo tyme to trete,   6089
All maner love and frenshippe was forgete,
The kyng' in his conseite he was stronge,
he thought noman shuld fight with hym so long'.   6092

and Generydes'
shield was
broken.

Hee strake Generides vppon the sheld,   6093
It all to brast in peces to and fro,
The handdell it fell in to the feld,
A grace of god that he askapyd soo,   6096
That with that stroke his arme was not a twoo !

'Go now,' said
the king.

Thanne seid the kyng', 'if thu wilt leve in rest,
Goo now thy way and hold it for the best.'   6099

Generydes
was wroth,

Generides wrothe was in his maner,   6100
That he shuld byd hym voyde owt of ye place,
Remembryng' whiche was to hym soo dere,

That fayre lady, that mayde Clarionas,   6103
he thought to ease his hert as in this case,
And ther with aH, withoute more taryeng,   *and struck him on the helmet,*
Vppon) the helme he smote Gwynan the kyng,   6106

And the helme to brast that was good and strong,
A quarter of it feH vppon) the grene,   *cutting off a quarter of it,*
The swerde ranne down) and clave y⁰ sheld along,   *and cleaving his shield*
And ij fynger⁹ he smote[1] of quyte and clene,   6110 *and two of his fingers.*
Thanne was he bare his visage mygHt be sene,
AH discomfeyte and aH forbled Also,
That in noo wise he wist not what to do.   6113

Thanne spake the kyng, and seid in y¹ᵉ maner,   6114 *'Who are you?' said the king.*
'what maner a man), be ye? I prae yow say ;
ffor I wiH figHt with yow noo longer here,   *'I will fight no more.*
My swerd and aH I yeld it vppe this daye ;   6117 *Here is my sword.'*
What is your name?' quod he, 'I prae you say '
'Trewly my name,' quod he, 'I wiH not layn),   *'My name is Generydes.'*
Generides men) calle me for certayn).'   6120

The kyng toke hym) his swerd, and seid ayeyn),   6121 *Gwynan gave up his sword, and said,*
'Though I have ben) Ayenst yow in this case,
yet am I not blame worthy in certayn),   *'I am not to blame,*
By yow only my fader slayn) was,   6124 *you slew my father.*
Butt now it is for govyn) certayn) y⁹ trespas,
And this I wold desire of yow also,   *Let me go to my land, and I will*
In to my land that I may savely goo.   6127

AH this I wiH ensure yow be myn) othe,   6128 *never trouble the Sultan more.'*
ShaH I neuer the Sowdon) trobiH more,
hym nor his land ; and for his ayris bothe,
I wiH be sworne like as I seid before,   6131
ffor I saw neuer that day sithe I was bore[2],
Atte my fuH age and was att mannys mygHt,
That euer I medled with soo good a knygHt.'[3]   6134

[1] MS. *swete*.   [2] MS. *born*.   [3] MS. *kyng*.

Generydes in
jest asked,
' What say you
now about
Clarionas ? '

Generides in Iapyng⸱ said agayn),   6135
' What sey ye now as for Clarionas ? '
' Syr,' quod the kyng⸱, 'with grete trobiłł,

' You have bought
her full dear,'
said the king ;
' she is yours.'

ffułł dere ye haue hir bought, this is ye case ;   6138
Now is she yourez by fortune and by grace,
And I am wełł content that it be soo,
And as for my part now ther with I haue doo.' 6141

Peace was
proclaimed,

After ałł this whanne pece was made and Ałł,   6142
The kyng therof sent tydinges to his ost,
Thanne were thei glad his men in esspeciałł,
Among them) Ałł whiche of them) myght be most,
The pece was cryed abought in euery cost,

and they rode
together to
Monperson.

The kyng⸱ and he no longer ther abode,
To monpersone to geder thanne they rode.   6148

Theder were come the kynges men) before ;   6149
As sone as he hym) see he seide anon),
' Now serys,' quod he, ' withoute eny more
I wold^t that ye went homeward euerychon) :   6152
The pece is made and ałł the werre is gon).
Now hye yow fast, I canne noo ferder say,
And I shałł come as sone as euer I may.'   6155

The Sultan had
dreamed that
Gwynan and
Generydes fought,

Now speke we of the Sowdon) in this case,   6156
Whiche hard^t no maner thing⸱ of Ałł y^is pece,
And in this mater dremyd sore he was ;
hym thought kyng⸱ Gwynan and Generides   6159
had fought hand to hand, yet neuer the lesse

and that Gwynan
was thrown into
a river.

Right this hym) thought it happid atte last,
That in A Ryuer Generides hym) cast.   6162

The kyng⸱ hym) thought for mercy yanne he prayde,
Generides thanne toke hym) vppe to grace ;
Whanne this was do, this dreme Aforescid

he told them) AH in to fayre Clarionas ;   6166
Thanne was the lady present in the place,
whiche with Generides spake on) the way,
She had forgete hir erande for to say.   6169

Full vmbely of pardon) she hym) prayde,   6170
' To yow I haue offendid, ser,' quod she,
' ffor Amessage the whiche I shuld haue seide ;
Ther is a knyght come in to this contre,   6173
To yow he recomaundid hym) be me,
his name he wold not telle me, ne what he hight,
Of Surre he[1] was born) the gentiH knyght.   6176

Right wele armed this knyght is also,   6177
And gladly wold haue sene yow or he went,
Butt nedis he must owt of this contre goo.'
Thanne was Clarionas not weH contente,   6180
ffor wele she vnderstode in hir entent,
And euer in one she thought stiH opece,
That it shuld be hir love Generides.   6183

And for by cause she had hym) in mystrost,   6184
Allway she demyd the[2] wold hir quyte,
hym) to Absente awhile while that hym) list,
And so to putte his comyng in respite ;   6187
Thanne ferthermore, as my auctour doth wete,
The kyng and Generides for ther disporte and play,
Att Mounperson) to geder bothe thei lay,   6190

Att ther pleasure ij dayes or a litiH more,   6191
And thanne to Mountoner he toke the way ;
Sygrem was made the messenger before,
Onward to goo as fast as euer he may   6194
To the Sowdon), commaundyng them) to say :
" The warre is att anende, and aH is pece
Betwix kyng Gwynan and Generides,   6197

Side notes:
He tells it to Clarionas, and then the lady who had spoken with Generydes

remembered the message of the strange knight.

[leaf 33, back]

Clarionas guessed who it was.

Gwynan and Generydes stay at Mounperson two days or more,

and then go to Mountoner, sending Sygrem before to say that the war was over.

---
[1] MS. _of he,_ but _of_ is struck out.   [2] So MS. for _that he_ ?

Neuer to vex the Sowdon and his land,   6198
With grete suerte in euery maner thyng.'

Sygrem delivers
his message,

'Now hath Sygrem this message take in hand,
To the Sowdon the tidyngges doth he bryng';   6201
Thanne was he glad, as eny man leving,

and the Sultan
goes and tells
Clarionas.

hym self he goth onto Clarionas,
And told hir all these tidyngges hough it was;   6204

And hough the kyng and he shuld mete Also,   6205
In the forest appoyntid betwix them twayn :
'Butt trow ye, ser¹, that it be now soo?'
'yae, dought ye not,' quod he, 'it is certayn;   6208
Sygrem is come which is bothe trew and playn,
ffro thense he come, he knowith all in fere,
he shall tell yow the trougth of this mater.'   6211

Now goth Sygrem as fast as euer he may   6212
To hir chaunber, and told hir this processe ;
'The warre is done,' quod she, 'this here I say ;'
'Madame,' he seid, 'for certayn all is pece ;   6215

She asks
'Where is
Generydes ?'
'At Mounperson,'
said Sygrem.

'Butt now,' quod she, 'where is Generides?'
'ffor sothe,' he seide, 'I left hym with yᵉ kyng,
To Mounperson he is withoute feyneng.'   6218

'And is he not
coming here ?'

'Butt will he not come heder now?' quod she;   6219
'Madame,' quod he, 'of that I canne not say,
ffor atte this tyme I trow it will not be ;

'No, madam,
he is going back
again to India as
fast as he can.'

his purpose is to ryde another waye,   6222
ffourth in to ynd as fast as euer he may,
ffor to his ost he must take hede among,
his people after hym think full long.'   6225

From hir he went withoute wordes moo,   6226
To the Sowdon furth he goth his way ;
'My lord,' quod he, 'it is good tyme to goo,

¹ MS. *serp*.

ffor ye wiłł mete witł hym) I dare wełł say.'   6229
Now gotł the Sowdoų furtł in good array,
With lordes and witł knygłtes many oų),
Toward the forest rode thei euerychone.   6232

The Sultan and his lords ride forth to the forest to meet him.

In this meane while abode Clarionas   6233
Iu hir chaunber, noo thyng¹ in hartes ease,
Gretly musyng¹ and in fułł hevy case,
Whanne she be thougłt hir oų Generides;   6236
And Alway she remembryd stiłł opece,
hougł she had mystrostid hym) before,
Supposyng¹ wełł he¹ wold se hir nomore.   6239

Meanwhile Clarionas was ill at ease in her chamber.

To Mirabełł thanne tolª she ałł hir hart,   6240
Iu euery thing¹ as it felle in hir mynde;
'Madame,' quod she, 'for eny wo or smerte
That euer he had, I wist hym) neuer on kynde,   6243
So vncurtese ye shałł hym) neuer fynde;
And ferthermore I warantt yow,' quod she,
'Or it be long¹ here witł yow wiłł he be.'   6246

Mirabell consoles her,

saying, that Generydes will soon be here.

To the forest the Sowdoų dotł ride,   6247
And first of ałł he mette Generides,
Thanne came the kyng¹ along¹ by yᵉ forestes side,
And whanne that thei were mett in ałł yᵉ prese,   6250
And made betwix them) bothe a fyniałł pece,
And witł a suraunce swornų) in broderhode,
Togeder bothe in grete frendshippe thei rode.   6253

The Sultan met Generydes and the King in the forest,

and peace was made.

Thanne they departid bothe the kyng¹ and he,   6254
In ałł maters to beų of oų assentt;
The kyng¹ gothe homeward in to his contre,
The Sowdoų streigłt to Mountoner he went;   6257
Generides ther was witł hym) present,
And praycth hym) of licence for to goo,
The Sowdoų mervelid why he shuld do so.   6260

The King goes home,

and Generydes asks leave to depart.

¹ MS. *I.*

'Will you not
come and see
Clarionas?'

'Wyll[1] ye not come and see Clarionas?'   6261
'Noo trewly, ser,' he seid, 'that may not be;
I must praye yow of pardon in this case,

'No, sir, I must
go back to India.'

ffor in to ynd now must I goo,' quod hee :   6264
Another tyme I purpose hir to see ;

[leaf 34]

And in certayn, herof ye may be sure,
I love hir best of eny creature.'   6267

Fro the Sowdon Generides is gon,   6268

He then sends his
men back to
Mouperson,

And to his men he seid this for certayn ;
'To Mounperson I will that ye goo euerychon,
And ther to Abide in to the tyme I come Ayeyn ; 6271

and he and
Sygrem go
secretly to
Montoner,

Sygrem and I, this is the mater playn,
To Mowntoner we will goo sekyrly,
In secrete wise noman but he and I.'   6274

Now is Sygrem gon with Generides,   6275
To Mountoner he take the way full right,
Savyng thei twoo ther was non other preese,

and at night he
stands in the
garden, near her
chamber,

Theder thei came be thanne[2] it was nyght;   6278
Generides whanne it was sterre light,
hym self anon gothe vnto Clarionas,
Thorough owt the gardeyn wher hir chaunber was. 6281

and hears a
woman's voice
complaining.

Whanne he came ther he hard a womannes voyce, 6282
In pytues wise complayneng more and more,
Save only deth ther was non other choyse,
She had so meche hevynes in store,   6285
vnkyndnes had greuyd hir so sore,
That Generides was in the countre her,
Butt see hir wold he not in noo maner.   6288

And whanne Generides had hard hir speke,   6289

He knew it was
Clarionas,

Thanne wist he wele it was fayre Clarionas,
ffor very payn hym thought his hert wold broke,

        ¹ MS. Uyll.   ² MS. be twanne.

And in hym self discomfcyte sore he was,   6292
Spoke myght he not as for a certcyn space,
Butt down he fell and ther withall he cryed ;   and for very pain
Myrabell hym hard and sone hym had Aspyde.   6295   he fell down with
                                                        a cry.

'Myrabell,' she seid, 'what may this be ?   6296   Mirabell heard
Whanne I hym hard mervell it was.'   him, and said,
'In hevy plight my lady is,' quod she.
'Whom speke ye to ?' thanne seid Clarionas :   6299
'Madame,' quod she, 'in sothe this is the case,   'Here is
Now shall ye fynde me trew in my seruice,   Generydes at the
here atte wyndow is generides.'   6302   window.'

Thanne with thoo wordes arose Clarionas,   6303   At these words
And to the wyndow came she all dismayde ;   Clarionas came to
Generides full redely ther he was,   the window,
Ther was kyssyng butt noo wordes were seid ;   6306   and then there
Eche of oyer wer full well apayd :   was kissing,
Anone thei putt All hevynes away,   but not a word
And thanne Clarionas beganne to saye :   6309   said.
                                                               Then Clarionas
                                                               began,

'Generides, why are ye so vnkynd,   6310   'Generydes, why
In this contre so long As ye haue be ?   are you so
Me thought I was full litill in your mynde,   unkind ?'
And all be cause ye wold not come to me.'   6313
Thanne seid Generides, 'Madame,' quod he,   'Madam,
'I yow beseche of pardon in this case,
In very trought a litill thyng ther was.   6316

Ye wend that I had be weddid in certayn   6317   you thought
To lucidas, whiche grevid me full soore ;   I was married to
To yow alway I haue be trew and playn,   Lucidas.
¹Now haue I lete yow wete why and wherfore,   6320   I have always
And yet I am mystrostid euermore,   been true to you,
In easyng of myn hert I haue don this,   and yet you
ffor now is all for geven that is amys.   6323   mistrust me.
                                                               But all is forgiven.

¹ This and the following line should be transposed.

Off yow I must haue licence for to go   6324
ffurth in to ynd, and therof haue I nede ;
My felisshepe they wote not who to do,
The treson of ser Amelok I drede :   6327
In all the hast homeward I will me spede,

ffor euer the sonner that I goo certeyn),
Meche the sonner thanne I will come ayeyn).'   6330

Quod she ayeyn), 'my reson) doth me bynde,   6331
And as ferre furth as I canne vnderstonde,
I canne wele think your' goyng' in to ynd
Shalbe wurchippe and profight to your' land,   6334
Your' pepill glad to wete yow so nygh hande :
wherfore,' quod she, 'if I me well avise,
I may nott be ayenst it in noo wise.'   6337

That nyght they were to geder as I rede,   6338
Nor sownyng' to [no] villany ne shame,
In grete pleasure and in all goodlyhede ;
She made hym) chere and he dede hir ye same,   6341
In feithfull wise withoute spotte or blame,
Anone with all withoute spotte or evill fame bothe ;[1]
Whanne it was day, though thei were neuer so loth.

To Mounperson) rideth Generides,   6345
In company with hym) Sygrem is gon),
his men) were ther abideng' still opece,
like as he had commaundid hym) before ichcon), 6348
Thei made no taryeng' but furth anon),
With hors and harnes in ther best Array,
Streight in to ynde thei toke the [redy] way.   6351

Whanne he was come ther as the pepill lay,   6352
Thanne were thei Ioyfull euery creature ;
Ser amelok full bold he was that daye,

---

[1] This line is corrupted by the copyist from the preceding.

ffor vnder a trete at All aventure   6355
Of ser DareH he thought he had be sure :
Butt of his werkyng ser DareH knew it welI,
And so he brake his purpose euery dele.   6358

Generides rode streight into the feld   6359
With his knyghtes, for noo thyng wold he lette,
his stede was blak, his spere and eke his sheld,
Anone with alI with Sampson ther he mett ;   6362
Generides fuH fresshely on hym he sett,
Owt Atte bak he bare hym quyte and clene,
Sampsone felle down and dyed vppon the grene. 6365

Thanne came ser Amelok into the prese,   6366
And thought he wold a be avengyd for his sake,
Vppon the hede he smote Generides,
A quarter of his helme ther with he brake :   6369
Generides ther with to hym he spak,
'Thu wend,' quod he, 'that I had lakkid sight,
ffor now I may se better thanne I myght.'   6372

And ther with aH he smote ser Amelok   6373
Vppon the hede, and brast [his] helme in twayn ;
Downe by the cheke his ere away he strake,
AH quyte and clene it felle vppon the playn ;   6376
And with that stroke, I say yow the certayn,
his Arme was smette fro the body clene,
So from his hors he felle vppon the grene.   6379

Thanne was ser Amelok fuH woo begon,   6380
AH ouer come for angwissh and payn ;
his men were ther and reskewyd hym Anon,
vppon his sheld thei brought hym home ayeyn,   6383
AH for wondid and sore in euery vayne :
Thanne seid he this, complayneng passing sore,
'I haue deseruyd this though it were more.'   6386

Generydes rode straight into the [leaf 34, back] field,
and runs Sampson through.
Up came Sir Amelok to avenge him,
and struck Generydes on the head, cutting off a quarter of his helmet.
In return Generydes cleaves his helmet,
and cuts off his ear and arm,
so that he fell.
His men rescued him, and took him home.

Sir Darell knew
not of Generydes,

Syr Dareƚƚ wist not of Generides,   6387
B[utt] Alway demyd that[1] it shuld be he;
To Sygrem thanne he came in to the prese,

and asked Sygrem
who the knight
was on the black
horse.

'Sygrem,' seid he, 'teƚƚ me the very sertente,   6390
What knyght is that that I may yender see?
his stede is blak; good Sygrem, teƚƚ me this,
I canne weƚƚ think Generides it is.'   6393

'It is Generydes,'
quoth Sygrem.

'Syr,' quod Sygrem, 'it is as ye haue rede,   6394
Generides it is withoute fayle;
he come butt late and right weƚƚ hath he spedd,
Wherby his honour gretly doth prevayle,   6397
ffor he hath wonne kyng' Gwynau in bateƚƚ;
The corde is made, the mortuaƚƚ werre is sese,
Betwix hym and the Sowdon Aƚƚ is pece.' 6400

Sir Amelok,
on his bed,
repented of the
time past,

Now lith ser Amelok vppon his bed;   6401
Of tyme past fuƚƚ sore he doth repente,
Wery and feynt, his wondys Aƚƚ for bled,
A basshed passyng' sore in his entent,   6404

and sent for
Serenydes,

And for Serenydes anon he sent,
Whiche in hir mende fuƚƚ gretly was dismayde;
Whanne she was come right thus to hir he seid: 6407

'Madame,' quod he, 'ye vnderstonde fuƚƚ weƚƚ, 6408
Sithe I beganne to love yow first of Aƚƚ,
I haue my hert, my seruice, euery dele,
To yow allonly in especiaƚƚ;[2]   6411

and told her they
had both done
wrong.

And now reasone constreyneth me to caƚƚ
Vnto my mend and to my remembraunce this,
Bothe ye and I haue done ferre Amys.   6414

'I made you
leave my lord
Auferius

Ye were the wyff of auferius the kyng',   6415
Whiche was my very lord and soucreyn,
And trayturly first Atte begynneng'

---

[1] MS. *that that.*   [2] MS. *especially.*

I made yow to forsake hym̄ in sertayn̄, 6418

And thanne vnder a false compassion̄ trayn̄, and the land to rebel.

The lande anon̄ and I were atte accorde,

To be rebeH ayenst our̄ soueryn̄ lord. 6421

I take noo hede of aH this werk before, 6422

Wherfore I am in bytter paynes strong';

And though that I shuld suffer[1] meche more,

In very trouth I thinke it were noo wrong', 6425

As for my dayes thei wiH not now be long',

And fayne I woH my consciens were clere,

Wherfore anon̄ do calle a messenger, 6428

And to ser DareH chargid hym̄ to goo, 6429 Send now to Sir Darell

Besechyng hym̄ that he wiH speke with me ;

After his counceH gladly wold I doo,

To pray the kyng' of grace and it wold be, 6432 to pray the king of grace.'

On me to shew his mercy and pitee.'

A CarefuH woman̄ was Serenydes, Serenydes was sad, and wept.

And euer wept that no man̄ cowde hir sese. 6435

To lucydas she seid in this maner, 6436 To Lucidas she said, ' Daughter,

'Doughter,' quod she, 'this is now myn̄ entent ;

Your̄ fader wold, as towchyng' this mater,

That to ser DareH a messenger were sent ; 6439 send Sygrem to Darell,

It were weH done that Sygrem theder went,

And to your̄ fader prae hym̄ for to come, and pray him to come to your

In aH the hast, loo this is aH and som̄.' 6442 father.'

Now on̄ this message Sygrem furth [is] went, 6443 Sygrem goes on his message to Sir Darell,

To[2] ser DareH and this to hym̄ he seid ;

'The mayde lucidas now heder me sent,

And hir commaundement I haue obeyde ; 6446

ffor hir fader now good hath so purveyde,

A febyH man̄ he is, I yow ensure,

And in this liff he may not long' endure. 6449

---

[1] MS. suster.   [2] MS. And to.

This is the effecte of my massage,   6450
That ye will doo so mekill as take ye payn,
To come so ferre hir fader for to se,
The whiche gretly shuld counfort hym certayn; 6453

[leaf 35]
To speke with yow truly he wold be fayn,
That wote I wele, and she wold purvey so,
That ye shall savely come and savely goo.'   6456

Off these tidynges was he well contente,   6457
And part also as for his hartes ease;
Yet he remembryd hym or euer he went,
who asks leave of he wold haue licence of Generides,   6460
Generydes,
ffor in noo wise he wold not hym displease;
And her vppon he made noo lenger space,
To hym he goth and told hym all the case   6463

Off ser Amelok and of his repentaunce: 6464
Generides answerd, and this he seid;
'If I may fynde his wordes of substaunce,
In very trougth I will be well apayde.'   6467
'ffor my comyng his doughter hath so purveyde,
Ser,' quod Darell, 'and that in suche wise
I shall goo save and come o warantise.   6470

And to be playn to yow in euery wise,   6471
This is the cause that he hath sent for me;
telling him of his I owe his doughter trewly my seruice,
love for Lucidas.
So ye were well content ther with,' quod he;   6474
'Ellys will I not goo in very certente.'[1]
Off his wordis Generides was full fayn,
And smyling softely answerd thus ageyn: 6477

'Darell,' quod he, 'I know this very sure,   6478
She is not long owt of your remembraunce,
Ye love hir best of eny creature;

---

[1] MS. *certentente.*

Wherin, god woote, I take noo displesaunce,   6481
ffor AH that may be for your foryeraunce,
I am contente to helpe yow to the same ;
Wherefore,' quod he, 'goth on in goddis name.' 6484

To the Castell ser Darell now is gon,   6485
Whanne he was come first atte begynneng,
his doughter lucidas mette hym Anon,
And thankfully she gave hym his welecomyng, 6488
Thanne furth with aH withoute eny more taryeng,
She brought hym to hir fader ther he lay,
Seke and febyH, full nye his endyng day.   6491

Syr amelok was glad of his comyng ;   6492
'Ser DareH, I prae yow, bere me witnesse,
This I desire above aH other thyng,
ffor to haue my pardon of Generides : 6495
I haue affendid sore, yet neuer the lesse
Of AH thynges that is past what euer it be,
Besechyng hym now of mercy and pite ; 6498

And of his fader auferius the kyng,   6499
If it wold be, fayne I wold haue his grace ;
ffor more vntrew ther was neuer non levyng,
Thanne I haue ben to hym as in this case : 6502
My life woH now endure butt short space,
Besechyng yow to prae Generides,
That he wold with his fader to make my pece. 6505

And for to do your dever in this case,   6506
Remembryng this mater euery dele,
here is,' quod he, 'my doughter lucidas,
The whiche, if I may vnderstonde and fele, 6509
That ye with hert and thought yt ye love hir wele,
She shaH be youres, lo this shalbo your wage,
And aH my land with hir in mariage. 6512

Pray also that
Serenydes may be
forgiven.'

And also, DareĦ, as for Serenydes,   6513
This I beseche yow hartely,' quod he,
'That ye spoke witĦ hir that she may haue hir pece,
And so to leve in rest and it wilbe :   6516
And pray Generides to spoke witĦ me,
So wold god that he were here present,
loo her is aĦ the effecte of myn) entente.'   6519

To lucidas he seid in this maner ;   6520
'Doughter,' quod he, ' here is a nobiĦ knyght,
his aunccetours were men) of grete powre ;
And of princes he is descendid fuĦ right,   6523
Ye shaĦ be his, this I haue hym) be hight,
In marriage, this is the mater playn),
And of my land I say yow for certeyn).   6526

And be ye so agreyd ther to,   6527
And as ye think now teĦ me your' avise.'
Lucidas agrees.
' Syr,' quod she, ' as it plese yow to do,
I am contente ther witĦ in euery wise,   6530
like as ye wiĦ appoynte it and devise ;
In euery thing' to folow your' entent,
I am hooly atte your' commaundment.'   6533

Darell goes back
to Generydes,
Thanne ser DareĦ departid home ayeyn),   6534
Vnto Generides the redy way,
And ther he told hym) aĦ to geder playn)
Of ser Amelok, and in what plight he lay ;   6537
' And this,' quod he, ' he prayde me to say,
In vmbiĦ wise, desireng' tenderly
That ye wold come and see hym) or he dye.   6540

and at length
prevails upon him
to visit
Sir Amelok.
He was in great
distress,
Wyth long' prayour he brought hym) atte last   6541
Vnto ser Amelok ther as he lay,
In grete distresse musyng' of tymes past,

And to Generides this ganne he say, 6544 [leaf 35, back]
and cried
'Mercy, mercy,
gentle Generydes,
let me have peace
with you
like as a man) had ben) half in affray ;
'Mercy,' quod he, 'mercy, gentiH Generides,
Graunt me that I witH yow may haue my pece, 6547

And witH your' fader auferius the kyng', 6548 and with Auferius,

whom I have
specially offended.
ffor hym) I haue offendid specially,
To non) so moche a creature levyng',
This land I hym) be raft fuH traytourly ; 6551
To god and hym) I yeld me now gilty, I yield myself to
God and him.
Pray hym) of grace and ellys, I wote certayn),
My sowle shaH lye in euer lastyng' payn). 6554

And o thyng' I wold, this is the case, 6555
Ye myght haue knowlage or [I] feryer goo,
DareH shaH haue my doughter lucidas Darell shall
marry Lucidas.
In mariage, and aH my land also, 6558
Besechyng' yow to be good lord therto, Be good lord to
them,
And shewe your' grace onto Serenydes,
That sne may prae for yow and leve in pece. 6561

And ferthermore, now I remember me, 6562 and forgive me
for smiting you
in the court.'
how I smote yow witH villany and shame,
Withynne the courte that euery man) myght see,
NougHt remembryng' the wurchippe of your' name, 6565
And therfore on) that side I am lame,
ffuH vmbely besechyng' your' goodnes,
That of aH this I may haue forgevenes.' 6568

With that he feH in swounyng' for very payn), 6569
Wherof Generides had grete pitye,
And whanne he sawe he[1] was awake ayeyn) ;
'Ser Amelok,' he seid, 'now as for me, 6572 'All that is past,
Sir Amelok,
AH that is past shaH clene forgevyn) be,
And witH my fader I shaH make your' pece, and I will make
your peace with
my father.
ffor yow and also for Serenydes. 6575

[1] MS. *hym he.*

But before you die, forgive me.'
And or ye dye this I desire also,[1]   6576
 That ye for geve me or I ferther passe.'

'That may soon be done,' said Amelok, 'for you have done me no wrong.'
'Trewly,' quod he, 'ser, that may sone be doo,
As for to me ye haue do noo trespace ;   6579
And [as] ferfurth as god will geve me grace,
With all the world, with highe and low degree,
I shall departe with loue and charite.'   6582

Serenydes tears her hair,
A Carefull woman) was Serenydes ;   6583
She rent hire here, a petuose thing to see,[2]

and with a naked sword comes to Generydes and begs him to slay her.
And with a nakyd swerd came to Generides,
'I yow requere for goddis loue,' quod she,   6586
'haue here this swerd, and make an ende of me
Now or ye goo, and bryng⸱ me owt of payn),
ffor I haue well deseruyd it for certayn).'   6589

'God forbid, madam,' he said,
'Do away, Madame,' quod he, 'god defende ;'   6590
Ther with he toke hir in his armys twayne,
'All that is amys,' quod he, 'may be amend,
And so ye must comfort your⸱ self ayeyn),   6593

'I have promised to make peace for you.'
ffor this I haue promysed for certayn),
Vnto my lord and fader for to goo,
To make the pece for yow and hym) Also.'   6596

Generides departid furth his way,   · 6597
Ser amelok lay in angwissh and in payn),
Sighyng⸱ full oft vppon) his bed he laye,

Sir Amelok died within a day or two,
And shortly to say yow the certayn),   6600
he dyed anon) withynne a day or twayne.
Thanne who was hevy butt Serenydes,
ffor more and more hir sorow ded increase.   6603

And ouer wharte his body ther [s]he lay,   6604
All in swoune, grete pite to be hold,
And in noo wise she wold not thens away,

---

[1] MS. *desire of yow also.*
[2] MS. *rent hire a petuose thing to here*

Moche sorow was made of yong' and old: 6607   and in an hour
                                                                         after Serenydes
With that hir face wex all to geder cold,   died of grief.
helpe was ther non, reskewe ne socour',
Bothe he and she were dede withynne An owre. 6610

A woofull creature was fayre lucydas, 6611   Fair Lucidas was
                                                                        very sad,
To se the maner of ther departeng',
And bothe to geder in a full litill space ;
So all the day alone she sate wepyng', 9614   and sat all day
                                                                       weeping and
She had noo comfort of erthely[1] thyng',   thinking of
                                                                      Darell.
Save euer more was ser Darell in hir mynde,
he was to hir so curtes and soo kynd. 6617

Generides sent furth a messenger, 6618   Generydes sent to
                                                                       the king
To telle the kyng' his fader tideng',   to tell him of
                                                                       Sir Amelok's
hough ser Amelok hath yeld vppe All in fere   repentance.
The Reme of ynd, and knowith hym for his kyng', 6621
With petuese wordes gretly repentyng',
And of all his offence and trespace,
full vmbly besechyng' yow of grace. 6624

Off these tidengys the kyng' was well apayd, 6625   The king was
                                                                        well pleased,
And toward Surre dressid hym to ride,   and prepared to
                                                                       ride to Syria,
Thanne to the messenger right[2] yuus he seid ;
'Sey to my sonne that he here abide, 6628   leaving Generydes
                                                                       to rule India.
And sette the lande in rewle on euery side,
hole to be and vnder his obeysaunce,   [leaf 36]
And take it as his owen inheritaunce.' 6631

Kyng' auferius fell seke anon vppon, 6632   Anon after he fell
                                                                       sick,
Yet not withstondyng so as it myght be,
With hym he tooke his knyghtes euerychon,
Tho streight way toward surre rideth he, 6635   but went back to
                                                                       Syria,
And whanne that he was come in to y[t] cuntre,
Tydynges he hard whiche grevid hym right sore,   where he found
                                                                       queen Serexne
Tho quene Sereyne was dede a day before. 6638   had died the day
                                                                       before.

[1] MS. etherly.
[2] MS. this right, the former word being marked for erasure.

Grete hevynes ther was for hir deceas,   6639

He went where she lay, and swooned twice,

The kyng' went to the place ther she laye,
And twyes he swouned among' the prece,
ffull sory were his men to se that day,   6642
Be one assent thei had hym) thens awaye,
And furth with all in to his chaunber y⁰¹ hym) brought,
All disfortles he was and full of thought.   6645

And alway still he febelid passyng' sore,   6646
So what with thought and feyntid with sekenes,

and within two days died,

Withynne ij dayes he dyed or litill more ;
Thanne was the lande in grete hevynes,   6649
To think vppon) so noble a princez
That dyed be fore, and ther kyng' Also,
So woo thei were thei wist not what to do.   6652

and they were both buried.

For hym) and hir was made grete ordenaunce,   6653
Prelettes, prestis, syngeng' ther seruice,
And grete lordes doth ther obseruaunce,
ladys also in full lamentabill wise,   6656
Euerychon) of them) in blak as is ther gise ;
Now late ys leue them) in rest and pece,
And speke wee ferther of Generides,   6659

Generydes, in India, set the land in order,

Whiche is in ynd, and doth grete diligence   6660
Thorough owt the land to sette good ordenaunce,
In ponyssheng' of them) that doo amys,
Suche as be good of witte and gouernaunce,   6663
Them) to charisshe and putte to fortheraunce,
All this remembert he both day And nyght,
And for to see that euery man) haue right.   6666

So wele he dede in euery maner thing',   6667
The land of hym) were passyng' well content,

and was crowned king.

As rightwise ayre thei toke hym) for yer kyng',

And Crownyd hym be aH the hooH assent ; 6670
Thus were thei AH att his commaundment,
he was soo good soo curtese and soo fre,
he had the loue of aH the hoole contre. 6673

The same forster that came on to [the] kyng', 6674
And told of AH the treson that was do,
he lost his office ther and his levyng',
And with quene Sereyne he went Also ; 6677
Ther for his trowth withoute wordes moo,
A C pownde of fee he had ther fore,
With his office like as he had before. 6680

Owt of Cesare thanne cam barons iij, 6681
And in ther Iurnay thei rode passing' fast,
To teH ser DareH the very certente,
hough his fader owt of his life[1] is past ; 6684
Desireng' hym to come in aH the hast,
And by the Assent of aH his baronage,
Of that contre to cleyme his eritage. 6687

Whanne thei had told ther message hole and playn,
Ye may weH wete ser DareH was not glad ;
Vnto Generides he went certayn,
And told hym of the tidynges that he had, 6691
Besechyng' hym, with countenaunce right sadde,
Of licence in Cesare for to goo ;
Generides consentid weH ther too. 6694

And whanne his leve of hym thus takyn was, 6695
ffor aH the payñ he sufferyd and the smert,
Ye shaH weH knowe the fayre mayde lucidas
Right endly was inprentid in his hert ; 6698
Vnto hir chaunber sone he made a stert,
And curtesly of hir his leve he toke,
With kysseng' fele as witnes[eth] the book. 6701

The faithful
forester was
rewarded with
100 pounds,

and restored to
his office.

Three barons of
Cæsarea bring
tidings to Darell

of his father's
death.

He asks leave of
Generydes to go
home,

and sorrowfully
parted with
Lucidas.

[1] MS. list.

In to Casare now ser Dareḧ is goon),   6702
The countre hole was glad of his comyng̔,
And for ther prince thei toke hym) euerychon),
And gave hym) ther troutḧ withoute feyneng̔,   6705
he was soo good to them) in euery thing̔,
Shewyng̔ them) favour' and grete gentilnes,
he had the hartes hoole of more and lesse.   6708

Whanne he had sett the rule and gouernaunce,   6709
Thorougḧ owt the land to mayteyn) rest and pese,
And made his officers to his plesaunce
Suche as hym) thought his honour wold encrease, 6712
Thanne ageyn) he went onto Generides,
And in his Iurnay rideth he fuḧ fast,
ffurtḧ in to ynd in aḧ the possibiḧ hast.   6715

Now is the prince of Cesare come ayen),   6716
Vnto the kyng̔ of ynde Generides,
The whiche in sothe of his comyn),
ffor he abode his comyng̔ stiḧ opece ;   6719
And for to teḧe yow shortly the processe,
Withoute delay or lenger space,
The prince was weddid onto lucidas.   6722

And whanne the fest was aḧ to geder do,[1]   6723
ffor tender love and speciaḧ remembraunce,
Witḧ hym) and here he gave the lande also,
Whiche was hir faders old̔ inheritaunce ;   6726
The prince also, his honour to avaunce, ·
he gave hym) fuḧ powre signyd witḧ his haude,
In his absence to gouerne aḧ his lande.   6729

Now gotḧ Generides, the kyng̔ of ynde,   6730
Toward Surre withoute more delay ;
And in the story leke as I do fynde,

[1] MS. donc.

Too Counstables ther mette hym þe the way, 6733   and is met by two
One of them twayne, tho very trouth to say,   constables,
Of all Surre cheff gouernour he was,
The toder kept the Citee of Damas.   6736

All sad thei were, and made full hevy chere,   6737   who told him
Generides had mervell what it ment;
To his presence he bad thei shuld come nere,
That he myght knowe the effecte of *yer* entente, 6740
And vppon þat A streight commaundment,
Gevyng them charge to tell hym all the case,
Trewly and playn what maner a thyng it was.   6743

Full lothe thei were to tell the certente,   6744
ffor hevy tidinges came to sone Alway,
Butte whanne thei sawe it myght non oyer be,
To hym thei spake, 'ser, please it yow,' quod thei, 6747   of the death of
'To take it in pacient that we shall saye,   his father and
     mother.
The kyng your fader dede is for certeyn,
And your moder also the quene Sereyne;   6750

Bothe he and she, withynne iij dayes of space: 6751
It is grete hurt to the land were it goddes will.'
And whanne Generides wist hough it was,   He fell from his
Down from his hors in swounyng ther he fell,   6754   horse in a swoon,
To tyme he was awake ther lay he still;
Thanne euery man dede grete diligence and payn,
And vppon his hors thei sette hym Ageyn.   6757

They brought hym to the Cite of Damas   6758   and was carried
And passing seke in his pales he laye,   to Damascus,
      where he lay sick.
All pale and wanne, owt of likeng he was,
his fressh colour it fatid al away,   6761
And thanne to Natanell this ganne he sey,
'Goo now, I prae yow hartely,' quod he,   He sent for
'And sey to Segrem that he come to me.'   6764   Sygrem,

and gave him a
ring to take to
Clarionas,

Whanne he was come thanne seid Generides,   6765
'Sygrem,' quod he, 'I haue sent for yow here ;
God wote I am noo thing' in hartes ease,
And very seke ye se, and in what maner ;   6768
Goo to Clarionas myn owen lady dere,
haue here this ryng', bere it here for me,
I am aferde I shall hir neuer see.   6771

Tell ye hir soo in very certente,   6772
Me recomaundyng' in full humble wise,
beseeching her to
pray for him. Besechyng' hir that she will pray for me,
I aske no more for all my trew seruice ;'   6775
  Ser,' quod Sygrem, 'right as ye will devise,
What I shall do or say for your entent,
I am redy att your owne commaundment.'   6778

Sygrem goes into
Persia Now goth Sygrem withoute wordes moo,   6779
ffurth in to Perce he ridith on a pace,
To Mountoner Citee now is he goo,
On his massage As he commaundid was,   6782
and tells Clarionas
all. So Streight he goth on to Clarionas,
And ther he told hir all the circumstaunce
Of his sekenes with hevy countenaunce.   6785

And whanne Sygrem had all to geder seide,   6786
She swoons, Anon she fell in swounyng' for very payn with all,
Where with Mirabell gretly was dismayde,
and Mirabell
counsels her 'Madame,' quod she, 'what thing' that euer fall ?' 6789
And on hir lady fast beganne to call,
'hurt not your self, I prae yow, in this case ;'
With thoo wordes a woke Clarionas.   6792

'All way your comfort is full good,' quod she,   6793
'Butt in this case I wote not what to sey.'
'Madame,' quod she, 'woll ye do After me ?'

'Gladly,' she seide, 'aH that I canne or may.'   6796
'Be my councell thanne shaH ye take your' way
To Surre warde,' quod she, 'be myn Avyse,
In pore clothing and in fuH secrete wise.   6799

to go to Syria secretly.

And haue witH yow Gwynot your chaunberleyn,   6800
And one to kepe your' hors it shaH suffice,
Take vppon yow the labour and the payn,
And ye shaH make hym hoole o warantice.'   6803
'I will,' quod she, 'do like as ye haue devico,
And certenly, withoute eny wordes moo,
To morow erly forward wiH we goo.'   6806

She agrees,

Fro Mountoner gothe Clarionas,   6807
With hir rode Sygrem to hir gide,
ffuH secretly as she appoynted was,
That noman of the Cite hir aspide ;   6810
ffurth on ther way to surreward thei hied,
And in aH goodly hast as it myght be,
ffuH sone thei came to Damas the Citee.   6813

and goes from Mountoner with [leaf 37] Sygrem,

till they come to Damascus.

Sygrem from hir departid furth with aH,   6814
Streight to the CasteH gothe Clarionas;
Vppon the porter she beganne to calle,
And he ayenward askid what[1] she was :   6817
'ffor certeyn, ser,' quod she, 'this is the case,
The kyng is seke, it is infourmyd me,
I trost to god to make hym hole,' quod she.   6820

Clarionas goes straight to the castle,

and tells the porter she is come to cure the king.

'In strenthe or erbys that ben profeitable,   6821
In them I knowe the vertu that is sure,
In euery kynd whiche is most comfortabiH,
And accordeng to euery creature,   6824
And often tyme I haue putte it in vre ;
Wherefore, I prae yow, do my craunde,[2]
That I may see the kyng now or I goo.'   6827

[1] MS. *was*.   [2] So MS. ? *my craunde to do*.

'Damesell,' quod he, 'your erande shall be do [1];' 6828

The porter brings Natanell,

With that the porter goth vnto the place,
And spake with Natanell a worde or twoo,

who does not recognize her.

And brought hym furth onto Clarionas,   6831
Vnknowen to them bothe what that she was;

'What is your will?' said he.

'Ye are right welcom, suster myn,' quod he,
'What is your will? I prae yow telle it me.'   6834

'I am a poor woman,

'Trowly,' quod she, 'I am a pore woman,   6835
The kyng is seke, whom gretly I complayne;

and wish to make the king whole.'

And I wold Shewe suche connyng As I canne,
Trosting to god to make hym hoole ayeyn.'   6838

He saw the ring on her finger, but still did not know her,

Thanne he beheld hir ferthermore certayn,
A ryng he knew whiche on hir fynger was,
Yet wist he not that it was Clarionas.   6841

and went straight to the king,

From hir he went streight onto the kyng,   6842
'Ser, please it yow to vnderstonde,' quod he,
'Ther is a woman whiche is full connyng
In euery sekenes and, as thinkith me,   6845
By here wordes her semyth so to be;
here atte Castell gate with hir I spakke,
To make yow hoole this wolle she vndertake.   6848

'On hir fynger ther is a ryng,' quod he,   6849
'The whiche in sothe me think a straunge case;
And this I wote in very certente,
Ye gave suche on vnto Clarionas,   6852
And in myself I mervell hough it was.'

who bade him bring her in.

Thanne seid the kyng, 'I woll now y[t] ye goo,
Bryng hir to me withoute wordes moo.'   6855

Now Natanell goth to the Castell gate,   6856

She came in closely veiled,

And brought this woman streight onto the kyng,
Butt she was wympelyd soo that woote ye what,

[1] MS. don.

That he had no maner knowlaching, 6859 so that he did not
                                         know her,
With that anon) he had aspyed the ryng,
The whiche hym) thought he gave Clarionas,
Yet for all that he wist not what she was. 6862

'I pray yow, ser, be of good chere,' quod she, 6863
'And if it please your goodnes for to here
I am a woman) of ferre contre ;'
And ther withall, in full curtes maner, 6866 and offered to
                                               kiss him.
She proferyd hym) to kysse with louyng chere ;
'Nay, suster myn),' quod he, 'with goddes grace,
I must pray yow of pardon) in this case : 6869

For I will kysse no woman) be ye sure, 6870 He refused to
                                               kiss any one
Though she myght make me hoole as euer I was, but Clarionas.
Butt only hir whiche is that creature
That I loue best, the mayde Clarionas ; 6873
And if that she were present in this place,
If I here kyssid, I think, so god me save, She, perhaps,
                                              could cure him.
It were the best fisykke that I cowde haue.' 6876

'I haue,' she seid, 'brought with me hir ymage :' 6877
'Ye,' quod the kyng, 'I prae yow, late me see ;'
Anone she dede vnWympill hir visage, She unveiled
                                          herself,
'Withoute fayle I am the same,' quod she : 6880
Thanne seid the kyng, 'Aye, Benedicite !
hough haue ye take vppon) yow all this payn) ?'
Ther with he toke hir in his armes twayn). 6883 and he took her
                                                 in his arms

Thanne he kyssid hir withoute more taryeng, 6884 and kissed her,
And all that nyght, till day beganne to rise, and they sat
                                                 together till
They twayne were sett withoute departeng, daybreak.
As glad and mery as thei cowde devise, 6887
To bothe ther pleasurez in all goodly wise ;
And on) the morow, sothely for to say, On the morrow
                                           she went back to
To mountoner sho toke the redy way. 6890 Mountoner.

Generydes recovered,	And hole he was and very well att ease, 6891
	And atte his hartes rest in especiall;
and was crowned king,	The iij^{de} day after Generides
	Was crownyd kyng⸳ of Surry furth with All; 6894
	Thanne the lordes echon in generall,
	With very dew and feithfull obseruaunce,
	Dede hym omage with vmble obeysaunce. 6897

Whanne he had sette the land in gouernaunce, 6898
ffurth in to perce he takith his Iurnay,
In grete estate And in grete ordenaunce,
With his lordes and in suche array, 6901
Thus rideth he the redy way
To Mountoner, ther as the Sowdon was,
Ther for to wedde the mayde Clarionas. ·6904

Whanne he was come, the Cite was full fayn, 6905
ffor att all tymes of necessite
he toke on hym the labour⸳ and the payne,
And was ther sheld from all aduersite; 6908
So thanne withynne the space of dayes iij,
As rially as thei cowde device,
The mariage was made in solempne wise. 6911

Gwynan the kyng⸳ was atte mariage, 6912
The kyng⸳ of Trace also withoute lese,
Whiche callid was Ismaell the savage,
Broder he was onto the kyng⸳[1] Generides, 6915
And so to gide and gouerne all the prece
Appoynted was, likke as thei thought it best,
The prince of Cesare cheff stiward of ye fest. 6918

And other grete estatis ther were moo, 6919
Bothe of lordes and ladyes many on,
Grete Iustis ther the Sowdon made also,

[Side notes: "and soon after set off for Persia," "to wed Clarionas." "[leaf 37, back]" "Gwynan was there," "and Ismael the Savage," "and Darell was steward of the feast," "and many others."]

[1] Omit *the kyng*.

And aH tho plesure that cowde be thougfit vppon);
And to be hold the pepiH euerychen),
Whiche came to se the fest of yong¹ and old²,
It was a very wonder to be hold².   6925

Sone after whanne tho fest was don) and AH,   6926   Soon after,
And euery man) gon) home in to his cuntre,   when all had gone
                                                              home,
Withynne a while, as aventur² gan) faH,
Tho Sowdon) dyed, whiche was grete pite ;   6929   the Sultan died,
Grete mone was made of men) of the Cite,
Save ther comfort and trost in¹ euery thyng¹,
Was only on) Generides the kyng¹,   6932

Whiche sesid aH the lande in his demeane,   6933   and Generydes
                                                              took his land,
Be right wise titeH of his mariage,   by right of his
                                                              marriage.
Takyng¹ homage, as lord and souereyn),
Thorough owt the lande of aH the Baronage :   6936
Bothe yong¹ and old² and euery man) of age,
As glad thei were of hym), I yow ensure,
As euer was land of eny levyng¹ creature.   6939

He was to them) so lovyng¹ and so kynd,   6940
The laugfi abseruyd wiH bothe ferre and nere,
No man) had Wrong that eny man) cowd fynde,
ffewe compleyntes or now) that men) myght here,   6943
GentiH ther with, curtes in AH maner,
If eny man) wold wrong¹ oyer day or nygfit,
he was redy for to forfete his rigfit.   6946

And for be cause it shuld not owt of mynd,   6947   He married
                                                              Natanell
The good seruice so feithfuH and so playn)   to Mirabell,
Off NataneH, whiche he had founde so kynde,
And for his love hadde grete labour² and payn),   6950
he thougfit he wold remember it ayeyn),
In suche a wise as hym) thougfit honorable,
And maryed hym) to the made MirabeH.   6953

¹ MS. *was in.*

Too hym) and her he gave a faire Citee,   6954
Withynne the Reme of Surre callid Sevre,
A bought the town) a dosen) myle fre
Vnto hym self, and yerly of valour[1]   6957
vj thousand pownde, to maynteyn) yer honour;
And of that land he made hym) cheff Iustice,
To maynteyn) in euery maner wise.   6960

Syr Anasore with hym) was not for gete,   6961
he made hym) lord of A grete baronye,
The whiche was fallyn) in perce be eschete,
Whanne lucas dyed that was of ydonye;   6964
And for grete trost that he hadde specially
In hym), Al myn) Auctour reherse,
he gave hym) ther the Stiwardshepe of perce.   6967

Sygram also was in his remembraunce,   6968
Vn to the lavender weddid ther he was,
Whiche vtterly for soke hir acqueyntaunce,
And toke hir Iurnay with Clarionas;   6971

and had a fair
lordship given
him by the king.

The king hym) grauntid, of his special grace,
A fayre lordshippe onto them) bothe in fere,
The whiche was wurth an Cli be yere.   6974

Thus quyte he them) that were to hym) so kynd,   6975
And, for to seie[2] yow in shorte conclusion),
A better prince was neuer had in mynd,
Thanne he was on) that euer bare crown);   6978
And thus he was a man) of grete renown),
Sowdon) of perce with al his signory,
And also kyng of ynd and of surre.   6981

In grete wurchipe Clarionas and he   6982
Good lyff thei ledde to geder many a yere,
In hartes ease and moche prosperite,

---

[1] MS. valowe.   [2] MS. seia.

Issue they had whiche was to them full dere,   6985 and had issue.
Right grete lordes and ladyes thei were,
Whiche on of them of xv yere of age,   The daughter was
                                               married to the
The kyng of Egipt had in mariage.   6988 king of Egypt,

The remenaunt grew to grete honour,   6989 and the others
                                               grew up in great
And thus I make an ende of this processe,   honour.
Besechyng hym that is our saviour,
All oure synnes of pardon to relese,[1]   6992
And in the Ioy and blisse that[2] is endlese,
he graunt vs a place perpetuall,
In paradise where all his seyntes dwell.   6995

      Explicit the boke of Gene-
      rides and of his faire lady Clarionas.

---

[1] MS. *be relese*, but the first word is struck out.   [2] MS. *this*.

VARIOUS READINGS FROM THE PRINTED FRAGMENTS OF SIR GENERYDES,

GIVEN IN THE PREFACE AND POSTSCRIPT TO MR FURNIVALL'S EDITION
OF THE HELMINGHAM MS. FOR THE ROXBURGHE CLUB.

2016. *claymeth it of*] they clayme this
2017. *Also to be made*] Aud also to be
„ *your*] his
2018. *roward*] forwarde
2019. *of right it longith*] it longeth of ryght
2021. *so it*] me so
2022. *may withoute*] may bere without
2025. *it is but*] for it is
2026. *full ourtes*] curteys
2027. *they ganne*] gan they
2029, 30. *withoute ... Batell*] withou[t dowte] Unto the kynge of kynges to gyue a strou[te]
2031. *ganne them*] gan
2032. *princes*] knyghtes
2033. *other dyuerce*] dyuers
2034. *Dukes and Erles*] erles
„ *anon*] many one
2035. *that they hadde vppon*] so that they shone
2036. *perlys*] grete perles
2037. *in the frossost*] on the best
2038. *through owt in*] thrughe
2040. *enmys for*] enemyes
2042. *ffro*] Forth of
2043. *rideth*] rode
„ *to his pavilion*] vnto his tente
2044. *With ... rome*] With his lordes aboute hym wente
2045. *redy*] all redy
2046. *a companye*] company
2047. *were*] brought
2049. *All redy to gye*] to guyde truly
2052. *att his demenyng*] in his ledynge
2056. *he was baneer*] dyde the baner bere

2058. *ij thousand ... companye*] [Sir Crove]s with thre thousande in theyr company
2059. *nard*] batayll
„ *ser Anasore*] anazere
2061. *they were thore*] that there were
2062. *withoute*] withouten
2064. *bothe the rule of more*] the reule more
2067. *all*] and
2072. *by and by*] ryght hardely
2073. *after hym*] after
2075. *begely*] vgly
„ *bothe in*] in
2105. *was Baner*] bare the banere
2314. *they twayne*] they
2345. *sheld and thu goo*] shelde agayne and go
5339. *on fortune*] a fortune
5343. *Amelokkez*] syr Amelokes
5344. *It was ayenst*] This was
5345. *cause*] case
„ *certente*] certayne
5351. *also he*] he
5352. *late*] let
5354. *where euer*] where that
„ *eny lande*] ony londe
5355. *noo lenger myght she*] she myght no lenger
5356. *for very payn*] for grete doloure
5357. *ageyn*] that houre
5359. *that she*] she
„ *vp ayeyn*] agayne
5361. *refrayn*] restrayne
5365. *full sure*] sure
5371. *shuld kepe*] kepe
5372. *here*] lo here

5374. *that*] elles that
5375. *full hastely*] hastely
5378. *with the shall neuer*] shall neuer with the
5379. *haue*] kepe
5382. *vppon*] on
5383. *as he*] as euer he
5384. *the chaunber*] her chaumbre
5386. *full of horynes*] and full of perplexcyte
5387. *alway now*] alway
5388. *of his vnstabilnes*] his duplycyte
5389. *not gilty*] giltles
5390. *alway*] had alway
5392. *do be*] done by
5394. *a kevynes*] mornynge
5396. *also gentilnes*] as a gentyll kynge
5690. *here you spoke*] here you
5692. *I am sure*] be ye sure
5694. *ferthermore*] forthermore
  „ *this*] so
5696. *o*] one
  „ *is*] is also
5701. *these wordes*] this worde
  „ *ganne*] began
5702. *goth*] wente
5703. *late*] let
5704. *hastith*] hasted
5705. *So*] And so
  „ *hir*] his
5706. *into*] in
5707. *the*] that
5708. *onto*] to
5709. *redy waye*] way redy
5711. *this to hym gan say*] to hym sayde preuely
5712. *the dore*] this dore
  „ *I yow praye*] I pray you hertely
5714. *to now*] tyll nowe
5715. *the neer he was*] the nerer he coude
5716. *otherwise*] other
5720. *onto the*] to hir
5721. *vpon*] open nowe
5722. *Thanne Darell*] When he
  „ *and*] he
5723. *onto fayre*] vnto
5724. *ffrom ynd . . . contre*] Fro ynde I come now as faste as I can [te]
5725. *on to*] to
5726. *now this*] this
5727. *be dremyd*] ben drenchyd
5728. *hym noyeth*] and nyghtly is

5731. *quod*] nowe quod
5732. *lesyng*] lesynges
5733. *yow*] it
5736. *this message*] the erande
5737. *not to don*] done
5738. *why*] quod he why
  „ *yow*] ye
5740. *onto*] to
5742. *is he*] he is
  „ *this dare I*] I dare well
5744. *I shall tell yow trougth*] in very trouthe
5752. *wote ye*] wote I
5753. *Serenydes*] Senerydes
5754. *he was*] was
5755. *ffor*] Fro
  „ *for*] fro
5756. *betwix*] bytwene
5757. *the trowth*] trouthe
5758. *that*] that euer
5759. *she*] the
5761. *and I had it*] if I had
5762. *shuld me mystrost*] mysdeme me sholde
  „ *my*] ony
5763. *not A take vppon*] nat taken on
5767. *ser Darell*] hym
5768. *now quod*] quod
  „ *yow*] ye now
5769. *he seide suche*] suche
5770. *very certente*] certente
5772. *nerrer*] nere
5775. *to say*] I say
5780. *it*] them
5782. *to*] vp to
  „ *hand*] honde
5784. *right wele*] well
5785. *he*] that he
5786. *eny maner*] ony
5788. *preiudice*] dyspyse
5789. *nede*] great nede
5790. *canne goo*] may gone
5791. *doo*] done
5793. *both good*] euer gode
5794. *is homeward in*] [home]warde gothe on
5795. *now*] a newe
5796. *cowde*] knewe
5799. *Citee*] towne
5800. *went*] sente
5802. *his own*] his
5803. [   ]nes to hym verament
5804. *that*] theyr

GLOSSARIAL INDEX.

ALOW, *adv.* in a low voice, 5717.

ALTO, *adv.* altogether, 1559. ALL TO, 4272, 6094.

ALWAY, *adv.* always, 415, 490, 899, 1044. In 3948 it appears to be an error for 'all away.'

AMELOK, the false steward of Auferius, and usurping King of India, 28, 2129. AMALOK, 2381.

AMEND, *pp.* amended, 6592.

AMONG, *adv.* 'Euer among,' continually from time to time, 1373, 1853. Palsgrave gives, 'Amonge, parfoys.' See also Prof. Zupitza's note to Guy of Warwick, l. 950.

AMYSELL, sworn brother to Ananyell, 4833.

ANANYELL, brother of Amelok, slain by Generydes, 4825, 5016, 5830, 5844.

ANASORE, a knight of Persia, keeper of the prison, 1460, 5575, 6961. Son of Croves, 1906. ANASAR, 1471. ANASOR, 1503. ANOSORE, 2852, 3023, 3029.

ANCERS, *sb.* anchors, 3653.

ANCETORS, *sb.* ancestors, 3139.

AND, *conj.* if, 214, 354, 889, 3415, 4436, 6432.

AN HUNTYNG, 37.

ANONE VPPON, *adv.* immediately after, 78. ANON VPON, 141. See VPPON.

A PASE, *adv.* apace, swiftly, 988, 4453. A PACE, 2316, 3076.

APAYDE, *pp.* pleased, 848, 3485, 4206, 4419, 5072. APAYD, 1932. APAYED, 856, 1162, 2430, 2828.

APAYN, an error for 'and payn,' 5915.

APOYNTEMENT, *sb.* arrangement, 5424.

APOYNTID, *pp.* arranged, 5347. APOYNTED, 5589. APPOYNTED, 5624. APPOYNTID, 5887.

APPARELL, *sb.* provision, 641. In the next line the word is repeated, apparently in error, perhaps for 'peril;' or it may merely be used in the other sense of 'preparation,' like Fr. *appareil*.

AQUYTE, *v. pret.* requited, 1876.

ARABYE, Arabia, 1901.

ARAY, *sb.* condition, 1193. ARRAYE, 1238.

ARAYED, *pp.* 'Thus hath arayed me,' hath made me in this guise, 515.

ARKADYE, Arcadia, 1952.

ARMYS. 'To do armys' = to do battle, 6078.

AS, redundant in the phrases 'as for that nyght,' 138, 152, 383; 'As for a nyghtis space,' 230; 'as in this case,' 442, 582; 'as for a space,' 568; 'as after hir avise,' 702; 'as for a tyme,' 902; 'where as,' 1191; 'as for his hartys ease,' 1354; 'as for the landes right,' 1846; 'as for more witnesse,' 2382; 'As now,' 2409; 'as towching,' 2805, 5443; 'as after myn avise,' 2892; 'as for a daye or twayne,' 2990; 'as for this landis right,' 3345; 'as for a litill space,' 3789; 'as for this day,' 3887; 'as for that nyght,' 3897; 'as this nyght,' 3902; 'As for the cheve guerdon,' 3912; 'as for on nyghte reste,' 4030; 'as for Generides,' 4623; 'As late me see,' 5233; 'as yesterday,' 5278; 'as for a certeyn space,' 5313; 'As for a dreme,' 5634; 'as for a certeyn space,' 6293; 'As for to me,' 6579.

ASKAPYD, *v. pret.* escaped, 6096.

ASKRY, *v.* to descry, 5999. ASKERYE, 6014.

ASPIED, *v. pret.* espied, spied, 437.

ASPIED, *pp.* 2476. ASPYED, 2674.

ASPYE, *v.* to spy, watch, 1357, 1409, 2600.

ASSE, *v.* to assay, 6074.

ASSEMELYD, *pp.* assembled, 1317. ASSEMELID, 2046.

ASSENT, *sb.* 'Ar of hir assent,' are in league with her, 983.

ASSIRYE, Assyria, 2166. ASIRYE, 2545.

ASTATE, *sb.* state, 389.

ASTERTE, *v.* escape from, avoid, 173.

ASTOINYD, *pp.* astonished, stunned, 2498.

ASTOWNYD, *pp.* astounded, 3506, 4013.

A SURANCE, *sb.* assurance, 5450.

AT, *pron.* that, 591, 4388. ATT, 347.

ATT, *prep.* In the phrase 'toke good hede att hym,' 660.

ATTE, at the, 2797, 2947, 4106, 6912.

ATTE, in the phrase 'atte after none' = in the afternoon, 3715.

A TWOO, *adv.* in two, 6097.

AUCTOR, *sb.* author, 6002.

AUFERIUS, King of India, father of Generydes, 7, &c.

AUFRIKE, Africa, 16. AUFERYK, 2138.

AUNCETOURS, *sb.* ancestors, 6522.

AVAILE, *sb.* advantage, 4259. AVAYLE, 4487.

AVAUNCE, *v.* to advance, 489, 2021, 3417, 4840, 5060.

AVAUNSED, *v. pret.* advanced, 650. AVAUNSID, 2214, 2673.

AVAUNTE, *v.* to vaunt, boast, 1008.

AVENTURE, *sb.* adventure, fortune, 370, 2597, 4893, 4969, 6928. 'Att all aventure' = at all events or hazard, 3494, 6355. 'At aventure' or 'Att aventure,' by chance, 1238, 2791, 4414.

AVISE, 258, 981, 1402, 1762, 2683; or AVYSE, *sb.* advice, 101. 'Toke gode avise,' considered well, 449; consideration, 702.

AVISE, *v.* to advise, 6063.

AVISEMENT, *sb.* advice, consideration, 4761.

AVOYDE, *v. i.* to remove, disappear, 4239.

AVOYDID, *pp.* cleared away, removed, 3293.

AVOWE, *v.* to avouch, acknowledge, 894.

AWAITENG, *pr. p.* waiting, 648.

AWAYWARD, *adv.* away, 3813.

AWISE, in the phrase 'maner awise' = maner wise, 4797.

AWREKE, *v.* to avenge, 508, 5122.

AWYSE. In 146 'sothe awyse' is probably an error for 'soche a wyse.'

AXKID, *v. pret.* asked, 309.

AYE, *adv.* again, 4426.

AYEN, *adv.* again, 133, 1098.

AYENST, *adv.* against, 5472, 6122.

AYENWARD, *adv.* again, 128, 1876, 3366, 3944, 4492.

AYERIS, *sb.* heirs, 2016.

AYEYN, *adv.* again, 2718, 2735, 3942.

AYRE, *sb.* heir, 5187, 6669; *pl.* AYRIS, 6130.

BALAM, King of Damascus, 1957, 2090.

BANYERE, *sb.* standard-bearer, 2014. BANEER, 2055. BANER, 2105. BANERE, 2128, 2213, 2963.

BARACHIAS, King of Europe, 2147.

BARONAGE, *sb.* the barons as a body, 4218, 6936.

BATELL, *sb.* a body of troops, 2077, 2101. BATAYLL, 2090.

BE, *pp.* been, 352, 811, 1209, 5220, &c.

BE, *prep.* by, 412, 635, 2445, 2761, &c.; with regard to, 610.

BE CAUSE, *conj.* in order that, 4279.

BEDDE, *v. pret.* bade, 1336.

BEFALL, *pp.* befallen, 1087, 3388.

BEFORN, *adv.* before, 521, 3139, 4603.

BEGELY, *adv.* bigly, hugely, 2075.

BEHAVINGE, *sb.* behaviour, 433.

BEHEST, *sb.* promise, 4499, 4690.

BEHIGHT, *v.* to promise, assure, 812, 2231, 2695, 3508.

BELEN the bold, King of Egypt, 1735. BELLEYN, 2451. BELLYN, 3291. BELYN, 3285. BOLEYN, 3059. BELLYNG, 3463. BOLYN, 3074.

BEN, *v. inf.* be, 2685; *ind.* 3 *pl.* 2738.

BE RAFT, v. pret. bereft, 6551.

BERY, v. to bury, 5883; pret. BERIED, 5877.

BESEN, pp. bosoon, provided, 1978. BE SENE, 2068.

BESETTE, v. to set, bestow, 5021.

BESY, adj. busy, 5303.

BESYNESSE, sb. in the phrase 'did all ther besynesse' = busied themselves, exerted themselves to the utmost, 1167.

BE TROST, pp. trusted, 1049, 3615.

BETWIX, prep. between, 108, 905, 3117, 5259.

BE TYME, adv. betimes, in good time, 522.

BEWRAYED, pp. exposed, 3885.

BE WREYE, v. to expose, betray, 4155.

BLAME, sb. 'To take a blame' = to take blame, 1628.

BLANCHARD, the name of King Belen's steed, 2458; given to Gwynan, 2265; and won by Generydes, 2247, 6066.

BLODE, ON. 'Braste on blode,' burst out bleeding, 546.

BLYSSYNG, sb. blessing, 236. BLISSYNG. 'On his blissyng,' as he expected to receive his blessing, 5346.

BOLDITH, v. pres. emboldens, 5803.

BOLEYN, BOLYN. See BELEN.

BOORE, pp. born, 5635. BORE, 6132.

BOTE, sb. use, advantage, 4681, 5853; v. 'It botith not,' is of no use, 4901.

BOTELER, sb. butler, 424.

BOUNDEN, pp. bound, 1458.

BOUSTOUS, adj. boisterous, rough, 2152.

BRAKE, pp. broken, 3489.

BRAST, v. pret. broke, 2326, 2677, 3047, 4926, 6094, &c.

BRASTE, v. pret. burst out, 546.

BRAYDE, sb. a sudden movement, a start, 2218, 2342, 2736, 6069.

BRAYDED, v. pret. started, 165.

BREDE, sb. breadth, 2075.

BRODER, sb. brother, 4826, 6915.

BRODEREN, sb. brethren, 2656.

BRODERHODE, sb. brotherhood, 6252.

BROWGTH, pp. brought, 4874.

BUSCOMMEST, adj. buxomest, most compliant or obedient, 2505.

BUSSHMENT, sb. ambush, 950. BUSCHEMENT, 5977.

BUT IF, conj. except, 322, 332.

BY AND BY, adv. 2048, 2072, 3287, 4766.

BYTWIX, prep. between, 2188.

BY WARE, v. beware, 4590.

CALLED or CALLID, reputed; in the phrases 'called passing wight,' 4573; 'callid good,' 4994. See 5186.

CAME, v. pres. come, 6745.

CAPADOCE, Cappadocia, 2087.

CAPADOOR, Cappadocia, 1954. Elsewhere CAPADOCE.

CAREFULL, adj. full of care, sorrowful, 4161, 6434, 6583.

CASARE, elsewhere CESARE, 6702.

CAST, v. to intend, purpose, 4423; pret. 3654.

CAWDE, could, 373. A scribe's error for 'Cowde.'

CERTAYNE. 'In certayne,' 462, 476, 4856; 'For certeyn,' 419; 'For certayn,' 4934; 'The certayn,' 2036, 6600.

CERUICE, sb. service, 4675.

CESALL, one of the Sultan of Persia's allies, 1965.

CESARE, Cesarea, 1926, 6681.

CESELL, Sicily, 2070.

CHARGID. Perhaps for 'chargeth,' the imperative, 6429.

CHARISSHE, v. to cherish, 6664.

CHARITE, OWT OF, 502. SEYNT CHARITE, 4282.

CHASE, v. pret. chose, 1325.

CHASTELYN, sb. the keeper of a castle, 1520, 1609. CHASTELAYN, 1632.

CHAUNBOUR, *sb.* chamber, 1407.

CHAUNBYR, *sb.* chamber, 69; CHAUNBER, 71, 3792, 4629.

CHEFF, *adj.* chief, 5893, 6735.

CHER, *sb.* aspect, countenance, 129; condition, 2594, 6031. CHERE, 239, 433, 2953; happiness, 2580. 'To make chere' = to be cheerful, 571; 'To make better chere' = to treat better, 2660; 'To take chere,' 751; 'To make frendly chere' = to treat in a friendly manner, 5764; 'To make chere' = to cheer, 6341; 'Made hevy chere,' were sad in countenance, 6737.

CHERYDONE, Prince of Cesarea, and father of Darell, 1928.

CHESE, *v.* choose, 1232, 1316.

CHESE, an error for 'Chek,' 4778.

CHEVE, *adj.* chief, 3912.

CHOSE, *pp.* chosen, 5230.

CLARIONAS, daughter to the Sultan of Persia, 686, &c.

CLARIONAT, a town in Persia, 3677.

CLARYET, the name of Generydes' sword, 3481.

CLAYMETH, *v.* 3 *pl.* claim, 2016.

CLEFE, *v. pret.* clave, cleft, 4598.

CLEUE, *v. pret.* clave, 3035, 3523.

COME, *v. pret.* came, 3017, 3042, 3829, 4214, 4281, 5204, 6396.

COMENAUTE, *sb.* the commonalty or commons, 254.

COMFORT, *v. pret.* comforted, 3854.

COMMANDITH, commendeth, 444. COMMAUNDITH, 5725.

COMNE, *pp.* come, 9.

COMPANABLE, *adj.* companionable, 2261.

COMPASSING, *adj.* 'False compassing' = with a false design, 4163.

COMPASSION, 6419; an error for 'compassing.' See 4163.

COMPLAYNE, *v. t.* to lament for, 6836.

CON. 'To con thanke' = to thank, 878.

CONFORTABLE, *adj.* comfortable, able to help, 2212.

CONFORTYNG, *pr. p.* comforting, 2514.

CONNYNG, *adj.* skilful, wise, 338.

CONNYNG, *sb.* skill, wisdom, 404, 1020.

CONNYNGLY, *adv.* wisely, 398.

CONSEYTE, *sb.* imagination, opinion, 696, 6091. CONSAITE, 4352. CONSEITE, good opinion, favour, 4638, 4739, 4902.

CONTENAUNCE, *sb.* 'Made no contenaunce,' did not change the expression of her face, 5116.

COPPE, *sb.* a cup, 4406.

CORAGEUS, *adj.* courageous, 2093.

CORDE, *sb.* accord, 6399.

CORNYSSH, the native county of Sampson, 6054. Called CORNYTH in the MS. l. 3137.

CORYNTH, Corinth, 3137. The MS. has CORNYTH, and elsewhere CORNYSSH.

COST, *sb.* coast, border, 6146.

COSTOM, *sb.* custom, 2974.

COSTYNG, *part.* traversing, 5923.

COUENAUNDE, *sb.* covenant, agreement, 3807.

COUERTURE, *sb.* pretext, 4596.

COUMFORT, *v.* comfort, 1019; *sb.* comfort, 1023.

COUNFORT, *sb.* comfort, 61, 3565.

COUNFORT, *v.* to comfort, 76, 1014.

COURSE. 'Toke ther course, or coursis,' a term of tilting, when the combatants rode at each other with their spears, 2462, 2627, 3360, 3383; 'Rode a course,' 5098.

COWDE, could, 381.

COWD GOOD SKILL, was skilful, 932.

CRAFT, *sb.* 'A craft' = a cunning contrivance, 4233.

CREDENCE, *sb.* 'To take credence' = to believe, 4680.

CROPPE, *sb.* the top of a plant or tree. "Croppe and rote," 4940.

CROSSYNG HYM THE WAY, crossing his path, 5814. See 6076.

CROVES, King of Arabia, 1901.

CRYED, *pp.* proclaimed, 5573, 6146.

CRYES, *sb.* proclamations, 4757.

CURTESLY, *adv.* courteously, 166, 392, 602, 694, 5091, 6700.

CURTEYS, *adj.* courteous, 3, 307. COURTEYSE, 338. CURTES, 425, 2026, 6617, 6866. CURTESE, 1946, 6672.

DALAY, *sb.* delay, 1842.

DAMAS, Damascus, 4744.

DAMASK, Damascus, 3140.

DANGER, *sb.* 'Made danger = made a difficulty, hesitated, 5073.

DARELL, a knight of Persia, son of Cherydone, Prince of Cesarea, 1505, 1929, 5058.

DAUID, eldest son of the Prince of Turkey, 1920.

DAY, *sb.* space of time; in the phrases 'ij monethis day,' 5882, 5888; 'a moneth day,' 1717, 1890.

DAYLE, a mistake for 'daye,' 3959.

DEBATE, *sb.* quarrel, strife, 2296, 5221.

DEBONERLY, *adv.* 279; perhaps for 'deboner' = debonair.

DED, 'Don to ded' = put to death, 1487.

DEDE, *v. pret.* did, 692, 1327, 5216; 'Dede of' = put off, 4343. DED, 3925, 4798.

DEFAUTE, *sb.* fault, 875.

DEFENDE, *v.* to forbid, 900, 4479, 6590.

DEFENSABLE, *adj.* 'In defensable wise,' in a defensive manner, fully armed, 1888.

DELAY. In l. 5300 'ony delay' is found to rhyme with 'batell,' where it must be a mistake for 'fayle.'

DELE, *sb.* a part or portion. 'Euery dele,' every bit, 112, 605, 892, 2717; 'Some dele,' somewhat, 261. DEELL, 698.

DEME, *v.* to judge, 461, 1614; *pret.* DEMYD, 1455, 4710.

DEMEANE, *v.* to deal with, treat, manage, 788, 4622.

DEMEANYD, *pp.* 'To be demeanyd' = to behave, conduct oneself, 1719.

DEMEANYNG, *sb.* demeanour, 398, 2195, 5981. DEMEANENG, 662, 5179. DEMEANING, 929. DEMENING, 1345. 'Att his demening,' under his command, 2052.

DEPARTE, *v. t.* to part, separate, 2747, 5851; and *i.* to share, divide, 3418; *pp.* DEPARTID, 3080, 6254.

DEPARTENG, *sb.* parting, separation, 209, 2661.

DETERMYTTE, *v. t.* to put an end to, 1695.

DEVER, *sb.* endeavour, 6506.

DEWTE, *sb.* 'Of dewte,' as their due, 2016.

DIGHT, *v.* to make ready, prepare, 382, 1110, 2027; *pp.* prepared, 3636.

DILIGENCE, *sb.* 'Dede diligence' = was diligent, 6756.

DISCOMFETE, *pp.* discomfited, 2411.

DISCOMFETURE, *sb.* 'Were att discomfeture' = were discomfited, 2511.

DISCOMFEYTE, *pp.* discomfited, distressed, 6112, 6292.

DISCOMFORTID, *pp.* deprived of comfort, 5913.

DISCOMFORTURE, *sb.* discomfiture, 2571.

DISENTE, *sb.* descent, 1314.

DISFORTLES, an error for 'comfortles,' 6645.

DISMAY, *v.* used as a reflexive verb, 5328.

DISPLESAUNCE, *sb.* displeasure, 4268, 4691, 5189, 5319, 6481.

DISPORTE, *sb.* sport, 36, 3836. 'Disporteng place,' pleasure ground, 647.

DISSENTE, 956; apparently an error for 'assent.' See 983.

DISSESE, *sb.* discomfort, 292, 713, 878.

DISSEYUED, *pp.* deceived, 959.

DISTEYNE, *sb.* destiny, 1097.

DISTEYNEY, *sb.* destiny, 175.

Do, in the phrases ' do ordeyne ' = arrange, 748; ' Do calle ' = call, 6428.

Do, *pp.* done, 11, 416, 555, 606, 960, 1179, 2881, 2955, 4646, &c. Doo, 3249.

Do AWAY = put it away, 6590.

DOBILNESSE, *sb.* duplicity, 3890.

DOLVYN, *pp.* dug, 5207.

DON, *v. inf.* to do, 5737.

DOON, *adv.* down, 4094.

DOTH, 3 *pl.* 6655.

DOUGIIT, *v.* to doubt, 661.

DOUTELYS, *adv.* doubtless, 430.

DOWTE, *v. i.* to fear, 2519.

DRAWE, *pp.* drawn, 1778, 3398.

DREDE, *v. pret.* dreaded, 996.

DREMYD, WAS, *pret.* dreamed, 5464, 6158; *pp.* BE DREMYD, 5727.

DRESSE, *v.* make ready, prepare, 1164, 3587, 4602; prepare to go, 3769, 3981; *pret.* DRESSID, 2028, 2477, 2830, 4563, 6626.

DROW, *v. pret.* drew, 1000.

DUBED, *pp.* endured, continued, 4618.

DURENG, *part.* continuing, 2766.

DYAMAUNTEZ, *sb.* diamonds, 2036.

EGIDIAS, a city of Egypt, 4200.

Ellipsis of verb of motion, 2901, 6947.

ELLYS, *adv.* else, otherwise, 4859, 5693.

EMBOSED, *pp.* embossed, foaming at the mouth. A hunting term, 80.

ENBATELL, *v. t.* to set in battle array, 2904. ENBATELID, *pret.* 2919. ENBATELYD, *pp.* 2925.

ENBROWDERYD, *pp.* embroidered, 3287. ENBROWDRED, *v. pret.* embroidered, 3253.

ENCONTINENT, *adv.* incontinently, immediately, 1769. ENCONTYNENT, 2819.

ENDLY, *adv.* inwardly, thoroughly, 849, 4844, 6698. See INLY.

ENDURYD, *v. pret.* continued, 2976.

ENGENYS, *sb.* engines, 2887.

ENMY, *sb.* enemy, 4951; *pl.* ENMYS, 2005, 2082, 2524, 4605.

ENSURE, *v.* assure, 169, 223, 431, 893, 2751.

ENTENT, *sb.* endeavour, 954. See INTENT.

ENTENT, *sb.* design, thought, 4668. ' To ther entente,' 220; ' To ther intent,' 1323; ' To myn entent,' 808; ' In ther entent,' 924; ' After ther entente,' 1070, 2099; ' As to his entente,' 2666; ' Aftur your own entent,' 2868; ' In his entent,' 2880, 6404; ' In myne entent,' 5286; ' The effecte of his entente,' 4217, 4275, 5810. See also 6740.

ENTRETYD, *pp.* treated, 3428.

ERANTE, *adj.* arrant, 1007.

ERITAGE, *sb.* heritage, 3115, 4642.

ERMONES, the King of Higher Ind, 2150, 3017; slain by Generydes, 3053. See HARMONES.

ERMONYE, 1958.

ERTELY, *adv.* heartily, 4057.

ESAUNCE, King of Nicomedia, 1945.

ESCIIETE, *sb.* escheat, forfeiture, 6963.

ESCIIEW, *v.* to avoid, 1377.

ESKEPYD, *pp.* escaped, 2374.

ESPECIALL. ' In especiall ' = especially, 5739, 6411.

ESTATIS, *sb.* persons of state and dignity, 6919.

ETIIIOPE, Ethiopia, 1947, 3143.

EUER IN ON, *adv.* continually, 5594. EUER IN ONE, 6182.

EUERYCIIONE, *pron.* every one, 5866, 5872.

EXCEPT, *v.* to accept, receive, 406.

EYNE, *sb.* eyes, 1483, 4398.

EYTHER, *pron.* each, 3447.

FADER, *sb.* father, 134.

FALL, *pp.* befallen, happened, 5487.

FALL, rhyming with 'will' and 'still,' 5858.

FALOW, *sb.* fellows, 1766.

FALSED, *sb.* falsehood, 958.

FALSHEDE, *sb.* falsehood, 1539, 5221, 5267.

FANTESIES, *sb.* fancies, 4652. FANTESYCE, 4676.

FARDE, *v. pret.* behaved, seemed, 4786.

FARE, *sb.* course of life, 4495.

FATID, *v. pret.* faded, 6761.

FAWTE, *sb.* fault, 4386, 5686.

FAYNE, *adj.* glad, 27, 3801, 5649. FAYN, 1145, 1284, 2329, 4560.

FEBELID, *v. pret.* grew feeble, 6646.

FELASHEPE, *sb.* company, 1667, 1956. FELASSHEPE, 2855.

FELAW, *sb.* companion, 134, 4833.

FELD, *sb.* field. To 'sette a feld' is to put an army in order of battle, 2914, 2921, 4806; 'Made ther feld,' 4813; 'made a feld,' 4817; 'To make a feld,' 5301.

FELE, *adj.* much, 6701.

FELISCHEPE, *sb.* company, 1886. FELISSHEPE, 2540, 4830, 5982, 6326. FELISSHEPPE, 2869, 2969.

FENDE, *sb.* fiend, 3069; *pl.* FENDEZ, 2520.

FENYALL, *adj.* final, 5038.

FER, *adv.* far, 911.

FERD, *adj.* afraid, 3389. FERDE, 4425.

FERDER, *adv.* further, 6154.

FERE. 'In fere' or 'in feere' = together, 422, 527, 728, 1326, 1378, 2113, 4353, 4604, 6210, 6620, 6973.

FERLY, *adv.* strangely, wonderfully; and hence, impetuously, 2203, 5815.

FERRE, *adj.* far. 'Ferre in age,' advanced in life, 66, 228, 3666; *adv.* 3118.

FEYNTID, *pp.* rendered faint, 6647.

FISYKKE, *sb.* physic, 6876.

FLATRISE, *sb.* flattery, 4042.

FOR BECAUSE, *conj.* because, 2959, 6947.

FOR BLED, *pp.* weakened by loss of blood, 4946, 6112; bleeding, 6403.

FOR BLODE. It is difficult to say whether 'sore for blode' (3528) signifies 'sore for loss of blood,' or 'having bled sore.' Most likely the latter. Compare 'sore forblod,' 4946.

FOR DY CAUSE, *conj.* because, 6037, 6184.

FORDER, *v.* to further, 336.

FORGETE, *pp.* forgotten, 2352, 5367, 5558, 6090, 6961.

FORGEVE, *pp.* forgiven, 4730.

FORGEVYN, *pp.* forgiven, 6125. FORGEVEN, 6323.

FORGROWE, *pp.* misshapen, 3667.

FORMEST, *adj.* first, foremost, 1998, 2023, 2971.

FORS, *sb.* care. 'Gave butt litill fors,' took but little care, 2268.

FORSAKE, *pp.* forsaken, 4671.

FORSOKE, *pret.* gave up, abandoned, 5674.

FORSTER, *sb.* forester, 975, 4803, 6674.

FORTHERAUNCE, *sb.* furtherance, advancement, 6664.

FORTHERMORE, *adv.* furthermore, 103.

FOR THOUGHT, *v. pret.* repented, 1456.

FORTUNE, *v.* to chance, happen, 3977, 4234, 5895.

FOR WHYE, *conj.* because, 996.

FOR WONDID, *pp.* severely wounded, 6384.

FORYERAUNCE, *sb.* furtherance, 6482.

FOR YETE, *pp.* forgotten, 1916.

FOUGHTEN, *pret.* 3 *pl.* fought, 3512.

FOUNDEN, *pp.* found, 5614.

FOUNDRED, *v. pret.* were worn out with fatigue; used of horses, 3385.

FOURTHNYGHT, *sb.* fortnight, 5342.

FOYS, *sb.* foes, 2491, 5157.

FRAUNCHESSE, *sb.* franchise, 1273.

FRE, an error for 'fore' or 'faire,' 5100.

FRELY, adv. 2415; perhaps for 'ferly.'

FRENDLEHEDE, sb. friendship, 5170.

FRESSEST, adj. freshest, 2037, 3562.

FRO, prep. from, 792, 5712. FROO, 3483, 3945.

FURMABELY, adv. formally, conformably to precedent, 1728.

FYENCE, sb. affiance, trust, 5611.

FYLLE, v. pret. fell, 4095.

FYND, v. to provide, 1013.

FYNE, sb. end, 1757.

FYNIALL, adj. final, 5427, 6251.

GADERID, v. pret. gathered, 2917.

GADERYNG, sb. gathering, 1335.

GAILE, sb. gaol, 1696.

GALAD, King of Assyria, 2167, 2545.

GANNE, v. pret. began, 243, 390, 933, 1998, 4870, 5701. GAN, 5711.

GEERE, sb. gear, equipment, 2104, 2670. GERE, 2857, 4563.

GENERYDES, son of Auferius and Sereyne, 291, &c.

GETE, v. imper. get, 6063.

GETEN, pp. gotten, begotten, 187.

GEVE, v. to give, 4249; pp. given, 3581, 4642.

GIDE, sb. guide, 4803.

GIDID, v. pret. guided, 4800.

GIRDE, pp. girt, 3557.

GISE, sb. guise, 2974, 4203.

GLAD, sb. gladness, joy, 1255.

GLYNT, v. pret. glanced, 2421; flashed, 6088.

GOFFORE, the Sultan of Persia, 651.

GOO, in the phrase 'goo sett,' 2914.

GOO, pp. gone, 4003, 4783, 6781.

GOOD, sb. goods, possessions, 237.

GOOD, interj. 2770.

GOODLYHEED, sb. goodness, 679. GOODLY HEDE, 2803, 6340.

GOOD MAN, sb. master, proprietor, 1122.

GOTEN, pp. begotten, 4287.

GOTH, v. imper. go, 6484.

GOUERNAUNCE, sb. government, 674, 1094, 1948.

GOULYS, adj. gules, 2306.

GRAMERCY, int. Fr. grand merci, great thanks, 452, 2653.

GRAUNT, pp. granted, 1671.

GRE, v. to agree, 1141.

GRE, sb. pleasure; to take in gre = to be pleased, 103, 998.

GREE, v. to agree, 5294.

GREKE, sb. Greece, 356, 402.

GRESELY, adj. grisly, 2153.

GRESES, sb. steps, 1531.

GRISSELL, the name of Generydes' horse, 3301.

GROW, pp. grown, 804. GROWE, 1343.

GUSARE, an Ethiopian in the service of Serenydes, 5245.

GWYNAN, son of Belen, King of Egypt, 2127, 3595, 5787. GUYNAN, 2238, 4198. GWAYNAN, 2241.

GWYNOT, chamberlain to Clarionas, 2688, 3244, 6800.

GYE, v. t. to guide, 2049.

HAKENEY, sb. hackney, 1249.

HAN, an, 5269.

HAND. To 'bere in hand' = to treat, 2780.

HAND BE HAND = hand to hand, 1827.

HANDE. 'Of his hande,' 1930; 'Of his handis,' 5186; 'Aside hand of' = beside, 2453, 2825.

HANGED, adj. 'An hanged bodde,' a bed with curtains, 71.

HAP, v. to happen, 156.

HAPPYD, v. pret. happened, 435, 3622. 'Hym happyd in,' he lighted upon, 57. HAPPID, 3524, 6161.

HARD, v. pret. heard, 516, 659, 2740, 3347, 3663, 5730. HARDE, 49.

HARD, pp. heard, 897.

HARKENYD, v. pret. heard: followed by 'of,' 2949.

HARKYN, v. to hear: followed by 'of,' 4016.

HARMES, sb. arms, 614, 2305. HARMYS, 2405.

HARMONES, the king of higher Ind, 2956.

HARNES, sb. armour, 605, 2028, 2965. HARNESSE, 2945. HARNEYS, 6088.

HAROWED, sb. a herald, 2249.

HARTID, pp. encouraged, 2418.

HATH, 3 pl. 2659.

HAUE. In the phrase 'have here' = take here, 6587, 6770. 'Had hym awaye,' took him away, 6643. HAUE, apparently for 'hath,' 1710.

HEDYR, adv. hither, 75. HEDER, 168, 5667, 6219.

HEERE, sb. hair, 545. HERE, 501, 6584.

HELME, sb. helmet, 6106, 6107.

HELVYS, sb. helves, handles, 2162.

HEM, pron. them, 5931.

HEM SELF, pron. himself, 4786.

HERE, pron. her, 4247.

HERE BEFORE, adv. heretofore, 1134.

HERIS, hers, 4675.

HEVILLY, adv. sorrowfully, 5513.

HEVY, adj. sorrowful, 239, 595, 2665, 3038, 5847, 6602.

HEUYNESSE, sb. sorrow, 887, 2548, 2604, 2987. HEVYNES, 2969, 3585, 4625.

HIDE, sb. head, 2342.

HIGH. 'On a high' = on high, aloud, 2456.

HIGHE, v. to hie, go, 4067.

HIGHT, v. pret. was called, 21, 639, 1291; v. pres. am or is called, 2756, 4144, 4159, 4694, 5063.

HIR, pron. their, 635, 4789; adv. here, 5892.

HIRE, v. to hear, 576.

HIS, is, 4675.

HOLD, pp. holden, 493, 1710, 1930.

HOLPYN, pp. holpen, helped, 5862.

HOLTYS, sb. holts, woods, 43.

HOLY, adv. wholly, 76.

HONOUR, sb. 'Hir honour' = for her credit, 4511.

HOO, adv. how, 868. HOUGH, 1068.

HOOLE, adv. wholly, 124.

HOOLE, adj. whole, sound, 5205.

HOOLY, adv. wholly, 32, 6533.

HOUGH, adv. how, 1069.

HOVYD, v. pret. tarried, 4028.

HUDE, sb. hue, colour, 1560.

HUSHT, adj. hushed, silent; and so, secret, 320.

HYE, v. to go, 41, 1955, 3056, 5153, 5934.

HYM, pron. them, 2919, 3280, 4542, 6150, 6348.

HYMSELF, pron. themselves, 3083.

HYNG, v. pret. hung, 5236.

IAPE, sb. a jest, 3377.

IAPYNG, sb. jesting, jest, 6135.

ICHE, pron. each, 2662, 4381.

ICHEON, each one, 1800, 1942. ICHON, 1691.

IE, 1980. IEE, sb. eye, 1874, 2772.

IENTILEST, adj. gentlest, 929.

IENTILL, adj. gentle, 3, 307, 664.

IENTILLES, sb. gentles, gentlemen, 1326.

IENTILLY, adv. gently, 1261. IENTELLY, 3428.

ILL FARYNG, adj. ill-conditioned, ugly looking, 2152, 3020, 3025.

IMAGENINGE, sb. plotting, devising, 122.

IMPORTABILL, adj. intolerable, 1477.

IN. 'In swounyng,' 1257, 6754, 6787; 'In falling,' 4425.

INCONTENENT, adv. incontinently, immediately, 2865.

INDE, sb. India, 2.

INDERLY, adv. 675. Like INLY.

INLY, adv. inwardly, thoroughly, 3361, 4986. See ENDLY.

I NOW, adv. enough, 2006, 3637.

2671, 6019; *v. i.* to stop, ceaso, 2470.

LEVE, *v.* to believe, 186, 1389; to live, 589, 1074, 5948; *imper.* LEVITH, 5619.

LEVING, *part.* living, 4210.

LEVER, *adv.* rather, 5616.

LEYNE, *v.* to conceal, 2284.

LEYSER, *sb.* leisure, 358, 838. LEYSERE, 3276.

LIFF, *sb.* life, 3181. LYFFE, 2699.

LIFT, *v. pret.* left, 4131.

LIGGING, *pr. p.* lying, 2475. LIGGENG, 3027.

LIGHT, *v. pret.* lighted, 3046.

LIKE, *v.* to please; *pret.* LIKID, 5165, 5653.

LIKENG, *sb.* condition, 6760.

LIST, *v.* to desire, 154, 656, 5758. 'What hero lyst,' what she pleased, 266.

LIST, *sb.* pleasure. 'On my list' = at my pleasure, 2459.

LONDYD, *v. pret.* landed, 4193.

LONG, *adv.* 'To think long' = to long, 6225.

LONG, *v.* to belong; *pres.* LONGITH, 347; *pret.* LONGYD, 26.

LOSE, *sb.* a string or lace, 5236.

LOTHE, *adj.* loathsome, 4302.

LUCAS, a knight of Persia, slain by Gwynan, 1652, 6028, 6964.

LUCIDAS, daughter of Amelok, 4843.

LYBIE, Libya, 2171.

LYGHT, lieth, 1027.

LYSTE, *v. pret.* desired, 33.

LYVEZ. 'A lyvez creature' = a living creature, 3381. Compare Chaucer, Clerk's Tale.

MADANE, King of Thrace, 2144. In the Roxburghe Club version he is called King of Greece. MADAN, 2920.

MAGRY, *sb.* ill will, 877.

MALICHIAS, a knight of Persia, slain by Generydes, 938, 1484.

MANASSEN, one of the King of Egypt's allies, 2169. Slain by Lucas, 2482. MANESSEN, 2476.

MANER. 'Some maner trayne,' some kind of snare or plot, 83, 1438; 'In no maner a wyse,' 259; 'No maner harnesse,' no kind of armour, 2945; 'All maner vitayle,' all kinds of provisions, 3111; 'Some maner waye,' in some way or other, 4478; 'What maner thing,' 4708; 'All maner right,' 5472.

MANERLY, *adv.* in a becoming maner, 653.

MASEDEYN, Macedon, 1952. MASEDOYNE, 2085.

MASSAGE, *sb.* message, 364, 2377, 3165, &c.

MASSENGER, *sb.* messenger, 1892, 5162. MASSANGER, 3173, 3329. MASSINGER, 5152.

MASTEREYS, *sb.* efforts, displays of skill, 2778.

MEANE, *sb.* means, 594, 952, 3160, 6035.

MECHE, *adj.* much, 1275, 1670, 1949, 5146; *adv.* 3199, 3419, 3445, 5635.

MEDEN, Sereyne's maid, 264. MEDEYN, 274, 298, 299, 304. MEDEYNE, 281.

MEDLED, *v. pret.* 'Medled with' = encountered, 6134.

MEKILL, *adv.* much, 6451.

MEND, *sb.* mind, memory, 412, 1073, 3032, 6413; mention, 2506. 'Sithe tyme of mend' = since time within memory, 1772. MENDE, 3198, 3434, 4796, 6406. Rhyming with 'fynde,' 5698.

MENY, *sb.* retinue, attendants, 277; company, 3002.

MERCAUNDEZ, *sb.* merchants, 4203.

MERTHIS, *sb.* joyful songs and cries, 3563.

MERVELYS, *sb.* marvels, 109.

MESELL, *sb.* a leper, 4237, 4311.

MESSAVENTURE, *sb.* misadventure, 3848.

METELY, *adj.* Of good measure, tall, 432; moderate, 768.

ME THINK, methinks, 2362, 3243.

MEVE, *v. t.* to move, 1760, 4909.

MIRABELL, Clarionas's maid, 716, &c. MYRABELL, 797. MIRABILL, 3804.

Mo, *adj.* more, 2722, 3908.

MOAB, King of Cappadocia, 1954.

MONE, *sb.* sorrow, complaint, 2695. 'To make mone' = to complain, lament, 2662.

MONPERSON, a town of Persia, 5987. MONPERSONE, 6058. MOUNPER-SON, 6190.

Moo, *adj.* more, 955, 1110, 1977.

MORE, with a comparative, more bolder, 1628; more wrother, 1568; more stronger, 2160.

MORELL, the name of King Belen's horse, 3286.

MORTUALL, *adj.* mortal, deadly, 6399.

MOST, with a superlative, 929.

MOST, *adj.* greatest, 2708.

MOTE, *v.* may, 668. 'So mote I goo,' 2900, 4639, 5043.

MOUNTENER, the chief city of Persia, 639, &c.

MYDDES, *sb.* midst, 538, 852, 6042.

MYNDE, *sb.* 'To make mynde' = to make mention, 2131. MYND, 3016, 4866.

MYSGOUERNAUNCE, *sb.* misgovernment, 4873.

MYSTREST, *v.* to mistrust, 1399, 1413.

MYSTREST, *sb.* mistrust, 1673.

MYSTROST, *sb.* mistrust. An error for 'mystrest,' as it rhymes with 'list,' 5760, 6184.

MYSTROSTE, *v.* to mistrust, 5695, 5762; *pp.* MYSTROSTID, 6238.

NATANELL, tutor to Generydes, 337, &c.

NAY or NAYE. 'That is noo nay,' there is no denying it, 2277; 'This is noo nay,' 4159, 4288,

4539; 'Said nay' = opposed, 4755, 5456.

NAYED, *pp.* denied, refused, 1797. NAYDE, 5248.

NE, *conj.* nor, 4368.

NEDE, *v.* 'That hym nede,' that may be needful for him, 350; 'Them nede,' they needed, 4400.

NEE, *conj.* nor, 3317.

NEER, *adv.* nearer, 5715.

Negative, double, 3317, 3413, 4205, 5361, 5374.

NEW. 'We are new to begynne,' we have to begin anew, 3108.

NICOMEDE, Nicomedia, 1940. NY-COMEDE, 2073.

NONYS. 'For the nonys,' for the occasion, 3289, 5139.

NORISE, *sb.* nurse, 288. NORYSE, 286.

NOT FOR THY, *adv.* nevertheless, 235, 813, 917, 3127.

NOTHER, *conj.* neither, 1749, 1817, 3181.

NOTHER, *pron.* other, 1749.

NOWNBER, *v. t.* to number, 1561.

NOYETH, *v. pres.* annoyeth, 5728.

NOYTHER, *conj.* neither, 4470.

NYE HANDE, *adv.* near, 2273.

NYERE, *adv.* near, 2531.

NYGH HANDE, *adv.* near, 62, 6335.

NYHAND, *adv.* near, 951.

O. 'o length' = at length, 1778; 'o trough' = in truth, 4286, 4501; 'o my trowth,' 4723.

OBEISEAUNCE, *sb.* obedience, 1096. OBEYSAUNCE, 6630. OBYSE-AUNCE, 2435.

OBESEAUNCE, *sb.* obeisance, 652. OBEYSAUNCE, 2020, 6897.

OBETH, King of Sicily, 1934.

OBEY, TO, *v.* For this construction see 19, 5782.

OBSERVAUNCE, *sb.* 'To do observaunce' = to shew respect, 6655.

OF = for, in construction with 'beseech,' 325, 6315, 6498; 'thank,' 5093; 'praye,' 6263, 6432; = on, in construction with

GLOSSARIAL INDEX. 239

'avengo,' 565; 'Sory of,' 597; 'To bo of assent' = to assent, 3609; 'Abiding of,' 4328; 'Purveyd of' = provided with, 4649.

OF, *prep.* off, 2798.

OFFEND, followed by 'to,' 6171.

ON. In the phrases 'on huntyng,' 962, 965, 3765, 3775, 5966; 'On lyve' = alive, 3375; 'On sleppe' = asleep, 4063.

ON, *adj.* one, 1316, 4791; redundant in 2909, 6978.

ON, *prep.* in. 'On twayn' = in two, 2242, 2632, 4569, 4926; 'On twoo,' 2933, 4598. Of, 4597.

ON- in compounds = un.

ONCOPELYD, *pp.* uncoupled, 42.

ONFORTUNE, *sb.* misfortune, 5339.

ONHAPPY, *adj.* unhappy, unlucky, 4874; mischievous, 5561.

ONHORSID, *pp.* unhorsed, 2464.

ONNESE, *adv.* perhaps for 'vn-nethe,' scarcely, 3453.

ONNETHE, *adv.* scarcely, 977.

ONTO, *prep.* unto, until, 282, 1288, 3136, 5178.

ON TOKE, *v. pret.* took on, 3951.

ONTREW, *adj.* untrue, 120.

ONTROWTH, *sb.* untruth, 4896.

ONYS, *adv.* once, 1182, 2492, 2785, 4242, 4303, 5401.

O PECE, *adv.* quietly, uninterruptedly (? Fr. *en paix*), 1385, 1681, 2417, 2544, 2620, 2766, 3739, 3755, 3920, 4189, 4328, 4581, 4911, 5254, 5627, 6182, 6237, 6347, 6719. OPEESE, 2313. OPESE, 3391, 3500, 4512, 4618.

OR, *prep.* before, 1185.

OR, *adv.* before, 917, 1005, 2232, 2968, 6540. OR EUER, 6459.

ORDENAUNCE, *sb.* array, 2084, 2142; arrangement, 4769.

ORKENAY, Orkney, 1961.

OSTAGE, *sb.* hostelry, 64.

OTHER, *pl.* others, 1587, 3132.

OTRAN, king of Spain, 3064, 5937.

OUER, *adj.* upper, 2996.

OUERTHROWE, *pp.* overthrown, 4979.

OUER WHARTE, *prep.* across, 6604.

OUGHT. 'As hym ought,' as was due to him, 142.

OUREZ, *pron.* ours, 2989; *sb.* hours, 4201.

OUTRAYTH, outrageth, 2426.

OWE, *v.* to regard as owing or due, 922, 1329.

OWTTRAYED, *pp.* outraged, violently treated, beaten, 3491. OUTRAYED, 4841. OVTRAYDE, 6068.

OYTHER, *conj.* either, 2610.

PACIENT, *adj.* 'In pacient' = patiently, 6748.

PALES, *sb.* palace, 4247, 6759.

PARAUENTURE, *adv.* peradventure, perhaps, 2586.

PARDE, *int.* verily! Fr. *par dieu,* 731, 3441.

PARENTYNE, the chief city of India, 5771. PARENTYNNE, 378. PAREYNTYN, 970.

PARTID, *v. pret.* departed, set out, 2113.

PARTISE, *sb.* parts, 1706.

PASSITH, *v. pres.* exceedeth, 5954.

PAYDE, *adj.* pleased, 2246.

PAYN. 'On a payn,' in 1727, is on pain of something which is not mentioned.

PAYN, *sb.* pains, 68, 1018, 5213. PAYNE, 3412.

PECE, *adj.* quiet, 320.

PEERLYS, *sb.* pearls, 3306.

PEKYS, *sb.* pikes or pickaxes, 2509. See 2161.

PENSELL, *sb.* a small penon or flag, 2686, 2947, 3245.

PEOPILL, *sb.* a body of people, 2670.

PEOPLE. 'A greto people' = a large multitude, 5279.

PERAUENTURE, *adv.* perchance, 153, 781. PERAUENTOUR, 888.

PERCE, Persia, 6780.

PERISSHED, *v. pret.* pierced, 3367.

PERSE, *sb.* Persia, 620, &c.

PETEUOSE, *adj.* piteous, 3586.

PETEVOUS, 3953. PETUOSE, 5594, 6584. PETUESE, 6622.

PETEVOUSLY, *adv.* piteously, 1529.

PHARES, one of the Sultan of Persia's allies, 2097.

PIGHT, *v. pret.* pitched, 5134.

PITEVOUS, *adj.* piteous, 2954.

PLAYN, *adj.* honest, 6948.

PLEASE IT = may it please, 3720, 6843. PLESE IT, 4309, 5400. PLEASIT, 4060.

PLENTEUOUS, *adj.* plenteous, 620, 1031.

PLESAUNCE, *sb.* pleasure, delight, 31, 126, 654, 4650, 5114, 6711.

PONYSSHENG, *sb.* punishing, 6662.

Possessive case, mark of, omitted, 'Suster sonne,' 283; 'Hevyn kyng,' 2642, 4002, 4427; 'Sowdon powre,' 3420; 'maister harnes,' 3845; 'nyghte rest,' 4030; 'auferius right,' 4134; 'auferius comyng,' 4772; 'prince sonne,' 5185.

POSTRENE, *sb.* a postern, 2559.

POYNTE DEVISE, ATTE, perfectly, completely, 3307, 5995.

POYNTED, *v. pret.* appointed, 2125, 2149.

POYNTEMENT, *sb.* appointment. 'In ther poyntement,' under their command, 2100, 2178; arrangement, 3006, 3086, 4762.

PRATYE, *adj.* pretty, 302. PRATY, 4422.

PRECE, *sb.* crowd, 2453, 6641.

PREFF, *sb.* proof, 1453, 1496.

PRELETYS, *sb.* prelates, 3561.

PRESE, *sb.* press, crowd, 538, 852, 2708, 2726, 5311. PREESE, 2299, 6277.

PRESENT. 'In present' = present, 3104.

PREUYD, *pp.* proved, 4.

PREVYED, *pp.* provided, 5887.

PRICE, *sb.* value, worth, 2036.

PRIUITE, *sb.* secrecy, 263.

PROCESSE, *sb.* story, narrative, 1509, 4615, 5911, 6213.

PROMES, *sb.* promise, 1328; *v.* to promise, 4654.

PROWSE, *sb.* prowess, 4231, 4950.

PUESSENCE, *sb.* puissance, power, 3419.

PURCHASE, *v.* to acquire, procure, 877, 5198, 5260; *sb.* acquisition, 2812.

PURVAYE, *v.* to provide, 59, 1026, 1365; *pret.* PURVAYDE, provided, 1298. PURVAYED, 1288; *pp.* PURVAYDE, provided, 1771.

PURVEY, *v.* to provide, 6455; *pret.* PURVEID, provided, 5310. PURVEYD, 3220, 4276; *pp.* PURVEID, provided, 2082. PURVEYD, 1115, 2889, 3196, 4649, 5139.

PURVYAUNCE, *sb.* providence, 272.

PUSAUNCE, *sb.* power, 1951. PUYSAUNCE, 1970.

PUT TO, *v.* to apply, 4948, 5213.

PYTUES, *adj.* piteous, 6283.

QUARELL, *sb.* cause of quarrel, claim, 3536, 4561.

QUIETE, *v. pret.* acquitted, 2861.

QUYK, *adj.* alive, 2576.

QUYTE, *v. t.* to acquit, 1500; to requite, 3498, 5700; *pret.* requited, 2327; acquitted, 3013; yielded, gave up, 3608; *pp.* requited, 3495, 6975.

QUYTE AND CLENE, 6364, 6376.

REAMES, *sb.* realms, 4332.

REANE, *sb.* rein, 3474.

REBELL, *adj.* rebellious, 6421.

RECOMAUNDID, *v. pret.* commended, 5907, 6174.

REDE, *v.* to advise, 625, 871, 2575.

REDELY, *adj.* ready, 6305.

REDEN, *pp.* ridden, 5597.

REDY, *adj.* near, 3706, 6890.

REDYEST, *adj.* quickest, nearest, 3700.

REHERSID, *pp.* mentioned, 1114.

Relative omitted, 5272.

REME, *sb.* realm, 19, 496, 1028, 2649, &c.

REMEMBRYD, *pp.* reminded. 'Am remembryd' = remember, 619, 2690, 5290.

REMEVE, *v. t.* to remove from, 3223.

REMEVID, *v. pret.* removed, 3015.

REMEVYNG, *part.* removing, 5069.

RENNE, *v.* to run, 930.

REPORTE, *v.* to refer, 4526.

REPREFF, *sb.* reproof, 1451.

REQUERE, *v.* to require, 619, 6586.

RESAN, *sb.* reason, 1061.

RESKEWSE, *sb.* rescue, 4928.

RETEYNE, *v. t.* to restrain, 1543.

REUER, *sb.* river, 1151.

REWITH, *v. pres.* repenteth, 3971.

REWLE, *sb.* revel, 5592. The line is corrupt. Order, 6629.

REWLE, *v.* to rule, 5892.

REYNYNG, running, 3825.

RIALL, *adj.* royal, 1950.

RIALLY, *adv.* royally, 1308, 6910.

RIGHTWISE, *adj.* righteous, 1322; Rightful, 2960, 6669, 6934.

RISSH, *sb.* rush, 1680.

RODE, *sb.* rood, 2445; roadstead, 4106.

ROMANS, *sb.* romances, 1.

ROUGHT, *v. pret.* recked, cared, 50, 1076.

ROWNDE, *adv.* direct, straight, 3364; and so, swiftly. 'Ranne to rownde,' 2627. ROUNDE, 3362, 4922.

RUBEN, son of Manasson, 2170, 2792.

RUMBER, *sb.* turmoil, 1377.

RYALL, *adj.* royal, 245.

RYNESHED, *v. pret.* rinsed, 1182.

SAD, *adj.* grave, serious, 3926. SADDE, 5832.

SADNESSE, *sb.* soberness, gravity, 1346, 3141.

SAFF, *adj.* safe, 3147.

SAMPSON, one of the King of Egypt's knights, 6053; slain by Generydes, 6362, 6365. SAMPSONE, 3138.

SANYK, King of Africa, and father of Serenydes, 2136, 2931, 4864.

SAUGYS, *sb.* sages, wise men, 88.

SAVE, *adv.* safe, 6470.

SAVELY, *adv.* safely, 6127, 6456.

SAYE, *v. pret.* said, 6017.

SCOMFITE, *pp.* discomfited, 570.

SEASONE, *sb.* 'Take your seasone' = take your time, 5825.

SECHE, *v.* to seek, 3997, 4150, 5566. SECHEITH = seeketh, 2451.

SECHING, *part.* seeking, 5812.

SECRELY, *adv.* secretly, 3786.

SEIGH, *v.* to sigh, 1416.

SEKE, *adj.* sick, 714, 6632, 6759.

SEKERLY, *adv.* secretly, 359, 867, 5298, 5538; certainly, 2095, 2911, 3695, 3840, 5373. SEKYRLY, 6273.

SEME, *v.* 'Him seme,' appear to him, 1981; 'Me semyth' = it seemeth to me, 2427; 'Ye semes' = it seems to you, 6007; 'Her semyth' = she seemeth, 6846.

SEMELY, *adj.* comely, 1918, 2000, 4827.

SEMLANTE, *sb.* semblance, appearance, 4019.

SEMYD. 'Hym semyd' = it seemed to him, 40, 1988; = he seemed, 3311.

SEMYNG, *sb.* 'To his semyng,' as he thought, 4986.

SENDE, *v. pret.* sent, 1896.

SENT, sendeth, 445, 2812, 3334.

SEOSYNNE, *sb.* season, 271.

SERENYDES, wife of Auferius and afterwards of Amelok; daughter of the King of Africa, 21.

SEREYNE, the mother of Generydes, and Queen of Syria, 255; her death, 6638.

SERTEYN. 'In serteyn,' 4978.

SERUAGE, *sb.* servitude, 1848.

SERVAGE, *sb.* slavery, 3344.

SERYS, *sb.* sirs, 6018.

SESE, *v. i.* to cease, 941; *pp.* 6399.

SESE, *v. t.* to stop, 1489, 6435.

SESILL, Sicily, 1933.

SETT, 680. SETTE, *pp.* seated, 387.

SEVRE, a city of Syria given to Natanell on his marriage, 6955.

SILAPE, *pp.* shapen, 175.

SHENDE, *v. t.* to injure, ruin, 1657, 4403; *pp.* SHENT, 4669.

SHETT, *pp.* shut, 5773.

SHETTE, *v. pret.* shut, 5133, 5876.

SICHE, *adj.* such, 1126.

SIDE, *adj.* long and flowing, 4398.

SITHE, *conj.* since, 587, 800, 805, 1215. In 800 'a' is repeated in error.

SKAPE, *v. i.* to escape, 2534, 2849, 5781; *pret.* SKAPID, 4567.

SLEE, *v.* to slay, 520, 2367. SLE, 3913, 3927, 4591.

SLEPPE, *v. pret.* slept, 3934, 3937, 4037.

SLEPPYD, *v. pret.* slept, 161.

SMETE, *v. pret.* smote, 2388, 6110. SMETTE, 2355; *pp.* smitten, 579. SMETTE, 6378. SMETYN, 553.

SO, *adv.* as, 4837.

SOFTELY, *adv.* gently, quietly, 2528.

SOKYD, *pp.* 234.

SOMTYME, *adv.* at one time, 4801.

SONE VPPON, *adv.* soon after, 243.

SONNER, *adv.* sooner, 6329, 6330.

SORGEONS, *sb.* surgeons, 3572.

SOTHE, *sb.* truth, 507, 612, 4885. SOTH, 996.

SOTHFASTNES, *sb.* truth, 4834, 5612.

SOTILTE, *sb.* subtilty, 122; trick, device, 1538.

SOWDON, *sb.* sultan, 640, &c.

SOWNNE, *v. i.* to sound, tend, 1750. SOWNYNG, *part.* 6339.

SPACE, *sb.* 'While I haue lyffe and space' = while I live and move, 2699, 3181.

SPECIALLY, error for 'special,' 3570.

SPERKELYD, *v. pret.* dispersed, scattered themselves, 6049.

SPORYD, *v. pret.* spurred, 217.

STERE, *v.* to stir, move, 5156.

STERT, *sb.* 'Made a stert' = rushed, 6699.

STOND, *v.* to stand, 4373. STOND-ENG, *part.* 5323.

STORE, *sb.* story, 3481.

STORY, *sb.* history, 2167.

STOUND, *sb.* space of time, 5659.

STRAKE, *pret.* struck, 2793, 2794, 2946, 3366, 5126, 6375.

STRAYTE, *adv.* strictly, 1462.

STRENTHE, *sb.* strength, 6821. A doubtful reading.

STRIFF, *sb.* strife, 3160.

STROKE, *pret.* struck, 2628, 3514.

STRONGETH, an error for 'strongest,' 5779.

STRYFF, *v.* to strive, 3373.

SUERTE, *sb.* surety, certainty, 2264; security, 4444.

SURAUNCE, *sb.* an assurance, bond, 6252.

SURE, *adj.* secure, safe, 2732, 4575, 4605.

SURRE, Syria, 93. SURRY, 99.

SUSTELY, 5070. Perhaps an error for 'softely.'

SUSTER, *sb.* sister, 4937.

SWARD, *sb.* sword, 519, 3400, 3406, 3921. SWARDE, 3480. SWERD, 2707, 3486.

SWONNE, *sb.* swoon, 2359.

SWORN BRODER. Knights who had taken an oath of brotherhood to each other were called 'sworn brothers,' 4831.

SWOUNE, *sb.* swoon, 4095, 6605.

SWOUNYD, *v. pret.* swooned, 4099.

SWOUNYNG, *sb.* an error for 'swoune,' 6569; in swounyng, 1257, 6754.

SYGHENYNG, *sb.* sighing, 162.

SYGREM, a herald, 2256, 4987, 5001, 5044. SEGREM, 6764. SEGRYM, 5986. SEGYREM, 5983.

TAK, *pp.* taken, 887.

TAKE, *v.* to deliver, 361, 447. TOKE, *pret.* 907.

TAKE, *pp.* taken, 226, 946, 2566, 3240, 3977, 5472, 5763, 6882; *pret.* took, 4070, 5536, 6422.

TARED, *v. pret.* tarried, 1287, 2757, 2926, 3352, 4347. TARYD, 2240, 2950.

TARYNG, *sb.* tarrying, 1293, 2513.

TEGER, Tigris, 1738.

TENDER, *v.* to treat kindly, 3734; to propose, 5210.

THANK, *sb.* thanks, 2879, 5915. THANKE, 3093, 3645.

THAT, redundant in 'what thing that euer fall,' 6789; 'what that she was,' 6832.

THE, *pron.* thy, 4086.

THEDER, *adv.* thither, 217, 1337, 6278.

THEDERWARD, *adv.* thitherward, 1269.

THEE, *v.* to thrive, 668.

THEMSELF, *pron.* themselves, 2596, 3057.

THER AS, *adv.* where, 2668.

THERFRO, *adv.* therefrom, 893.

THERYS, *pron.* theirs, 2989.

THING, *sb.* things, 1153.

THINK. 'Me think' = I think, 3243, 5408. THYNK. 'Vs thynk' = we think, 1782; 'Thinkith me' = seemeth to me, 3337; 'Hym thought' = seemed to him, 5639, 6861.

THIS, *pron.* these, 4402. THISE, 1706.

THO, *pron.* those, 26, 2486. THOO, 888, 1965, 2958, 4090, 4525, &c.

THO, *adv.* then, 2828.

THORE, *adv.* there, 3394, 4316.

THOROUGH, *prep.* through, 557, 2452.

THOROUGHOWT, *adv.* throughout, 2946.

THOUGHT, *sb.* anxiety, trouble of mind, 2725, 2985, 3234, 4612, 6647.

THREFTE, *adj.* thriving, 280, 1342.

THREFTY, *adj.* thrifty, 1134.

THRETE, *v. pret.* threatened, 500.

THRETING, *part.* threatening, 539.

THRETYNG, *sb.* threatening, 4086.

THROUGHELY, *adv.* thoroughly, 388.

THYNG, *sb. pl.* things, 202, 466.

TIDE, *sb.* time, 5925.

TIDENG, *sb.* tidings, 1159, 6619. TIDING, 2512.

TO, *prep.* until, 2781, 5714, 6012. 'Stroke to' = struck at, 3514; at, 6218; for, 6808.

TO AND TOO, more and more, 3378. TO AND TO, 5550.

TO BRAST, *v. pret.* broke asunder, 2356, 2495, 5837, 6107.

TODER, *adj.* other, 67, 1504, 2338, 3002, 3012, 3454, 3929, 6736.

TO GEDER, *adv.* together, 179, 1440.

TOKE, *v. pret.* delivered, 683, 1184, 2716, 5238.

TOKENYNG, *sb.* token, sign, 2608. TOKENNING, 4626.

TOKKYD, *pp.* tucked, 4397.

TONE, *adj.* one, 1957, 2338.

TOO, *adj.* two, 5879.

TRACE, *sb.* Thrace, 1028, &c. The Roxburghe Club version reads 'Tharse' in these passages, and this removes the difficulty in 2144 compared with 2288. TRASE, 2920.

TRAPPOUR, *sb.* trappings, 3305.

TRAVELL, *sb.* labour, toil, 111, 159.

TRAYN, *sb.* stratagem, artifice, 1069, 2140, 4503, 5752, 6419. TRAYNE, 4027.

TRAYTURLY, *adv.* traitorously, 2272, 4038, 6417. TRAYTOURLY, 6551. This is probably the reading in 2130.

TRESONE COLOUR. If this be the true reading it seems to mean 'treasonable pretext,' 5474.

TREST, *sb.* trust, 4621.

TRETE, *v.* to entreat, 5853.

TRETE, *sb.* treaty, 6355.

TREW, rhyming with 'now,' 5793.

TREWAGE, *sb.* tribute, 1792. TREVAGE, 3343.

TREWSE, *sb.* truce, 5887. TREWYS, 3006.

TRIFFOLYS, *sb.* trifles, 4664.

TROBELYD, *pp.* troubled, 54, 3737. TROBOLID, 3730. TROBOLYD, 5550.

TROST, *sb.* trust, 265, 786, perhaps for 'tryst,' or 'trest,' as it rhymes with 'lyst.'

TROST, *v.* to trust, 994, 3760. 'That is to trost' = that is to be trusted, 4356. Perhaps we should read 'trest,' as it rhymes with 'wist' and 'list,' as in 4621.

TROUGTH, *sb.* truth, 107, 816, 2279, 3722, 4473, 5447, &c. TROUGHT, 5437, 6316.

TROW, *v. i.* to think, 1598, 5455, 5519.

TROWLY, *adv.* truly, 144.

TRUSE, *sb.* truss, 4425 ; truce, 5882.

TRUSHED, *v. pret.* trussed, packed up, 605.

TWAYN, *adj.* two, 65. TWAYNE, 108, 1218, 1763. THWAYNE, 155.

TWYES, *adv.* twice, 3952, 3969, 6641.

TYME. 'To tyme,' or 'To the tyme' = until, 2471, 2746, 4228, 6755.

VAILE, *sb.* valley, 216.

VALOUR, *sb.* value, 6957.

VARIAUNCE, *sb.* strife, 5756.

VELANYE, *sb.* villany, 1358.

VENGE, *v.* to avenge, 5149.

Verb of motion omitted, 5282, 6606.

VERY, *adj.* true, actual, 2623.

VIAGE, *sb.* journey, 3146, 3331, 5162, 5271.

VICE, a city of India, 4770, 5778.

VISITE, *pp.* visited, 4293.

VITALLE, *sb.* victuals, 3637.

VMBLY, *adv.* humbly, 600. VM-BELY, 6170, 6567.

VNCURTESE, *adj.* uncourteous, 6244.

VNDERTAKE, *v. t.* to be surety for, 3583.

VNKYLL, *sb.* uncle, 5017. VNKILL, 5028.

VNNETHE, *adv.* scarcely, 2534, 4946.

VNQUYTE, *adj.* unrequited, un-avenged, 6038.

VNWURCHIPFULL, an error for 'And wurchipfull,' 4850.

VNWYMPILL, *v.* to unveil, 6879.

VOWARD, *sb.* vanguard, 2018.

VOYDE, *v.* to avoid, remove one-self, 6101.

VPON, an error for 'open,' 5721.

VPPON, *adv.* after, in point of time ; in the phrases 'sone vppon,' 1926, 1041 ; 'anon vppon,' 6009, 6632. On, 2035. 'Came so hastely vppon' = came upon him so hastily, 4787.

VRE, *sb.* usage, custom, 2788, 4594; use, practice, 6825.

VTERLY, *adv.* entirely, fully, 3516.

WAGE, *sb.* wages, hire, 2441, 6511.

WALOPING, *part.* galloping, 3325.

WANNE, *v. pret.* won, 1133, 2130, 2237, 2609, 2814; conquered, 3688, 4766.

WARANTISE, *sb.* 'O warantise,' of a surety, 5938, 6470.

-WARD. 'As to me-ward' = as regards me, 4331:

WARE, *adj.* careful, cautious, 351, 1084 ; aware, 2315, 2625, 3040.

WARENTICE, *sb.* 'O warentice,' of a surety, 174 ; 'O warentyce,' 287, 6803.

WARK, *sb.* work, 1171.

WAWIS, *sb.* waves, 91.

WAX, *pret.* waxed, 2472.

WAY, *pl.* 5923.

WAYTITH AFTER = waiteth for, 2440.

WEDDER, *sb.* weather, 1403.

WEDE, *sb.* dress, 4258.

WEIGHT, *sb.* wight, person, 331, 3852.

WEIGHT, *adj.* active, nimble, 3361.

WELCOMYNG, *sb.* welcome, 392, 663.

WELE, adv. well, 5733.

WELEWILLYNG, adj. well-disposed, 964.

WELLYD, pp. 'Wele wellyd,' well-disposed, 2089.

WENE, v. to think, 4655; pret. WEND, 6317. WENDE, 3947. WENYNG, part. 2502, 5636.

WENT, pp. gone, 2667, 6443.

WERRE, sb. war, 898, 6153.

WERS, adj. worse, 1365.

WESHT, v. pret. washed, 1182. WESSH, 4316.

WETE, v. to know, 132, 180, 333, 714, 4153, 4432; pres. WOTE, 739, 777, 778 (read 'Ye wote ye what;' see 6858); WOOTE, 891; pret. WIST, 153; WYSTE, 53, 913; imper. 2 pl. WETE, 1300, 2739.

WEX, pret. waxed, 3349, 5065, 6608. WEXE, 5173.

WEXEN, pp. waxen, grown, 306, 430, 2765.

WHAT SOME EUER, pron. whatsoever, 4556.

WHAT TYME, whenever, 4225.

WHECHE, pron. which, 5389.

WHEDER, whether, 914.

WHELS, adv. whiles, 4037.

WHERE, adv. whereas, 1134.

WHO IS, whoso, 353.

WIDDED, pp. wedded, 1080.

WIGHT, sb. weight, 2163.

WIGHT, adj. nimble, swift, 3634, 4573, 5055.

WILL, adv. well, 371, 899, 1835, 3698, 6941. WILE, 581. WILL, 'And it wilbe' = if it may be, 6516. See WOLD.

WISE, sb. manner, 1036, 1045, 5780.

WITHOUTEN, prep. without, 341, 794, 1171, 3706; WITHOUTYN, 20.

WITHOUTEN, adv. without, 3917.

WITTE, sb. blame, 869.

WITTELY, adv. wisely, 1051.

WOLD, would, 376, 1036. 'And it

wold bo' = if it might be, 214, 6432; 'If it wold be,' 6500. WULD, 374.

WOLLE, v. will, 4403, 4432.

WONDER, adj. wonderful, 501, 1171, 1418, 2074, 4307, 5327; adv. wonderfully, 1414, 3447, 4696.

WONNE, pp. conquered, 6398.

WOO, adj. sorrowful, 915, 2371, 2578, 3484, 6652.

WOODE, adj. furious, mad, 2983.

WOOTE, v. pres. knoweth, 891; imper. know, 6858.

WORLD. 'A world to here,' 2205.

WORTH, in the phrase 'woo worth' = woe be to, 4871.

WOTE, v. to know, 2696.

WOWETH, v. pres. wooeth, 4442.

WRAUGTH, sb. wrath, 1373.

WREKE, pp. avenged, 1824.

WULL, v. will, 2807.

WURCHIPPE, sb. honour, dignity, credit, reputation, 35, 404, 616, 882, 2896, 2911, 3417.

WURCHIPPE, v. to honour, 5179.

WYMPELYD, pp. wrapped in a wimple or veil, 6858.

WYNNE, v. to conquer, 5159.

WYSE, sb. manner, 34. 'In lyke wyse,' in like manner, 102.

YAE, int. yea, 294.

YCHE, pron. each, 698.

YDONYE, a town of Persia, 6964.

YEDE, pret. went, 2503, 3458.

YEE, sb. eye, 4549, 4984.

YEFERUS, King of Ermonye, 1957. Called also Zeferus.

YEFT, sb. gift, 3441; pl. YEFTEZ, 3569. YEFTYS, 3094.

YELDE, pp. yielded, 4781. YELD, 6620.

YENDER, adv. yonder, 1027, 2318, 2425, 2869, 4552, &c.; adj. 2777, 3704, 6019.

YMAGENING, sb. device, plot, 5747.

YMAGENYNG, *pr. p.* plotting, designing, 963.

YND, *sb.* India, 375, 2505, 5598.

YNDLY, *adv.* 3096. See INLY.

YOUR, *pron.* yours, 5096.

YOUREZ, *pron.* yours, 2869.

YSORES, son of Sanyk, 4869.

YUELL the Barn, a knight of Egypt, 3618, 4167. IUELL, 3717.

ZEFERUS, King of Ermonye. Called also Yeferus, 2092.

ERRATUM.

p. 235, col. 2, line 12, under HUDE, *for* hue, colour, *read* hide.

CLAY AND TAYLOR, PRINTERS, BUNGAY.

CORRECTIONS FOR *ADAM DAVY*, &c.

No. 69, Original Series, E. E. T. Soc.

14/87. worthyng-niȝt. Prof. Skeat says "*Dele* hyphen. 'On worthyng niȝt' = as it was *becoming* night, at nightfall. *Worth* = to become." Mr. F. J. Vipan suggests that "'Worthyng-night' = Christ's worthyng-night = Night of Christ's coming into being (as a man) = Christmaseve. If the word were originally 'Christ's worthyng-night,' the word 'Christ's' would soon be dropped, as we speak of Milton's *Ode on the Nativity* without saying whose Nativity; so also we say the 'Day of the Assumption' without saying whose assumption. Thus 'Worthyng-night' is *the* 'worthyng-night' *par excellence*. It will be observed that Davy gives his dreams in the order in which he had them; the one next before that on 'worthyng-night' he had on a night 'next the day of seint lucie bifore cristenmesse'; that next after it 'on Wedenysday in clene lente'; therefore, if we interpret 'worthyng-night' as Christmaseve, the dream on 'worthyng night' will fall in its proper place." ¶

15/144. 'And, for me, they shall not be [shewn] to clerk,' etc.

34/316-17 : for *grene, ene*, read *greue (grief)* and *eue (Eve)*.

"63/*d*. 429. *Trine* = to touch; see P. Plowman, Notes, index, s. v. *tryne. Dele* the word *ouer* in MS. Laud, absurdly introduced.

"73/386 ; for *me bade* read *bade me*, to ryme with *dde (die)*.

"83/33. *Emforþ* = commensurately with, as much as : to your true friend as much yourself, you may speak. It is originally an adverb, but here a preposition. It is merely *even-forth*, contracted in the usual way. It occurs in P. Pl., B. xvii. 134. See *efencristene, evenworþ* (equivalent), in Stratmann, p. 175, ed. 1878."—W. W. S.

"89/254, Vndytt; Ydytte 89/242, are both from '*Dit*, to close, to stop up. (*A.S.*) Still used in the North. Sometimes the pa. past.

> And yn the middes a grete pytte,
> That al the worlde myghte hit not *ditte*.
> *Purgatory Legend, MS. Rawl.*'—Halliwell's Glossary.

"The lions were shut up in the pit, and at the end of the week the king had the enclosure undone."—H. Wedgwood.

p. 112, col. 2. *Meyny*, l. 4 : for *minus natu*, read *mansionatus*.

p. 114, col. 2 : for *Preijs*, read *Prijs*.

The Cotton text is very full of scribe's blunders, and was designedly printed as it was in the MS. without emendation. Mr. Vipan sends a few from his long list: 22/15, read *three* for *there* (*three* is given by the Vernon and Laud MSS. 21/14). 50/245, read *fro thee* for *for thee*; 73/387, read *fere* for *free*; 73/389, for *leuan* (or *lenan*) read *leman*.

CORRECTIONS FOR *WRIGHT'S CHASTE WIFE.*

Preface, p. vii (2nd ed.). Note 1, line 1, for *Chaucer* read *Adam ;* l. 2, for *he* read *Chaucer.*

" In Massinger's *Picture,* Ubaldo & Ricardo, two courtiers of the king of Hungary, make love to Sophia, wife of a knight of Bohemia. She treats them as the Wright's Wife treats her admirers : one of them has 'the door shut on him'; the other falls through a trapdoor ; the former is set to work at spinning ; the latter, being a ladylike youth, to the less laborious task of reeling. See *Picture,* iv. 2 & v. 1."

" There is another point of resemblance : that Sophia's husband, Mathias, before leaving her for the wars, procures from his friend Baptista, 'a general scholar, one deeply read in Nature's hidden secrets,' a model or picture of Sophia, the property of which is, that if the lady is tempted, it turns yellow : if she falls, black."

" 18/640. ? for *thryste* read *thryfte* in the sense of thriving, prosperity.

" *Women,* 24/36. ? for *moke* read *smoke* = smock. Stratmann says ' moke, ? rete.' "

Fredk. John Vipan.